MERCHANT MOSCOW

Merchant Moscow

Images of Russia's Vanished Bourgeoisie

EDITED BY

James L. West AND *Iurii A. Petrov*

WITH THE COLLABORATION OF

EDITH W. CLOWES

AND THOMAS C. OWEN

PRINCETON UNIVERSITY PRESS

PRINCETON, NEW JERSEY

Copyright © 1998 by Princeton University Press
Published by Princeton University Press, 41 William Street,
Princeton, New Jersey 08540
In the United Kingdom: Princeton University Press,
Chichester, West Sussex

Library of Congress Cataloging-in-Publication Data

Merchant Moscow : images of Russia's vanished
bourgeoisie / edited by James L. West and Iurii A. Petrov.
p. cm.
Includes bibliographical references and index.
ISBN 0-691-01249-0 (cl : alk. paper)
1. Businesspeople—Russia (Federation)—Moscow—Portraits.
2. Businesspeople—Russia (Federation)—Moscow—
History—19th century.   3. Moscow (Russia)—Social conditions.
4. Moscow (Russia)—Commerce—History—19th century.
I. West, James L., 1944– .
II. Petrov, ЇU. A. (ĪUriĭ Aleksandrovich),
kandidat istoricheskikh nauk.
HF3630.2.Z9M676   1997
305.5'54'094731—dc21   97-9077

This book has been composed in Berkeley Book Modified

Princeton University Press books are printed on
acid-free paper and meet the guidelines for permanence
and durability of the Committee on Production
Guidelines for Book Longevity of the
Council on Library Resources

http://pup.princeton.edu

Printed in the United States of America

2   4   6   8   10   9   7   5   3   1

To the Descendants of Merchant Moscow,
This Volume Is Dedicated

Contents

INTRODUCTION

The ruined stairs of the Riabushinsky estate
at Kuchino, outside of Moscow

Merchant Moscow in Historical Context

James L. West

In the village with the prosaic Soviet name of "Railroad" (Zheleznodorozhnyi) just outside of Moscow, there is a curious hillside above the river Pekhorka, just behind the buildings of the once supersecret Moscow Aerodynamic Laboratory. At first glance the steep terrain appears wild and overgrown, but closer inspection reveals traces of extensive architectural structures beneath the tangle of vines and brambles: a marble esplanade, flanked by stairs and balustrades, leading down to a lower terrace emplaced with fountains and pools, all long dry and derelict. This finely carved wreckage was once the central adornment of the summer home of the first family of Russian capitalism, the Riabushinskys of Moscow. These ruins serve as an architectonic symbol of the fate of the early Russian entrepreneurs: enormous creative efforts and impressive achievements destined to become a stairway to nowhere. Or so it seemed until recently.

For many decades, researching the past of Russian capitalism more resembled archeology than history. As if reconstructing some lost civilization, one had to strain to piece together the world of the Russian entrepreneur from scant and scattered remains: the worn and dilapidated factories that still dot the remote (and, until recently, inaccessible) countryside, the elegant city homes housing foreign embassies, once lavish emporiums renamed "Foodstore Number 3," a few laconic memoirs, fragmentary company records, and rare personal archives. Moreover, the public memory of these people had been so thoroughly blackened and effaced under the weight of a seventy-year campaign of vilification that most Russians had little notion even of their existence, except as "class enemies."

Following the stunning collapse of the Soviet system, however, the memory of these vanished people is returning, new sources of information are becoming available, and their long-neglected history is coming into sharper focus. The early entrepreneurs, once regarded as the marginalized "losers" in the Russian Revolution, now appear to many as early pioneers of Russia's democratic and free-market transformation.

Any first effort to rewrite the history of the Russian bourgeoisie seems naturally to focus on the city of Moscow. It was in the ancient capital of the Russian empire, far removed from the foreign influences and bureaucratic controls of Petersburg, that entrepreneurial capitalism had its finest hour in Russia. The echoes of that distant moment were long muted in the Soviet era. But the unrestrained and undisciplined economic transformation now occurring brings vividly to mind the Moscow of another day. Indeed, from today's perspective, one is struck not by how remote these people seem but by how persistent and pervasive their legacy remains. The aerodynamic laboratory that stands near the ruined stairway was founded by Dmitry Riabushinsky in 1904, whose installation of the world's first wind tunnel in that year marked the beginning of the scientific study of flight and of the Russian aerospace industry. The factories of the central industrial region involuntarily bequeathed by the Moscow entrepreneurs formed the foundation of the Soviet industrial infrastructure of that city: the Riabushinsky, Konovalov, and Prokhorov cotton factories are still in production, though in a state much degraded from the ordered perfection maintained by their private owners. The Abrikosov Chocolate factory still produces candy. The Moscow Commercial Institute, founded by merchant Vladimir Vishniakov in 1902, now trains the next generation of economists and managers. The Tretiakov Art Gallery, the Moscow Art Theater, and many more of Moscow's landmark institutions, now openly proclaim their origins as creations of Merchant Moscow.

Moscow's urban spaces were also indelibly shaped by the business needs and aesthetic tastes of the last generation of prerevolutionary entrepreneurs. Beyond the ancient Kremlin and the massive architectural ensembles of the Stalin era, the city we see today is largely the one that was planned and constructed by the merchant elite. Less visible but more profound than stone and concrete monuments, however, was the multigenerational effort these people initiated and sustained to construct a private sphere in Russia, to pioneer private industrial and commercial enterprise, and, most important, to envision a distinctively Russian road to capitalist development.

All these aspirations and achievements of the prerevolutionary era now seem to resonate strongly in the strivings of post-Soviet Russian society. No period in Russian history is richer in precedents and analogies for the emergent civil society and free-market economy than that of the turn of the century, when Moscow of the Silver Age became for one historical moment the architectural and cultural expression of an emergent bourgeoisie. That the ascent of these new people was dramatically cut off, that their influence was systematically expunged from public memory and the historical record, that their achievements were appropriated and concealed, all now seems less important than the effort they undertook long ago to establish a modern and open society in Russia.

I

The entrepreneurs of turn-of-the-century Merchant Moscow were perhaps the freest and most energetic people ever to live in Russia. They embodied the explosive coming of age of a group that for centuries previously had shown little promise. For most of its existence the *kupechestvo*, or merchant estate, despite its obvious economic function, seemed an unlikely candidate for the status of a modern entrepreneurial bourgeoisie. In fact, so deeply rooted were the impediments to the creation of any enclave of freedom and initiative that the mere existence of so vibrant a place and people appeared unlikely. And as it turned out, historical forces soon reasserted themselves in new form, and Merchant Moscow turned out to be only a brief but brilliant exception to a long history of privation, subservience, and oppression.

Many factors conspired to delay and impede the emergence of a vigorous entrepreneurial culture in Russia. From the time of the Mongols onward, Russia's principal trade routes ran east and south, toward Persia, Central Asia, and China. Muscovite merchants looked the part of Asian traders in caftans with extended sleeves, long beards, boots and Asiatic headgear. These sartorial styles persisted among merchants well into the eighteenth century, and in some cases into the nineteenth, as did the deferential and ritualized habits of mind that accompanied them.

The social structure that shaped merchant culture was equally static and inhibiting. As the autocratic state strengthened its centralizing and regimenting control over the territory of Russia, it decreed a social structure that served its fiscal and military needs. The entire population was divided into hereditary *sosloviia*, or estates, each of which was defined by its obligations to the state: *krestianstvo* (peasants), *meshchanstvo* (petty townspeople), *dukhovenstvo* (clergy), *kupechestvo* (merchantry), and *dvorianstvo* (nobility). The majority of the population, peasants and petty townspeople, constituted the "taxable population," subject to the *tiaglo* tax (from the word *tianut'*, to pull or extract). In addition, the peasants were gradually but ineluctably enserfed during the sixteenth and seventeenth centuries, while townspeople were locked by the Law Code of 1649 into the dwelling-place and trade of their fathers. The merchants were included in the elite of "nontax" *sosloviia*, along with the nobility. As such they remained free of the *tiaglo* obligation and immune from corporal punishment, and granted the right to own serfs.

Among the elite *sosloviia*, however, the *kupechestvo* occupied a precarious position: the title of "merchant" did not confer the security of heredity status, for it was a distinction that had to be purchased and continually renewed through payment of annual fees. Failure to pay in any given year meant immediate loss of commercial privileges and expulsion from the merchantry into the underlying stratum of urban traders and artisans. In this sense, the *kupechestvo* was a weak, dependent, and unstable entity.

For its part, the autocratic state treated the merchants like indentured servitors. The *gosti*, or merchant elite, were not only required on their own time to manage the state's monopolies; they were also continuously "invited" to make "donations" to its coffers and perform other onerous and expensive services at the pleasure of the authorities. Thus when Peter the Great founded his new city of St. Petersburg, he simply decreed that the richest merchants, along with other elites, should move there from Moscow, and that they would build private residences according to government specifications at their own expense. This charmed servitude to the whim of the autocrat embedded in the merchant mentality a close association between all forms of public service and the ruinous impositions that they often entailed.

What few perquisites the merchantry enjoyed were further eroded during several centuries of competition with the more socially and politically advantaged landed elites. Because the nobility was of supreme military and administrative importance to the state, its members were able to preempt the few privileges still enjoyed by the merchants. Thus in the mid-eighteenth century, nonnobles were excluded from the ownership of serfs. Such erosion of an already tenuous status set the social agenda of the most successful merchants for generations. Because wealth alone conferred no status in Russian society, and the commercial calling was more stigmatized than revered, the elite of the merchantry sought whenever possible to abandon their lowly vocation for the security and recognition of noble status. Personal and even hereditary ennoblement became more accessible to commoners in the nineteenth century, and these channels of upward mobility routinely skimmed off the cream of the merchantry.

Those unfortunate enough to remain in the merchant estate continued to suffer the indignity of near-universal disdain on the part of both elite and non-elite groups. In part this negative esteem was assiduously earned by the often reprehensible behavior of the merchants themselves: crude business practices and questionable professional ethics were adopted by some in order to survive in the primitive and mercurial Russian economy. All forms of deception and chicanery became firmly rooted in the popular image of the dishonest and predatory merchant.

Such negative stereotypes resonated with and reinforced a deeper prejudice embedded in the public mind. Russian aristocrats feared any activity that threatened to undermine the hierarchies of privilege, power, and deference; intellectuals, often enamored of socialist ideas, despised the bourgeoisie and its works; and peasants shared a common distrust of any behavior that infringed upon the collective norms of the community. Individual initiative, private entrepreneurship, and profit-making enterprise thus suffered near universal opprobrium, with predictably negative consequences for the economic development of the country.

As if these incapacities and disqualifications were not enough, the old merchantry of Moscow all but succumbed to the seismic disruptions of the Napoleonic invasion of 1812, when its citadal was apocalyptically burned to the ground. The old merchants never recovered from this blow, yet their demise opened the way for others. Into the charred ruins of Moscow poured peasant traders and artisans who soon filled the vacuum left by the decline of the old *kupechestvo*. Many of these newcomers were religious dissidents known as Old Believers, who were imbued with a determination and persistence lacking in others (see "Note on Old Belief" that follows).

It was from among these rough peasant-traders that most all of the founders of the great industrial dynasties of Merchant Moscow emerged. Well positioned in the 1820s to take advantage of the technological revolution of steam power then belatedly occurring in Russia, the most aggressive of these early entrepreneurs, a few dozen at most, rode a short-lived economic escalator to wealth and well-being quickly enough to pioneer a whole new industry in cotton production. In many cases they became rich enough to buy their way out of serfdom long before the Emancipation of 1861. Following the Great Reforms, the next generation of these industrial clans labored on to consolidate and expand Moscow's textile empire.

Public attitudes and perceptions lagged far behind these changes, for playwrights and intellectuals continued to propagate old stereotypes of merchant life even while these new people were transforming themselves and their world through their hard work and sense of mission. By the time the third generation of Moscow's industrial families came of age at the end of the nineteenth century, the stage was set for this unique group to make its presence known in the larger cultural and political arenas of Russian life. This volume chronicles that brief but splendid moment in their history.

II

This book makes use of new materials, new expertise, and new perspectives in an attempt to reconstruct the vanished world of Merchant Moscow. Among the new sources on the history of Russian entrepreneurship now becoming available are photographs, some printed in rare prerevolutionary publications, others carefully preserved by descendants of merchant families still living in Moscow. The majority of the images used here come from the collection of Mikhail Zolotarev, who over the past fifteen years has mined both sources to compile an impressive photo archive of merchant life in Old Moscow. His collection formed the basis of one of the first public exhibitions on merchant history in 1991, entitled "Merchant Moscow." That tentative public recognition of the early entrepreneurs in Russia, the first since the Revolution of 1917, supplied the initial inspiration for this project.

New expertise has also been called upon to narrate these images. The Russian historians included in this volume are saying their first word to a foreign audience. Their shared outlook contrasts sharply with that of their Soviet-trained elder colleagues, long dominant in the field, who in the best of cases had to refract the history of the bourgeoisie through the distorting lens of Soviet ideological orthodoxy. These young Moscow scholars represent a new generation of historians working to adjust the historical record both to the sudden availability of new sources and to the altered perspectives made possible by the collapse of Communism. Petrov, Ulianova, Potkina, Shatsillo, and Kalmykov exhibit the kind of meticulous scholarship and narrative style, reminiscent of the work of prerevolutionary historians, that may well come to characterize Russian historical method in the post-Soviet era.

Represented among the American contributors are both classical and experimental approaches to the history of Merchant Moscow. Owen and Brumfield present vignettes of business culture and merchant architecture of the kind that have made them authorities in their respective fields. West explores visions of the future capitalist order that the industrialists hoped to build in Russia. Ruane and Clowes mine new methodological seams that run between literary criticism and social history to produce fresh readings of familiar texts and old images. Bradley, Lindenmeyr, and Joffe bring to bear for the first time on the merchant culture the insights of the emerging fields of women's history and history of private life, leisure, and civic patronage. Finally, Karen Pennar, herself a descendant of the Morozovs, explores daily life in Merchant Moscow by drawing on her family's unpublished private archives.

III

The history of the Russian bourgeoisie was long hostage to the passions of the Russian Revolution and the calculations of the Cold War. As the proverbial "losers" of the Russian Revolution, the industrialists were long passed over by Western historians in favor of the more alluring revolutionary and liberal intelligentsias. Soviet interpretations ritualistically dismissed the industrialists as "exploiters" and "enemies of the people." It has only been in the last two decades or so that American historians such as Rieber, Owen, and Ruckman undertook to revive interest in what the pioneering émigré historian Valentine Bill rightfully called "the forgotten class," and to investigate the colorful and sometimes alien world of Russian entrepreneurial history. Late Soviet scholars such as Laverychev and Diakin also began to look "on the other side of the barricades," but their very solid archival work was submerged beneath layers of Marxist-Leninist terminology and marred by the obligatory denigration of any and all opponents of Bolshevism.

The history of Merchant Moscow in Western scholarship was long embedded in a larger debate over the "fate" of imperial Russian society before the

First World War. The classical Western liberal interpretation of Russia's progress immediately prior to the Great War, strongly influenced by émigré views,
held that Russia was making great strides toward European-style parliamentary government and free-market capitalism. All this progress was swept away
in the war and revolution.

This comfortable consensus was challenged in the 1960s by a revisionist
interpretation of the Russian Revolution less viscerally hostile to the Bolsheviks and somewhat more critical of their liberal and social-democratic opponents. The onset of this new wave was signaled by the famous "Haimson-
Yaney debate" in 1965. The "pessimist" Leopold Haimson argued that Russia's
rapid prewar development, as vibrant and multifaceted as it may have been,
was already placing intolerable stresses on a fragile civil and political order.
Thus he saw a society in revolutionary crisis even before the Great War, and
argued that the coming of hostilities actually postponed rather than accelerated the social collapse of tsarist society. The "optimist" George Yaney defended the liberal interpretation, countering that a degree of social disorder
and political struggle was endemic and natural to the process of modernization. In his view, it was only the war that finally rent the fabric of society in
a revolutionary way.

Haimson's challenge prompted the next generation of historians to re-
examine the history of the prerevolutionary period. Armed with new historical
methods, many sought to probe beneath the level of political and intellectual
history to explore the social and cultural dynamics of late imperial society.
While few today would accept uncritically Haimson's radical view that the
Bolshevik Revolution was somehow inevitable, much new scholarship tends
to support his central contention that not all was well in the years before the
war. Recent studies have revealed forces of disintegration and fragmentation,
strong and perhaps intensifying, beneath the surface of the already conten-
tious political discourse of the prerevolutionary period. In this view, the very
process of modernization itself, having come to Russia late and with disorient-
ing rapidity, was having chaotic and destructive effects on the cohesion of the
fragile civil society and embryonic social classes just then emerging.

Echoes of this larger debate resonate in this volume. For all their dedication
to the common task, the participants do not always agree. Some emphasize
the positive achievements of entrepreneurial culture, while others hint sugges-
tively at flaws and weaknesses in entrepreneurial organization and bourgeois
identity hidden beneath the brilliant surface of life in Merchant Moscow.
Ruane, for example, traces the growing sophistication of the merchants
through their styles of clothing; Brumfield documents the creative transformation of Moscow's urban spaces to fit the needs and tastes of the city's business elite; Bradley examines the "coming out from behind the walls" of the
last generation of the great entrepreneurial dynasties; Lindenmeyr and Joffe
explore the rapidly expanding horizons of merchant women; and Petrov and

Potkina demonstrate the growing financial and commercial sophistication of Moscow's business infrastructure. The spectacular and very real achievements of Merchant Moscow are evident in these essays.

Other participants, pursuing different lines of inquiry, offer more guarded assessments. Their work plays against the positive and hopeful images presented in the photographic record. Owen stresses the alien "look" of capitalism in Russia and its inability to strike a responsive chord among the masses; Clowes explores the ambiguous and uncertain self-image of the merchants as they transformed themselves into capitalists; Shatsillo traces the ominous trends in labor relations between employers and an increasingly peasantized work force; Ulianov explores the deeply traditional religious world of Merchant Moscow, juxtaposed uncomfortably with the modern economic role pioneered by the entrepreneurs; Kalmykov suggests that the "flowering" of Moscow's business elite might alternatively be read as an abdication of responsibility and a coming apart of an immature social class; and West investigates the intensifying divisions that ramified through the entrepreneurial stratum, even while groups such as the Riabushinsky Circle labored mightily to formulate a Russian capitalist myth designed to hold it all together.

IV

These cross-currents of interpretation raise legitimate questions about the reliability of photographic documents as historical evidence. Taken together, the pictures presented here reflect largely positive and hopeful images: they radiate vitality, sophistication, and human empathy. The people in them look much like us, and they share with us that sense of well-being and optimism that still manages fitfully to inform our own outlook despite the intervening century of catastrophe. The pictures portray a real if distant structure of human existence, and they invite a sepia-tinged nostalgia for a time long ago, a sympathy for and identification with their subjects and their achievements.

The photographic images clearly show that, however hard the last generation of Moscow's entrepreneurs worked during business hours, they lived leisured lives of wealth and ostentation after hours. Moving out of the cramped wooden structures of the Trans-River District (Zamoskvoreche) where their fathers and grandfathers began their careers, they consciously occupied the palatial city homes and country dachas of the aristocracy. Increasingly, they also commissioned the best architects to build spectacular private villas and country estates. These were not the timid merchants of yesteryear, nor were they the abstemious and retiring Old Believers of the past. Their dwellings and lifestyles bespoke a people on the move, forward-looking and self-assured.

Yet the lush style of living revealed in these pictures, one that Moscow's elite clearly felt it had earned, turned out to be a dangerous lure. In their haste to supplant Russia's traditional elites and to emulate their Western counterparts, the new merchants took on a distinctly un-Russian look, one that sharply demarcated them from the common people from whom their grandfathers had emerged. By appropriating the visible trappings of leisure and privilege, they unwittingly fueled popular suspicions that instinctively equated wealth with abuse and individualism with avarice. Unable to establish their social legitimacy or wrest real political power from the nobility, the flamboyant merchants self-fashioned themselves into an increasingly visible, and therefore vulnerable, collective symbol of the brutal disparities and inequities of early industrialization. The splendid settings captured in many of these photographs became the tangible targets of mass discontent once the restraining structures of the Old Regime crumbled in 1917.

For all that the photographs accurately reveal about the past, their use as historical "texts" carries with it inherent limitations and perils as well. The focus and field of vision of the camera are narrow. In the Russian case, beyond the photo's edge there spread a sea of peasant strangeness, decidedly unmodern and non-European. The merchants' world appeared ordered with a symmetry and cleanliness that bespoke the onset of modernity and a bourgeois ethos; but it remained an isolated, largely urban enclave in a disordered and potentially anarchic landscape of rural dilapidation, poverty, and resentment.

The camera's lens is also narrowly focused in another way: the images it captured were shaped by a sensibility that looked upward and forward. The light allowed through the aperture consciously and systematically obscured the darker side of capitalism in Russia. For every enlightened and compassionate Riabushinsky or Konovalov, there were hundreds of voracious and still-benighted factory owners who abused and exploited their workers beyond human endurance. Such people did not often take pictures of their handiwork. And even the workers in the well-ordered factories and mills of Merchant Moscow appear to the camera as little more than dutiful extras. Clearly the ultimate failure of the entrepreneurs to make good their claim to national leadership in Russia rested to a large degree on a massive public rejection of the predatory behaviors and social abuses that persisted to the end, invisible to the camera's eye.

The story of this underside of bourgeois achievement, the history of the working class in Russia, has been amply told in Soviet and Western historical literature. The history of provincial merchant life is only beginning to unfold. It is with full recognition of the failure of Merchant Moscow to bring the masses of the Russian people, or even the rank and file of the entrepreneurs, to its own high level, that this volume seeks to wend a thoughtful middle way between demonization and deification as it narrates the photographic record.

These pictures not only convey an image of history; they have a history of their own. They were in large part taken or commissioned by a new and rising elite anxious to preserve the memory of its collective youth. They were produced in a time when the conventions of photography were still more akin to those of portrait painting than journalistic reportage or political propaganda (see Neumaier, "A Note on Photography in Russia"). They were intended largely for private use; in a sense we are peeking into the scrapbooks and photo albums intended to preserve pleasant group and family memories rather than to document history. The pictures were selected and arranged often by the people depicted in them, according to personal criteria that we can only guess at. Then they were subject to the chaotic winnowing of a revolutionary upheaval, and those images that survived intact were selected again and preserved by relatives and descendants during the decades when it was tantamount to treason merely to possess them. Finally, these fragile and rare images were processed yet again by the collectors, historians, and editors of this volume.

While the photos do provide a window into the past, it is a portal that is both narrow and in some sense artificial. Understanding these constraints, the historian is obliged to look beyond and beneath the photographic image, even while deciphering its visible surface message. The reader is invited to enjoy the immediacy of the images, their direct visual evocation of personality, locality, and ambiance, while simultaneously listening to the voice of the historian, at times interpreting and amplifying the message of the photographs, at times offering a counternarrative to the impressions they convey.

Photographs alone provide a vision of history at once real and illusory. Documents alone often seem fragmentary and remote. Together, however, text and photograph provide vivid and complex evocations of a faraway time, restoring form, texture, and context to the lost world of Merchant Moscow.

A Note on Old Belief

―――

James L. West

Seal of Ioann, Archbishop of the Belokrinitsa Priestly
Old Believers, Rogozh Cemetery, 1910.

The history of Russian entrepreneurship and the history of Russian religiosity
are closely intertwined, as the numerous references to the Old Believers
(*Starovery*, *Staroobriadtsy*) in this volume testify. As happened in certain other
societies in the early stages of capitalist development, religious belief and economic circumstance intersected in powerful ways to produce a distinctive
religious subculture conducive to entrepreneurship and enterprise. The Old
Believers in Russia performed the role of economic pioneers fulfilled by the
Dissenters in England, the Huguenots in France, and the Jews in other parts
of Central and Eastern Europe. This variegated family of fundamentalist sects
served as an incubator of entrepreneurial values in Russia.

Old Belief was born in the seventeenth century, a time of natural calamities,
foreign invasions, enserfment of the peasantry, popular insurrections, and
"true tsar" pretenders. During the Time of Troubles at the beginning of the

century, Muscovy had nearly been extinguished as a sovereign realm by invading Poles and Swedes, and a Polish Catholic king had ruled briefly in the Kremlin. The Troubles marked the onset of Muscovy involvement in the destructive swirl of religious and military conflict known in Europe as the Wars of Religion. On all sides, alien and militant faiths, backed by powerful states, surrounded Muscovy: to the west, the Catholic Counter-Reformation surged in Poland; to the north, Protestant Sweden brandished its military power; and to the south, the Islamic Ottoman Empire loomed across the Wild Field of the southern steppes. Muscovites of all strata interpreted these tumultuous events as portents of the Apocalypse. Millenarian expectations and end-time prophesies were the religious currency of the era.

Old Belief arose as a protest movement in response to the church reforms of the imperious Patriarch Nikon in the middle of the century. Nikon's intention was to strengthen the Orthodox Church to withstand these many challenges to the religious culture of Muscovy. He came to the patriarch's throne in 1652 with a strong sense of mission to transform what he saw as the superstitious and widely varying religious practices of Old Muscovy into a coherent and homogeneous faith. Reformed Orthodoxy, he hoped, would be capable of mounting an ecumenical response to the secular and religious tides threatening to engulf Muscovy.

Nikon believed that the church he inherited was in sorry shape: centuries of what he viewed as lax observance, superstitious accretions, and errors of textual transcription had corrupted the original pure faith of Russian Orthodoxy. Nikon took it upon himself to refashion Muscovite ritual, liturgy, and scripture to bring them into conformity with the primordial Kievan faith inherited from the Byzantine Greeks at the dawn of Eastern Slavonic history. To aid him in his effort, he invited to Moscow religious scholars and holy men from around the Orthodox world, especially from the Kievan Academy in the ancient capital, newly conquered from the Poles.

Certain of the righteousness of his reformist mission, Nikon began almost immediately to decree on his own authority a veritable cascade of liturgical and textual changes: in the direction of processions around the church, in the number of loaves to be consecrated, in the spelling of the name Jesus, and, most infamously, in the number of fingers used in making the sign of the cross (Muscovites used two, Nikon decreed three, *troeperstie*). These changes set off the eruption within the Muscovite church known as the Great Church Schism.

Nikon's reforms cut to the heart of Muscovite religiosity. Medieval Muscovite faith was profoundly eschatological, in that issues of salvation and redemption were accorded absolute priority in the economy of human existence. In a religious culture where text had been largely absent and even churchmen were often illiterate, the physicality of icon, incense, and chant filled the void of inaccessible written scriptures as earthly markers of divine presence. Within this intensely literal religious tradition, ritual played a central role: exact observance of lengthy and complicated ceremony was considered the surest road to salvation. The tsar himself, as Intercessor for his people, was expected to follow a rigorous schedule of observances, and upon his piety depended the salvation of all his subjects. In Old Muscovy ruler, elites, and masses alike shared the same religious culture, the same cosmology, the same apocalyptical expectations, the same ritual.

The Nikonian reforms shattered the coherence of that religious world. To millions of pious believers, and to many in the elite as well, Nikon's alteration of sacred, time-honored ritual was apostasy, throwing into question the hope for salvation of every Orthodox soul. The resulting movement of religious protest interacted powerfully with preexistent popular resentments against the deepening enserfment of the peasant population to form a most potent and persistent current of protest. Those who refused to change their ways were called "Old Believers." Russia's Church Schism was thus something of a Protestant Reformation in reverse: it was the church, not the laity, that championed reform, and the common people, not the hierarchy, that rejected it.

Sensing the crystallization of widespread popular resistance to its authority, the government, with monumentally poor timing, summoned a Church Council to resolve the dispute in 1666. The Council upheld the Nikonian reforms and with characteristic severity anathematized those who resisted them. To the dissenters, only one reading of these momentous events was possible: the Apocalypse was at hand, a satanic process was underway in Russia, and the tsar was none other than the Anti-Christ prophesied in the Book of Revelation: "Let him who has wisdom count the number of the Beast, for it is the number of a man, and the number is six hundred, three score and six."

Faced with imprisonment, torture, and execution at the stake for their faith, hundreds of thousands of Old Believers physically and spiritually withdrew from Russian culture, fleeing to the far corners of the realm to escape the Anti-Christ and his agents: to the Far North, to the Wild Field of the southern steppe frontier, to the forests of Siberia. The subsequent reign of Peter the Great, with its massive infusion of Western influences, only confirmed the worst fears of the dissenters, while continued brutal persecution of their number solidified their determination to resist. In their self-willed eremitic isolation from the sinful world, they began to build a distinctive and indigenous culture of their own. The Old Believers thus consciously became the quintessential "outsiders" of Russian history.

Old Belief was the most profound and sustained antitsarist resistance movement ever to emerge in Russia. To a people who believed in Anti-Christ and Apocalypse, even death by burning was welcomed as martyrdom. Indeed, some more fanatical groups in the early years of the schism practiced self-immolation when threatened by authority. Thus the whole range of punishments and sanctions deployed by the tsarist state were largely ineffective against these most stubborn of dissidents. Despite the best efforts of the state and church to stamp out this "heresy," Old Belief grew steadily over the next two centuries.

The gospel of resistance sparked insurrectionary movements across the centuries. The *streltsy*, the musketeers of Old Muscovy, were rife with Old Belief when they violently confronted Peter the Great at the end of the seventeenth century. The "Ancient Piety" also played a catalytic and mobilizing role in the great Cossack-peasant rebellions of Bulavin and Pugachev in the eighteenth century.

In self-imposed isolation from the secular world, and often from one another, Old Believers adapted to their circumstances in a variety of ways. While all rejected the tsar's authority and blessed themselves with two fingers in the ancient way, the rites they practiced soon varied widely. The faith quickly divided into Priestly and Priestless sects (those with priests and those without), and the latter group, freed from the structures of ecclesiastical hierarchy, splintered into dozens of subsects (*soglasiia* or "concords"). New religious permutations, such as "Shoredwellers," "Wanderers," "Theodosians," "Filippians," and "Silent Ones," proliferated endlessly through the fractal history of Priestless Old Belief.

Scattered across the remote districts of the empire, often living in secret or clustered together for protection, the "schismatics" (as the government and official church called them) evolved a distinctive way of life that marked them off from the general population in practical as well as spiritual ways. They were an inquisitive and disputatious people, constantly debating among themselves the meaning of the scriptures, which in the absence of a hierarchy was left to them to interpret. Primacy of the written word meant that access to it was essential to the faith: Old Believer villages usually boasted literacy rates far above those of surrounding populations.

Old Believers were also hard-working, sober, and frugal. While there was nothing in their belief system that sanctioned enterprise per se, their ascetic ways fostered a strong work ethic. The hard-earned and carefully saved material wealth accumulated by dissident communities proved useful in bribing officials (thus deflecting or delaying persecution), while visible prosperity served to distinguish true believers in their own minds from the less fortunate, and less providential, "Nikonians." Over generations, the fundamentalist ways of the Old Believers served as an incubator of habits and attitudes consistent with an ethos of labor and enterprise.

The industrious nature of Old Believers and their tendency toward self-help and collective solidarity conformed well to the needs of peasant traders and peddlers, especially those who traveled through remote districts of the empire. The dissenting sects attracted to themselves some of the most energetic and independent strata of the trading population. The historical trajectories of Old Belief and of Russian capitalism crossed after the War of 1812. The disastrous Moscow Fire of "the French year" all but wiped out the fortunes of the established merchants of that city, and few such families recovered in the subsequent decades. In their place, a virtual flood of peasant traders and petty merchants swarmed in from the hinterland selling rags and cloth made in their villages. Many of these newcomers were Old Believers. It was from this motley population of itinerant peddlers that the new entrepreneurial dynasties of Merchant Moscow would arise: the Morozovs, Riabushinskys, Konovalovs, Guchkovs, Soldatenkovs, and Khludovs all traced their ancestry to followers of "the Ancient Piety."

The stronger, more energetic, and perhaps luckier members of this trading population managed to remain in business until a new technology, that of steam-powered cotton textile production, became available in the 1820s and 1830s. A goodly number of the cloth peddlers of 1812 became the cotton factory owners of later decades, and those who enjoyed the financial backing of Old Believer communities enjoyed an extra advantage in the primitive and unforgiving Russian economy. Cotton was particularly attractive to Old Believers because it was virtually the only sector of the economy that did not entail extensive contact with the state and its agents: its products flowed not to Petersburg but to the vast peasant market of the hinterland from which the new industrialists had so recently come. Thus it was that this most archaic and fundamentalist of Russian traditions paradoxically served as a catalyst for Russia's first "industrial revolution" and of its earliest private entrepreneurial sector.

The more successful Old Believer entrepreneurs soon tempered their apocalyptical beliefs. Some, such as the Khludovs and Guchkovs, joined the officially sanctioned halfway house of "Single Faith" (*Edinoverie*). The Priestly sect, funded by Moscow merchant families like the Riabushinskys, managed in the 1860s to establish a patriarchate across the frontier in the Bukovinian town known by the Latin name of Fonta Alba. This Belokrinitsa ("White Fountain") concord soon became the wealthiest and most influential of the Old Believer sects. While their bishops were sometimes arrested and their services proscribed and disrupted by the authorities, the Belokrinitsy managed to live more successful and public lives than many of their more radical Priestless brethren.

By the dawn of the twentieth century, Old Belief seemed to have faded into the cultural background as the religious passions of an earlier age were swept aside by the onrush of modernity. But the heritage of the Ancient Piety, and the character traits it engendered, still marked the leadership of the emergent bourgeoisie. After the Revolution of 1905, which ushered in Russia's first democratic and capitalist experiments, the personalities who rose to articulate the aspirations of Moscow's entrepreneurs and merchants were almost to the man drawn from Old Believer stock: the Riabushinskys, the Konovalovs, the Morozovs and the Guchkovs had all emerged from the "schismatic" tradition. Drawing on the traditions of resistance of their forebears, these people led the business opposition to autocracy in its final years. Their demand for economic and spiritual freedom and their nationalist vision of Russia's future were deeply permeated with the values of the schism.

Despite the decidedly forward-looking attitude of the modernized Old Believer entrepreneurs, some had clearly not abandoned their allegiance to the spirit of Old Russia. The reanimation of Old Believer culture that occurred after 1905 would no doubt have remained sectarian and self-absorbed but for the efforts of the Riabushinskys to cajole their co-religionists to look to the future rather than to the past. The Riabushinskys led an eleventh-hour effort to refashion the ancient faith, with its implicit work ethic, into a new nationalist-capitalist ideology. Their campaign constituted the last attempt to find a creative place for Old Belief in the modern world. Had the war and revolution not intervened to sweep away both Old Belief and the "Nikonian" church simultaneously, the Ancient Piety might well have had a role to play in the search for a distinctly "Russian road" to capitalism.

A Note on Photography in Russia

Diane Neumaier

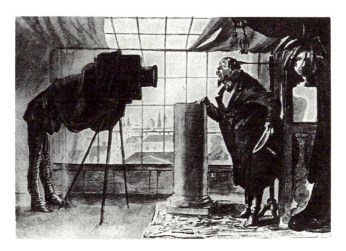

"A merchant of the 1870s" (cartoon from Slonov's *The Life of Commercial Moscow*, 1914).

The images in this volume date from, and in part illustrate, a remarkable period in the history of photography. During the decades that bracketed the turn of the century, Russian photographers, like photographers everywhere, used their cameras with ever-increasing frequency to capture the people and objects around them on plate and film. Without realizing it, these photographic chroniclers were in fact gathering data for future historians, inadvertently providing visual access to their own time in a way not possible for any previous age.

The historians in this book exploit a new corner of what is a long-neglected photographic heritage. Despite the abundance of Russian photographic materials, and the artistic and technological skill of Russian photographic pioneers, most studies of nineteenth-century photography focus primarily on Britain,

France, and America. This is in part because early commercial development of photography—starting with its nearly simultaneous invention in several places—was centered in London and Paris. Yet little known to Western historians, several significant technical developments in the field took place in Russia prior to similar innovations in Europe: experiments with pliable roll film in Russia pre-dated Eastman-Kodak's introduction of this technology, and the first photographs using artificial light were made there prior to a parallel development in France. Yet in the history of photography, as in so many other areas, the flow of information, knowledge, and technique seemed to move from Europe to Russia, and not the other way around. Hence Russian photography has been little studied in the West.

Ever since its invention in 1839, photography has played a multivalent role in the construction of culture. It can function, sometimes simultaneously, as a vernacular picture-making system, a method of fine-arts expression, and a tool of scientific observation. Photography is inherently ambiguous and multifaceted: its images, created for one purpose, often end up serving a multiplicity of others. For example, family photographs capturing intimate personal moments can, as evidenced by the pictures that follow, serve as records of social conventions and cultural traditions. Photographs intended to document private occasions often provide collateral evidence of public and historical events of which the photographer was completely unaware. The fact that most nineteenth-century portrait, landscape, and architectural photographs collected by art museums in the twentieth century were never intended to be artworks is another indication of the malleable character of the medium. This malleability makes photography a valuable, though subtle and elusive, resource for the historian.

In its early phases, photography was an elite craft. In Russia, as in Western Europe and America, early photography draped itself in the conventions of portrait and landscape painting (as the cartoon at the beginning of this section satirically illustrates). In Moscow, as in Paris, London, and New York, portrait photography of wealthy and middle-class subjects accounted for the majority of photographs produced. Likewise, burgeoning urban development and bustling commercial activity were extensively documented by commercial photographers patronized by private individuals, businesses, and the state.

Photography clearly had to await further technological developments in order to become in any sense a democratic medium. Little visual material exists from this early period that illuminates the lives of the poor in proportion to the enormous archive of bourgeois and aristocratic self-display. Tsar Nicholas II was an avid photo hobbyist (as was Queen Victoria); thus today we have remarkable access to the turn-of-the-century life of royalty, at least as it was orchestrated for the camera. As this volume illustrates, the emerging middle of Russian society enjoyed projecting its wealth and well-being into the camera's lens as well. In contrast, we have comparatively little visual access to the daily lives of common people outside this charmed circle of elites. Likewise, we have ample photographic records of the monumental technological achievements of the industrial revolution in Russia, but very little documentation of the social conditions of the workers who labored in the factories or the peasants who toiled outside them.

As with any mode of representation, those who control the means also control the meaning. In Russia that control was rigidly preserved: not only did the majority have little access to the tools of photography, there were also extensive restrictions on what could be photographed. Unofficial pictures of royalty, government and military installations, and other strategic assets were strictly forbidden. The later period covered by this volume saw a brief relaxation of some of these strictures, a photographic thaw that lasted from the Revolution of 1905 through the avant-garde Constructivist era of the early 1920s. Soviet authorities, however, soon reimposed restrictions with renewed intensity. As even casual tourists to Soviet Russia can no doubt recall, taking pictures of any scene that might suggest negative aspects of Soviet life was strictly prohibited.

Many early photographs unconsciously mimicked the conventions of painting. In Russia, this devotion to the fine-arts canon on the part of many photographers set their work apart from one of the most powerful artistic trends of the late nineteenth century in Russia, the realist aesthetic. Adapted from Western styles in characteristically intensified form, Russian realism played a powerful role in shaping artistic production in that country in the 1860s and after. The art of the *Peredvizhniki* (the "Itinerants" or "Wanderers"), such as Ilya Repin and Vasily Surikov, embedded powerfully charged ideological statements within realist artistic representations. Despite its potential for realistic portrayal of reality, Russian photography did not exploit its hybrid capacity simultaneously to record and interpret. Self-conscious art photography—genre scenes, staged tableaux, and still lives—was often loaded with bizarre, belabored, and sometimes irrational aesthetic principles that sought to define and confine photography as fine art. The impulse to pigeonhole photography—as art, as science, as record, as souvenir—kept it from being recognized as the multivalent medium that it inherently is. In the period covered by this volume, photography was only beginning to realize its broader potential to shape the world as well as record it. The journalistic and socially critical functions of photography were barely conceived of, and would have to wait until a later period to assume the conspicuous place in the visual record that they occupy today.

Ironically, one prominent application of photography as a chronicler of social life in Russia became entangled in the subjective threads of growing national self-consciousness. The camera became an important tool for geographic and ethnographic exploration. Such expeditions, usually conducted far away from Moscow and St. Petersburg, were often mounted in search of the

national "types" that inhabited the vast empire. Yet this effort to discover and
fix ethnicity and culture was undermined by an interesting contradiction inherent in the nature of photography: because of the camera's marriage to the
specific, it cannot be general, even when its subjects are intentionally selected
as exemplary or prototypical. While there could be Russian subject matter—
Russian people, Russian places, Russian objects—there really was no particularly Russian way of photographic seeing. The images that resulted from such
ethnographic research inevitably came to be judged by artistic standards that
were everywhere the same.

The evolution of photography was a truly international undertaking. At
numerous sites around the world, inventors and scientists, independently and
dependently, created, shared, and improved photographic processes and
practices at an accelerating rate toward the end of the nineteenth century.
Initially, academies of science and official organizations advanced the medium. Increasingly, however, photography escaped from official patronage to
become the focus of private initiatives symptomatic of a burgeoning civil society. Soon after the founding of the Russian Photograpic Society in Moscow in
1895, nearly a dozen photographic societies sprang up in Petersburg, Kiev,
Odessa, Kazan, and other cities. In 1896, the society convened the first Congress of Russian Photographers. By the turn of the century, several photographic journals were being published and periodic All-Russian Photographic
Exhibitions were being organized.

This expansion of interest in photography to a broader public was consistent with growing trends toward mass participation in many fields, but it was
also in part the consequence of late-century technological innovation. The
physical difficulty of producing photographs long limited the range of expression of the medium and the access the public could have to it. Many technological developments notwithstanding, until the 1880s the making of photographs remained a very cumbersome and expensive procedure. Metal plates,
such as Daguerreotypes and tintypes, existed as one-of-a-kind negative images; paper negative processes, which permitted the production of multiple
copies, were not rich in fine detail. Glass plates and the extremely sensitive
and temperamental collodion process were usually preferred, despite their
weight, fragility, and requirement for immediate on-site development. The
exquisite detail rendered through the collodion glass-plate process has yet to
be surpassed. It was not until the end of the century that truly portable photography was fully established. In 1888, the Eastman-Kodak pliable roll film
camera revolutionized the medium, particularly for amateur photographers.
With this innovation, the democratization of photography was dramatically
advanced.

Shaped by and yet distinguished from other picture systems, including
painting and lithography, the formats, technologies, and conventions of photography simultaneously evolved. Driven by emerging mass markets that ex-

ploited the ease with which photographs could be produced in multiple editions, photography quickly became a mass visual medium. As early as the 1860s, mass-produced stereo cards and cartes-de-visite (cardboard-mounted photographs of celebrities and tourist sites, for example) were among the first artifacts of mass popular culture. Commercial portrait studios offered increasingly affordable services. The photograph became at once an article of consumer culture and an emblem of modernity. By the 1890s, the invention of ever-faster portable photo processes and the halftone photo-reproduction technique facilitated the development of the commercial picture press. Simplicity, economy, and portability in turn revolutionized journalistic standards of newsworthiness, for the twentieth-century press would demand immediate, highly graphic, and narrative documentation of events.

The photographs in this volume represent a mixture of these late nineteenth-century forms. Some are rigid and formal studio portraits, often embellished with conventional props of easel painting. Others are informal snapshots, suggesting the use of new hand-held cameras. Still others are drawn from contemporary publications, publicity materials, and in some few cases, from newspapers. Thus inadvertently, this collection chronicles the growing multiplicity of photographic media that characterized the turn of the century in Russia and elsewhere.

As potentially rich as the Russian photographic archive is for historians, its resources must be exploited with great care. Photography's apparent devotion to reality—all photographs are records of light striking real things, in real space, in real time—promises to *represent* the truth transparently. In Russian, as in many other languages, the word for "lens" (*ob"ektiv*) is related to the word "objective." But photography by its nature also involves *distortion* of reality. The camera's transcription of what it sees is subject first to objective transformation of the image, such as the mechanical substitution of black and white for color, and two-dimensional vanishing-point representation of three-dimensional space.

Photography is also affected by subjective factors as well, such as the choice of subject, the decision as to when and where the camera is pointed and focused, and the process of framing to include certain subjects and exclude others. Because photography simultaneously insists upon and refuses objectivity, we must be innately suspicious of this familiar yet elusive medium about which we all assume we have some degree of expertise. The apparent ease with which visual materials can be uncritically "read" across time, space, and culture should not blind us to the distance that the medium inevitably inserts between the reality it purports to capture and the "document" it creates, the finished photograph.

Archival photographs are a rich primary source for historians. Yet the complexities and ambiguities of the medium itself, which specialists in photographic history continue to explore, should give healthy pause to anyone who assumes that it is a simple task to assign meaning to these seemingly self-evident visual artifacts. Further study of the technologies of photography, the canons of photographic taste, and the modes of publication and distribution of visual materials in this period will no doubt offer insights that will be exciting in themselves. But this new knowledge will also be useful in refining the analytical techniques of historians who, like the participants in this volume, venture beyond written documents in their effort to understand and interpret the past.

About the Photographs

Mikhail Zolotarev

Most of the photographs in this volume are drawn from my collection, which now contains more than thirty thousand images. This photographic archive began modestly as a project to study the history of my hometown, Bogorodsk, on the Kliazma River about forty miles from Moscow. This village is dominated by the sprawling textile mills that once belonged to the Morozov family. My interest in the past of this area naturally led me toward the Morozov clan and everything connected with them: their numerous family branches, their other factories in the Moscow region, their city houses, their social world, art collections, and civic projects. But because the Morozovs were only the most brilliant representatives of a whole entrepreneurial culture, I was soon drawn to collect photographs of other merchant families and their works.

My early collecting activities took place in the late Soviet period, when any fascination with the "big bourgeoisie" was viewed with suspicion and fraught with some risk. Things began to change in the era of "glasnost," yet it was only in the 1990s that I was able at last to begin sharing my images with the public and with professional historians. In the summer of 1991, a major photo exhibition mounted in Moscow included some six hundred of my photographs. This show, the first visual presentation in Russia of the country's entrepreneurial history since the revolution, attracted the interest not only of the general public but also of many specialists: journalists, archivists, surviving relatives of the merchants, and professional historians (including, of course, the editors of the present volume). The success of this project encouraged me to continue and expand my efforts to gather even rarer visual materials on merchant history, some of which appear in this book.

The Soviet era, with its destructive cycles of war, revolution, civil war, and Stalinist repressions, inflicted vast and irreplaceable losses on our history in terms of destroyed, lost, scattered, and confiscated visual and archival remnants of merchant culture. Today one can find in Moscow and elsewhere people bearing the most famous names of the old merchant dynasties who know of and revere their merchant ancestors yet possess little real knowledge about their heritage. Conversely, upon visiting the apartments of the most unlikely people who share my passion, I have found beautifully preserved family albums, boxes of photographs, and keepsakes that bring to life once again the visual reality of a long-concealed past. To these kind people who over the years have shared their hidden treasures with me, and now with the readers of this book, goes my deepest gratitude.

*Unless otherwise noted, all photographs in this volume
were drawn from the Zolotarev collection.*

MAPS

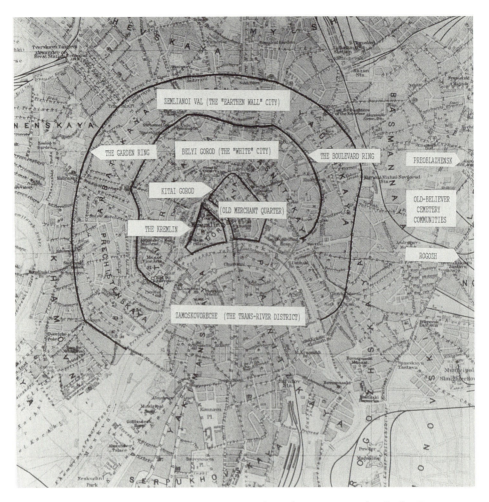

Map 1. The Concentric Medieval Structure of Merchant Moscow. The Garden Ring;
Zemlianoi Val (the "Earthen Wall" City); Belyi Gorod (the "White" City);
the Boulevard Ring; Kitai Gorod (Old Merchant Quarter); the Kremlin; and
Zamoskvoreche (the Trans-River District).
(Adapted from Baedeker's *Russia Observed* [1914].)

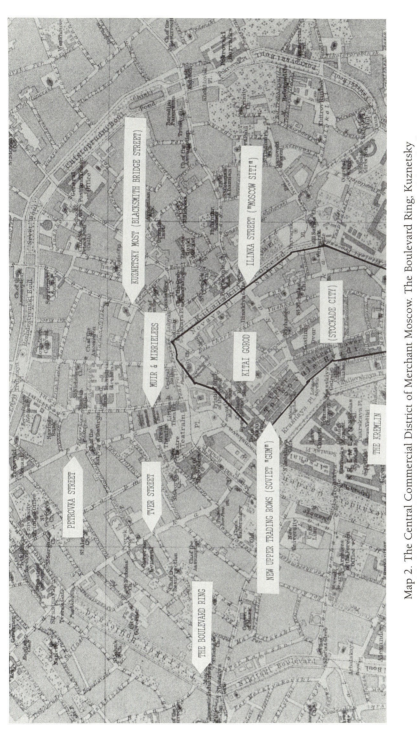

Map 2. The Central Commercial District of Merchant Moscow. The Boulevard Ring; Kuznetsky Most (Blacksmith Bridge Street); New Upper Trading Rows (Soviet "GUM"); Kitai Gorod (Stockade City); and Ilinka Street ("Moscow Siti"). (Adapted from Baedeker's *Russia Observed* [1914].)

PLATES

Plate 1. *The children of Mikhail Vasilevich Sabashnikov, May 1902.*

Plate 2. *The second wife of Pavel Riabushinsky, Elizaveta, with her children, Elizaveta and Pavel.*

Plate 3. *Maria Ilinichna Guchkova, the wife of Aleksandr Guchkov, with her children.*

Plate 4. *Olga Morozova, the daughter of Ivan Vikulovich Morozov, at the estate Odintsovo-Arkhangelskoe.*

Plate 5. *The children of Boris Dmitrievich Vostriakov, Kira and Igor.*

Plate 6. *Ivan Aleksandrovich Baranov with his daughter Elizaveta.*

Plate 7. *Rufa Mukhina, the daughter of a Moscow merchant in the flour trade, in her home on Elokhovskaia Street.*

Plate 8. *Aleksandra Mikhailovna Balashova. The prima ballerina of the Bolshoi Theater, she became the wife of Moscow merchant Ushkov.*

Plate 9. *Mariia Aleksandrovna Sorokoumovskaia* (née *Bauer in Hungary*), *wife of Nikolai Petrovich Sorokoumovsky.*

Plate 10. *Yekaterina Shchukina, the daughter of Sergei Ivanovich Shchukin.*

Plate 11. *In the home of Ilya Semenovich Ostroukhov. An elegant Edwardian lady sits beneath an ancient icon.*

Plate 12. *Arseny Abramovich Morozov and his wife, Vera Sergeevna.*

Plate 13. *Sergei Pavlovich von Derviz (Derwies) and his wife. The son of railroad magnate P. G. von Derviz, Sergei paid for the construction of the Great Hall of the Moscow Conservatory.*

Plate 14. *Pavel Buryshkin and his wife, Anna Organova.*

Plate 15. *Fedor O. Shekhtel, the architect of choice of turn-of-the-century Merchant Moscow. The entrepreneurial elite of the city coveted both his historicist and his modernist styles. His most famous buildings include the Riabushinsky Bank and the Riabushinsky Publishing House, the Yaroslav Railroad Station, and his Art Nouveau masterpiece, the home of Stepan Riabushinsky (now the Gorky Museum).*

Plate 16. *The Stepan Riabushinsky House on Malaia Nikitskaia Street, built by Fedor Shekhtel 1900–1902. In Soviet times it was the home of the writer Maxim Gorky, and today it still serves as the Gorky Museum. It is perhaps the most stunning example of the* moderne *(Art Nouveau) style in Moscow.*

Plate 17. *The house of Aleksandra Derozhinskaia, the first wife of Pavel Riabushinsky,
no. 13 Kropotkin Street. Built 1901–2, in the moderne style, by architect Fedor Shekhtel.
At present it serves as the Australian embassy.*

Plate 18. *Home of Matvei Kuznetsov, a manufacturer of porcelains and an Old Believer. Designed by architect Fedor Shekhtel, 1896. Located on First Meshchansky Street (today Prospekt Mira no. 43). The building still stands but is unrecognizably modified.*

Plate 19. *The home of Zinaida Morozova, wife of Savva Timofeevich. Neo-Gothic style, designed by architect Fedor Shekhtel, 1893. After Savva Morozov's suicide in 1905, the house was purchased by Mikhail Riabushinsky, who occupied it until the Revolution. It currently serves as a reception hall for the Ministry of Foreign Affairs.*

Plate 20. *Advertisement for the S. I. Zimin Dress and Costume Company, in the* moderne *style. "Our costumes are sewn from designs of operatic artists, and under their personal supervision."*

Plate 21. *The Brocard Perfume Company, in period sentimental style.*

Plate 22. *Advertisement for Abrikosov cocoa, Abrikosov Candy Company.*

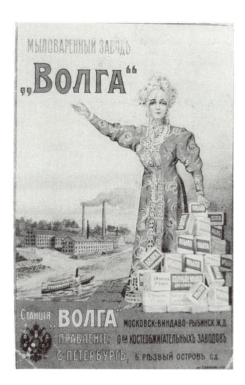

Plate 23. *"Volga" soap, showing a Muscovite princess incongruously lauding the modern factory on the Volga and its hygienic product.*

Plate 24. *Kalinkin Liquors, in the Old Russian style.*

Plate 25. *The Singer Sewing Machine Company, one of the most successful foreign enterprises in Russia.*

The Economic Engine of
Merchant Moscow—The Textile Industry

Plate 26. *The factory of Ivan Konovalov and Son Manufacturing Company, in the village of Boniachki. This four-story mill typified the textile complexes of the Moscow region. The photo shows as well the entrepreneurs' impulse to impose order and symmetry on the surrounding landscape.*

Plate 27. *The main warehouse of Ivan Konovalov and Son Manufacturing Company. This clean and orderly space belonged to one of the most profitable textile companies in Russia.*

Plate 28. *The factory grounds of the Trinity-Aleksandrovsk Textile Mill.*

Plate 29. *The spinning section of the Nikolsk Textile Mill, 1909.*

Plate 30. *The weaving section of the Prokhorov Mills.*

Plate 31. *The dyeing section of the Prokhorov Mills.*

PART ONE

From Street Fair
to Department Store:
Business Culture
and Practices

Doing Business in Merchant Moscow

Thomas C. Owen

Photographs of the central business district in Moscow under the last tsar suggest, at first glance, that European capitalist institutions—industrial corporations, banks, department stores, and commodity and stock exchanges—had become firmly rooted in the urban landscape. Moscow seemed transformed as it became the commercial and railroad hub of the Russian Empire and the center of its textile manufacturing industry, which ranked fourth in the world after that of the United States, Britain, and Germany. The proliferation of factories, the increase in the number of hired workers, the emergence of industrial cartels, and the financial involvement of the major banks in giant manufacturing corporations provided some evidence that Russian capitalism was approaching maturity on the eve of World War I. Soviet historians saw in these economic trends a justification of Lenin's allegedly "socialist" revolution of October 1917, while Western liberal historians stressed the evolution of Russian politics toward a liberal system based on the rule of law, but both groups accepted the premise of the triumph of capitalism in Russia.

These photographs from the Moscow business world at the turn of the century can be subjected to a different interpretation, however. Historians skeptical of both teleologies, the Soviet and the liberal, have recently stressed the survival of traditional cultural patterns into the industrial age and the resistance of Russians to European institutions. The most promising hypothesis now guiding social and economic historians in this field is that capitalist factories, banks, and stock exchanges came to Russia bearing many features distinctive to European civilization, so that capitalism appeared to Russians as an essentially foreign, even alien (*chuzhoi*) force. They could not ignore it because the Crimean War (1853–6) had demonstrated the need to borrow modern technology for the sake of maintaining the power of the empire in a future war; but could they adapt it to the needs of their native land without surrendering the essence of their Russian culture?

Several patterns were clear in the late tsarist period. First, corporate capitalism remained weakly developed because it evolved in a more repressive political environment on the eastern periphery of European culture than in the lands of its birth and maturation. Second, Russian companies, especially in the key sectors of railroad management and banking, depended on foreigners for success because few Russian merchants were skilled in European business practices. This need to depend on foreign expertise heightened the sense of capitalism as an essentially foreign phenomenon. Third, the difficulty of creating the new corporate elite limited the geographical proliferation of corporations in Russia, as three-quarters of all corporate headquarters were concentrated in ten cities, of which Moscow ranked second after the capital, St. Petersburg. Fourth, as a foreign entity, corporate capitalism encountered suspicion and resentment at all levels of Russian society, not least among Russian merchants, who sought to meet the potentially fatal challenge from European corporations with the aid of special favors from the autocratic state.[1] Finally, capitalist institutions succeeded best in Russia when they adapted to local realities, such as the cultural traditions of the semipeasant labor force.

The photographs suggest the difficulty of grafting European institutions onto Russian society. What at first glace seems a rapid accommodation to the universal forms of modern urban life in Moscow, from gas and electric lighting systems to department stores and banks, on closer examination turns out to be an uneasy borrowing of European institutions. That is, the Moscow merchants appropriated some outward forms of European capitalism, but they sought to do so in ways that allowed the perpetuation of their traditional ways. These included the concentration of their entrepreneurial energies in family-centered firms and the use of explicit appeals to Russian nationalism to enhance their own social prestige and to win tariff protection and financial favors from the ministries in St. Petersburg. An enlightened, self-confident, and politically liberal bourgeoisie did emerge among the Moscow merchants, but only at a very late date and in such small numbers as to undermine the notion of universal progress common to both Marxist-Leninist and liberal historiography.

By the turn of the century, handsome commercial buildings stood in the very center of Moscow. In 1888 and 1889, merchants founded corporations to build two arcades of shops opposite the Kremlin, called the Upper Trading Rows and the Middle Trading Rows.[2] The view from Red Square down Ilinka Street (Kuibyshev Street in the Soviet period) juxtaposed visual elements typical of both European and Russian culture: modern shops and an onion-domed church (figure 1.1).

By the early twentieth century, many of the negative stereotypes of the Moscow merchants in the dramas and novels of the mid-nineteenth century—their lack of education, penchant for dishonesty, cruel treatment of subordinates, and devotion to excessive eating and drinking—had faded. The most prominent merchant leaders now had a university education, supported philanthropic organizations, patronized the fine arts, and occupied high elective office in the municipal government. The portrait of Petr M. Kalashnikov, president of the Upper Trading Rows Company in the late 1880s, exemplified the striving of the Moscow merchant leaders for dignity and prestige commensurate with their financial expertise and wealth (figure 1.2).

Businesses took several forms under Russian law, ranging in complexity from single proprietorships to partnerships and giant corporations. The sign of "the manufacturer Sytov" in the Middle Trading Rows indicated that he sold brocades from his shop. As a single proprietorship, his business operated with a minimum of formality under Russian law: the purchase of an annual business certificate. The owner-manager bore personal liability for all debts of the business, which ceased to exist in the eyes of the law on his bankruptcy, retirement, or death.

Much of the crucial role of coordinating economic activity lay with unincorporated firms, called "trading firms" (*torgovye doma*), such as that of A. I. Abrikosov's Sons, which occupied the stall on the ground floor of the Upper Trading Rows across from Sytov's. Trading firms took two forms: the "full partnership" (*polnoe tovarishchestvo*), in which the owners managed the business; and the "limited partnership" (*tovarishchestvo na vere*, literally, "partnership based on trust"), in which nonmanaging investors held shares under the principle of limited liability but did not participate in the management of the firm. The managing partners in trading firms did not enjoy limited liability; in other words, the debts of the firm became their collective responsibility. Strictly speaking, any change in the composition of a trading firm—through the death or departure of a partner or the admission of a new partner—required the dissolution of the firm and the creation of a new one, but many firms kept the same name for generations as one partner replaced another.[3]

A handful of hardy trading firms survived for many decades despite the hazards of unlimited financial liability and impermanent organizational structure. Such longevity implicitly reassured customers of the acumen and trustworthiness of the firm's managers. Only a solid firm could survive amid the unfavorable financial conditions prevailing in Russia, particularly the lack of commercial credit at reasonable interest rates, the weakness of the contract law, and the danger of a contraction of the domestic market whenever a bad harvest deprived the peasantry of cash. For example, the firm of Pavel Sorokoumovsky and Sons, which specialized in the sale of fine furs, had existed since 1809 (figures 1.3–5).

Foreigners exercised great influence in the economy of the Moscow region through several small but powerful trading firms. Perhaps the most important trading firm in Moscow was that of Wogau and Company. In the half-century prior to 1914, the names of the Wogau firm's partners—Wogau (Vogau), Marc (Mark), and Bansa (Banza)—figured prominently in the lists of corporate founders and managers and on the roster of the Moscow Exchange Committee. Corporations in which the firm had an interest on the eve of World

War I included the Anchor Insurance Company, the Kolchugin Copper Company, the Moscow Electrolytic Company, and the Beloretsk Iron Company. Another German, Ludwig Knoop of Bremen, equipped over a hundred textile mills in central Russia with English machinery from the 1840s onward, and his sons, Andreas (Andrei) and Theodor (Fedor), controlled the Russian market for raw cotton and cotton textiles at the turn of the century. Wogau and Company, Ludwig Knoop and Company, and the other foreign firms in Moscow prospered not only because of their massive financial power, although they did enjoy easy access to European money markets. The key to success lay in their superior ability to unite capital, raw materials, labor, and managerial expertise in profitable combinations, especially in fields requiring knowledge of high technology imported from Europe.[4] Consequently, the business publications of the late tsarist period were filled with advertisements for foreign products (figure 1.6).

The largest capitalist institutions were, of course, corporations. Several flurries of corporate entrepreneurship in the Russian Empire—in the late 1850s, early 1870s, late 1890s, and 1908–13—created a modest network of companies: 1,354 corporations in 1905, and 2,167 (plus 262 foreign corporations authorized to operate in Russia) in 1914.[5] The Russian corporate law promulgated in 1836 stipulated the familiar structural elements of the corporation, borrowed from European practice. Large undertakings in industry, transportation, and finance required the contributions of many investors. The shareholders elected the board of directors (*pravlenie*) and, in the largest companies, a supervisory council (*sovet*). All participants enjoyed limited liability, so that, in the event of the liquidation of the enterprise, investors and managers lost only their invested capital. Shares circulated on the stock market in the exchange (*birzha*, from the French *bourse*, via the German *Börse*). Unlike the major European states, however, the tsarist government retained the principle of incorporation by concession, which required the approval of the tsar (or of the minister of finance in the case of small banks and pawnshops) instead of incorporation by registration. This restrictive system kept the numbers of corporations in Russia far lower than in Europe.

Capitalism in Moscow reflected the uneasy accommodation of traditional Russian culture to European business methods. Moscow ranked second among cities in the empire as a corporate center, with 329 in 1905 and 507 in 1914, but its corporations tended to have smaller capitalization amounts than in St. Petersburg because of the relatively simple technological requirements of textile production and the city's isolation from European capital markets. Even the largest textile companies in the central region had originated as family-owned firms and remained in the hands of a family for generations. Founders of such family-centered corporations typically set the price of shares very high—between one thousand and five thousand rubles each—to limit the circulation of shares on the open market. Indeed, the charters of such corporations often required shareholders to offer shares for sale to other shareholders before selling to outsiders. Typically, such family corporations took the name "share partnership" (*tovarishchestvo na paiakh*). In 1896, Nikolai K. Krestovnikov, one of the leading Moscow manufacturers, wrote that "the majority of our corporations retain their family character and can be considered corporate only in form; in essence they are run by individuals."[6] Had Russian corporate law contained a provision for the limited liability of managers in a partnership like the German *Gesellschaft mit beschränkter Haftung*, many family-owned companies in Moscow would probably have taken that form, but the tsarist government never authorized it.

Despite the formal distinctions in law, the line of demarcation between the trading firm and the corporation was not always clear. For example, the Abrikosov Manufacturing Company, producer of fine candies and jams, had two founders in 1880: the Abrikosov trading firm and Aleksei I. Abrikosov himself. This corporation fit the typical profile of a Moscow merchant's enterprise in light industry: a modest capitalization of five hundred thousand rubles of basic capital and shares (called *pai*) priced at one thousand rubles each to discourage circulation on the market.[7] Proof of the family-centered nature of the corporation lay in the fact that as late as 1914 two of its six managers were still members of the Abrikosov family. In this case, it was hardly possible to distinguish the trading firm from the corporation that it had engendered. Likewise, the brothers Aleksandr and Vladimir G. Sapozhnikov founded several corporations in the 1870s, but the silk and brocade enterprise bearing their name did not become incorporated until 1912. Its capitalization of 2.5 million rubles reflected the substantial growth of the enterprise as a trading firm before incorporation. As in most family-owned companies in Moscow, the shares of this company bore a high face value, five thousand rubles, which limited their circulation.[8]

The technical and entrepreneurial expertise of Europeans continued to give capitalist institutions in Moscow a distinctly foreign complexion. As the percentage of ethnic Russians among corporate managers in Moscow fell from 62.7 to 57.3 between 1905 and 1914, those of German subjects of the tsar rose from 15.4 to 17.0. Among the statistically significant ethnic groups were Jews, whose percentage rose from 4.4 to 9.1, and foreign citizens, whose role remained important despite a decline in this period from 7.5 to 4.5 percent. For example, the Siou Perfume Company, a share partnership founded and managed by Frenchmen,[9] typified the several small corporations that provided European luxury goods to wealthy Muscovites (figure 1.7).

To be sure, the very largest corporate enterprises—railroads, banks, and insurance companies—could not amass the requisite amounts of capital by appealing to a narrow circle of family members and friends. Even in Moscow, therefore, these large enterprises issued shares with a relatively low face value—between 150 and 500 rubles—to attract hundreds of investors. Typically, a low-priced share was called an *aktsiia* (from the French *action*; cf. German *Aktie*), and the corporation that issued *aktsii* generally bore the name "joint-stock company" (*aktsionernoe obshchestvo*, from the French *société par actions*).

Russian railroads, even those built by Moscow merchants and Slavophiles, required European investment capital. In 1868, the Moscow-Iaroslavl Railroad, managed by the Slavophile Fedor V. Chizhov and the merchant Ivan F. Mamontov, issued 5-percent bonds denominated in pounds sterling to ensure their sale on the exchanges of London, Berlin, and Amsterdam (figure 1.8). Almost three decades later, in 1897, this railroad, which had since reached the northern port of Archangel, floated a 4-percent bond with a face value of two thousand German marks (figure 1.9).

Despite their dependence on European expertise and their recourse to European money markets, corporate managers in Moscow felt the influence of European capitalism less than did those in St. Petersburg. The Moscow Exchange saw little trading in corporate stocks and bonds, in contrast to the St. Petersburg Exchange, which, from 1900 to 1917, operated the only real stock exchange (*fondovyi otdel birzhi*) in the Russian Empire. Banks in the two leading cities functioned differently as well. In St. Petersburg, the major banks served as informal stock exchanges. They invested their own basic capital in industrial and railroad stocks and bonds; accepted such securities as collateral for the benefit of investors who speculated on the exchange with borrowed capital; and held large packets of securities in their safe-deposit boxes. In contrast, banks in Moscow issued short-term commercial loans, primarily by discounting bills of exchange issued by wholesale commodity traders. The very name of the Moscow Discount Bank, founded in 1869, reflected this function.

The nerve center of the business elite in Moscow from 1839 onward remained the Moscow Exchange Committee (*Moskovsky birzhevoi komitet*). Composed of leading manufacturers and wholesale traders, primarily in the cotton and woolen textile industries, the committee was elected by delegates (*vybornye*) selected by merchants who traded on the exchange. The committee supervised the sale of commodities and expressed the views of the Moscow merchants to the imperial ministries on a variety of commercial-industrial issues.[10] Elections of committee members and debates on economic policy took place among delegates in the large meeting hall (figure 1.10). Brokers met to buy and sell commodities (and, to a limited extent, government securities and the stocks and bonds of a few large corporations) in an ornate main hall.

The most successful Moscow businesses combined European technology and capital with native raw materials in order to satisfy the needs of the domestic Russian market. The stock certificates of two banks founded in Moscow shortly before World War I provided fascinating visual evidence of this accommodation (figures 1.11 and 1.12).

Two members of prominent Moscow merchant families, Sergei I. Chetverikov and Aleksandr I. Konovalov, deserved the title "bourgeois" for their success in combining expert business ability in the Russian market and political liberalism, derived from their intelligent appropriation of European values. Chetverikov assumed control of the family's woolen textile business on the death of his father in 1871 and incorporated it two years later. The group portrait of the staff of the woolen mill at Gorodishche, in Bogorodsk district, Moscow province, showed the typical combination of European style, expressed in the fancy furniture and elegant clothes, and native Russian ways (figure 1.13).

Chetverikov demonstrated his entrepreneurial ability by establishing merino sheep farms in Siberia. The Vladimir Alekseev woolen textile company owned the largest herd of merino sheep in the Russian Empire, but in 1906 it lost its lease on state lands in the north Caucasus region. Chetverikov, president of the company, found a suitable site for three sheep farms in the Minusinsk region of Siberia the following year. He also bought a profitable copper mine in the foothills of the Altai mountains. These sheep farms supplied the Gorodishche and Vladimir Alekseev textile companies with Russian wool superior in quality to Australian wool. Two informal photographs documented his travels to Siberia (figures 1.14 and 1.15). When the Russian Revolution broke out, the farms contained forty-seven thousand merino sheep and five thousand sheep of mixed breeds. In October 1919, during the Civil War, shepherds abandoned the farms to the Bolshevik army, leaving the sheep to starve on snow-covered fields. In emigration, Chetverikov wrote in his memoirs: "I have reconciled myself to the loss of my fortune, the result of fifty years' activity, but the destruction of the Siberian sheep farms is a wound that I will carry, unhealed, to my grave."[11]

The Ivan Konovalov Manufacturing Company ranked thirteenth in size among 262 light industrial corporations in Moscow in 1914. The product of three generations of successful enterprise, it operated a fully modern cotton-textile complex in the village of Boniachki, near Moscow (plate 26). Like many in Moscow, the Konovalovs decorated their stores and warehouses with large, three-dimensional emblems of the imperial double-headed eagle, symbol of their strong Russian nationalism (figure 1.16).

From 1905 onward, however, the head of the company, Aleksandr I. Konovalov, bitterly castigated the tsarist government for its opposition to liberal reform. Confident in both his European education and his devotion to political and economic liberalism, Konovalov exemplified the tiny Moscow bourgeoisie. He represented the third generation of a remarkable family that had risen, like many in the textile industry, from serf origins. Photographs of his grandfather and father revealed a fascinating cultural evolution. The grandfather wore a beard with long hair parted in the middle and combed over the ears, in the typical Old Believer peasant style; the father, with a moustache and hair combed straight back, had a somewhat coarse expression that reflected his lack of education; but Aleksandr, an expert in modern textile production, expressed in his clothing and demeanor the proud self-consciousness of the liberal Moscow bourgeoisie (figure 1.17).[12] As minister of trade and industry in the Provisional Government in 1917, he simplified the system of incorporation by concession. The principle of incorporation by registration, never allowed by the tsarist regime, first appeared in the Soviet economy under the law on enterprises promulgated by Mikhail Gorbachev on June 4, 1990.[13]

NOTES

1. These themes are analyzed in detail in Thomas C. Owen, *Russian Corporate Capitalism from Peter the Great to Perestroika* (New York: Oxford University Press, 1995).

2. The charter of the Upper Trading Rows Company, confirmed on May 10, 1888, is in *Sobranie uzakonenii i rasporiazhenii pravitel'stva*, (1889), no. 466.

3. On the various forms of Russian businesses and the laws governing them, see Ivan A. Gorbachev, *Tovarishchestva . . . aktsionernye i paevye kompanii: zakon i praktika s senatskimi raz"iasneniiami* (Moscow: Pravovedenie, 1910).

4. On the Wogau firm, see Torgovyi dom Vogau i Ko., "Istoricheskii ocherk deiatel'nosti s 1840 po 1916 g." (Moscow, 1916), in "Istoriia monopolii Vogau," ed. I. F. Gindin and K. N. Tarnovskii, in A. L. Sidorov, ed., *Materialy po istorii SSSR*, 6:641–733. On Ludwig Knoop, the best source remains Gerhart von Schulze-Gävernitz, *Volkswirtschaftliche Studien aus Russland* (Leipzig: Duncker and Humblot, 1899).

5. Corporate statistics drawn from Thomas C. Owen, *RUSCORP: A Database of Corporations in the Russian Empire, 1700–1914*, rev. ed. (1992), distributed by the Inter-University Consortium for Political and Social Research, Ann Arbor, database no. 9142.

6. *Promyslovye sindikaty ili predprimatel'skie soiuzy: issledovanie prof. I. I. Ianzhula* (Moscow, 1896), p. 8.

7. Charter confirmed April 25, 1880, in *Polnoe sobranie zakonov*, series 2, no. 60843.

8. Charter confirmed February 25, 1912, in *Sobranie uzakonenii i rasporiazhenii pravitel'stva* (1912), no. 472. On this company see Chedomir M. Ioksimovich, *Manufakturnaia promyshlennost' v proshlom i nastoiashchem*, vol. 1 (Moscow: Vestnik manufakturnoi promyshlennosti, 1915), fourth pagination, pp. 1–14.

9. The five founders of this company and its four managers in 1914 all held French citizenship. *RUSCORP* database; charter confirmed December 30, 1906.

10. Moscow, Birzha, *Moskovskaia birzha 1839–1889* (Moscow: I. N. Kushnerev, 1889).

11. S. I. Chetverikov, *Bezvozvratno ushedshaia Rossiia: neskol'ko stranits iz knigi moei zhizni* (Berlin: Moskva-Logos, n.d. [1920s]), pp. 7–31, on Siberian sheep farms; on the events of 1919, see pp. 38–39.

12. Ioksimovich, *Manufakturnaia promyshlennost' v proshlom i nastoiashchem*, first pagination, pp. 95–107, gives a brief history of the company, based on jubilee volumes published in 1896 and 1912.

13. Article 6, section 3 of "Zakon SSSR o predpriiatiiakh v SSSR," *Vedomosti s"ezda narodnykh deputatov SSSR i Verkhovnogo soveta SSSR*, no. 25 (June 20, 1990), law no. 460, dated June 4, 1990, pp. 639–55; English translation in International Chamber of Commerce, *Foreign Investment in the USSR: Key 1990 Legislation* (New York: ICC Publishing, 1991), pp. 23–42.

Москва - Мoscou   Ильинка - Rue Ilinka.

Figure 1.1. *View of Ilinka Street from Red Square. The Upper Trading Rows (on the left) and the Middle Trading Rows (on the right) seemed to embody the commercial spirit of contemporary Paris. Indeed, their mansard roofs explicitly quoted the grand French style. However, the ornamental details on the buildings, motifs drawn from the time of Ivan the Terrible, expressed the Moscow merchants' devotion to their native Russian artistic traditions.*

Figure 1.2. *Petr Mikhailovich Kalashnikov, president of the board of the Upper Trading Rows in the late 1880s. He supervised the construction of the grand new commercial building on Red Square. His clothing, from the bowler hat to the striped trousers, was that of the prosperous European bourgeois. The walking stick, wire glasses, and cigarette reinforced the image of a dynamic man of business.*

Figure 1.3. *Petr Pavlovich Sorokoumovsky, head of the famous Russian fur-trading firm. The patriarch of the family posed for his portrait wearing all the clothes of a fashionable European businessman, including the bowler hat and a large watch chain. Despite his advanced age, he retained the stolid gaze of a merchant accustomed to great risk in an unincorporated family firm.*

Figure 1.4. *The retail outlet of Pavel Sorokoumovsky and Sons trading firm in Saratov. The sign emphasizes the company's unusual longevity, while the stuffed animals in the window demonstrate the firm's expertise in the sale and storage of furs. Imperial regalia lend prestige, with the proud claim "Purveyors to the Court of His Imperial Majesty." The repetition of the message in German lends a cosmopolitan character to this family-owned firm.*

Figure 1.5. *The staff of the Sorokoumovsky store in Saratov. European clothing and fine furniture, including the ubiquitous fabric over the table, testify to Western influences in business even in this provincial capital. The somewhat Asiatic features of one of the men provides a reminder of the geographical distance from Europe, however.*

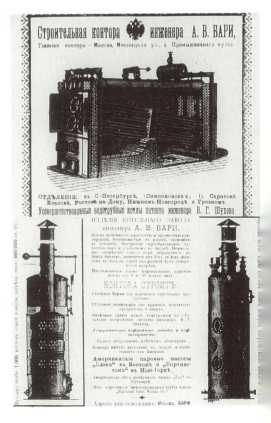

Figure 1.6. *An advertisement for the Alexander Bary (Bari) trading firm, 1897. Alexander's father, William Bary, an American Jewish merchant of Russian extraction, built a profitable machinery import firm in Moscow. Although this ad mentions steam boilers and iron buildings designed by Russians, references to New York, Boston, and Rutland, Vermont clearly imply the technical superiority of American equipment. The imperial eagle is incongruous here, for in 1910 Bari warned executives of the International Harvester Company that after thirty years' experience in Russia, he regarded the tsarist government as "absolutely unreliable."*

Figure 1.7. *Council of the Siou Perfume Company. This share partnership, founded in 1906, manufactured fine perfume and candy. The four founders were all Frenchmen: Armand, Adolphe, Charles, and Louis Siou (Siu). Other French perfume companies in Moscow were the Brocard (Brokar) and Rallet (Ralle) companies. The high price of shares of those corporations (5,000 and 750 rubles, respectively) indicated that some foreigners, like Muscovites, maintained tight familial control over their companies.*

Figure 1.8. *A bond certificate of the Moscow-Iaroslavl Railroad, 1868. Merchants and Slavophiles founded this railroad as an act of economic nationalism in 1859. The line was known as the Trinity Railroad, for it passed through Sergiev Posad, site of the Holy Trinity Monastery. The signatures of Fedor V. Chizhov, a Slavophile journalist and banker, and Ivan F. Mamontov, a Moscow merchant, symbolized the alliance of the two groups during the era of the Great Reforms. (Photo by permission of the State Historical Museum, Moscow.)*

Figure 1.9. *A bond certificate of the Moscow-Iaroslavl-Archangel Railroad, 1897. The intention of the company's management to sell its bonds in Europe was clear from the Dutch and German translations of the Russian text and the denomination in German marks, with Dutch, British, and Russian equivalents. (Photo by permission of the State Historical Museum, Moscow.)*

Figure 1.10. *Hall of meetings of the Moscow Exchange Society, 1889. A huge portrait of the reigning autocrat, Alexander III, dominated the wall behind the podium. The picture expressed the merchants' awareness that the imperial government exercised unlimited control over economic policy.*

Figure 1.11. *A stock certificate of the Moscow Bank. This firm was founded in 1911 by prominent members of the Moscow "Young Group," including the Riabushinskys and Aleksandr Konovalov. The low price per share (250 rubles) and the marginal text in French and German indicate that this bank adopted a fully European form of financial management. This became the largest of the eight banks in Moscow and the eighth in size among the forty-seven in the empire on the eve of the Great War. (Photo by permission of the State Historical Museum, Moscow.)*

Figure 1.12. *A stock certificate of the Moscow People's Bank, issued in 1912. This bank, founded in 1911 by a member of the gentry named Vladimir A. Pereleshin, provided loans to small credit institutions and cooperatives. The ornate decoration and stylized script, based on medieval Russian handwriting, boldly proclaimed the founder's devotion to historical tradition. Note the initials of the artist, Ivan Bilibin, who produced many works of art celebrating Russian folk traditions. In this certificate, these neo-Slavic artistic elements coexisted with the essential structures of a capitalist enterprise: joint-stock organization and a low share price (250 rubles). (Photo by permission of the State Historical Museum, Moscow.)*

Figure 1.13. *The staff of the Gorodishche Manufacturing Company's main warehouse on Ilinka Street. Sergei Chetverikov, director of the company, sat second from the right. The office, located in the Northern Insurance Company building in the heart of Merchant Moscow, contained numerous objects typical of European bourgeois culture, from the tasseled chair to the folding Chinese screen. The only hint of traditional Russian culture was the hairstyle of the foreman standing at the far right.*

Figure 1.14. *Moscow merchants, guests of Sergei Chetverikov, on the Yenisey river in Siberia, c. 1910. In this photograph, the merchants enjoyed a glass of tea, brewed in a traditional Russian samovar. Some signs of European culture are also unmistakable: the bowler hat, the straw hat, and at least three cameras, two on the bench and one in the hands of the photographer. (Photo from S. I. Chetverikov, Bezvozvratno ushedshaia Rossiia: neskol'ko stranits iz knigi moei zhizni [Berlin: Moskva-Logos, 1920s].)*

Figure 1.15. *Sergei I. Chetverikov, the prominent Moscow woolen textile manufacturer, on one of his Siberian sheep farms. He proudly displays a championship female merino sheep born on his farm. At the time of the Revolution, the farm contained fifty-two thousand sheep. As the Red Army approached the farm during the Russian Civil War in late 1919, the shepherds fled, leaving the untended sheep to starve in the snow. (Photo from S. I. Chetverikov, Bezvozvratno ushedshaia Rossiia: neskol'ko stranits iz knigi moei zhizni [Berlin: Moskva-Logos, 1920s].)*

Figure 1.16. *A warehouse of the Ivan Konovalov Company in Kharkov. The prominent three-dimensional emblems of the double-headed eagle, symbolic of the two gold medallions awarded to the firm by the government, expressed the pride of the owners in both company and country.*

Figure 1.17. *Aleksandr Ivanovich Konovalov, president of the board of the Ivan Konovalov Company. Educated at Moscow University and trained in textile production in Mulhouse, Alsace, he became a prominent public figure and spokesman for Moscow industrial interests in advocating sweeping liberal economic and political reforms. His family had risen in three generations from serf Old Believer origins. An expert in modern textile production, Konovalov expressed in his clothing and demeanor the proud self-consciousness of the liberal Moscow bourgeoisie. Minister of Trade and Industry in the Provisional Government, he surrendered the Winter Palace to the Bolsheviks on October 25, 1917.*

CHAPTER 2

Moscow's Commercial Mosaic

———

Irina V. Potkina

At the turn of the century, Moscow's commerce astonished visitors with its jostling profusion of forms, colors, and sounds, combining "the modern age and the age bygone." This commercial mosaic included wholesale stores and warehouses, remnants of medieval bazaars, commodity exchanges and fashionable arcades, tiny shops and modern department stores, open-air markets, and ubiquitous street vendors. Such a capricious combination imparted a unique charm to Merchant Moscow, with both the fragrance of the past and the fresh air of modernity. Yet this hybrid commercial system managed to serve the varied social strata of a sprawling urban population surprisingly well.

By the late nineteenth century, Moscow was the largest center of wholesale and retail trade in the Russian Empire, the major point of internal commodity turnover, the internal hub from which goods were carried by rail to the provinces and abroad. In terms of absolute volume of goods traded, textiles stood at the top of the list, while foodstuffs ranked second. International trade made Moscow the second most important customhouse in Russia, and through it passed a constant flow of raw materials and semifinished products, foodstuffs (mainly tea and wine), and manufactured products (mainly machinery and spare parts). Moscow's arteries of trade linked the city with the towns and factory settlements of the Central Industrial Region and the Volga Valley, and also with Central Asia, Siberia, and Transcaucasia.[1]

At the turn of the century, the city of Moscow, which was already a voracious consumer of industrial goods and agricultural products, also became the main supplier of merchandise for the eastern and southern borderlands of the country. Large Moscow-based distilleries, textile, confectionery and tobacco factories, including those of Hubner, Nosov, Guchkov, Sapozhnikov, Smirnov, Shustov, and Bostanzhoglo, shipped their products all over Eurasia. At the same time, more than seventy enterprises of the capital, most of them textile firms, traded at the Nizhny-Novgorod Fair, which operated from July 15 to September 10 each year. By the end of the nineteenth century, this ancient form of commerce had acquired the new vitality, as the fair began to operate as an exhibition ground and commodity exchange. The prices established at the fair constituted the benchmark values for the entire commercial year. So important was the fair that when it was open, financial and commercial establishments often shifted their operations entirely to its territory (figures 2.1 and 2.2). It was also there that the Moscow merchants carried out their largest annual transactions, thus confirming the centrality of the fair in the business life of the Moscow region.

Despite the continued importance of Nizhny-Novgorod, the forces of business modernization pressed for the introduction of new and more promising forms of trade, such as the permanent retail shop. As a rule, Moscow businessmen preferred to have their own stores in the capital, as well as in other towns of the empire, in order to trade their products independently of the fairs (figures 2.3 and 2.4). The tendency to open retail shops where goods were sold at factory list prices became predominant in the last third of the nineteenth century. Among the pioneers of such new forms of merchandising were Moscow industrialist families like the Alekseevs, the Morozovs, and the Tretiakovs, all of whom owned several retail outlets apiece.[2]

In period of the Great Reforms in the 1860s and 1870s, the proliferation of commercial establishments in Moscow was remarkable; it was accompanied by pivotal changes in the geography of urban trade that finally took definitive shape by the turn of the century. The construction of railroads linking the capital with the major economic regions of the country contributed to the expansion of wholesale trade. In this respect, the western, northern, and eastern suburbs were the leading venues. By the end of the century, siting of open-air markets had been completed: wholesale trade in meat, grain, and firewood had shifted from north of the Moscow River to the vicinity of the railway stations. Thus, for example, in the northwest of Moscow, close to the Brest railroad line, there was a concentration of wholesale and retail trade enterprises dealing in timber materials and firewood.[3]

The geography of retailing underwent considerable change from the socioeconomic point of view as well. Large retail stores of wealthy Russian and foreign merchants concentrated in Kitai Gorod ("Stockade City") and Bely Gorod ("White City"), the ancient central districts close to the Kremlin (see map 1). The downtown district witnessed a proliferation of imposing and expensive department stores marketing a variety of top-quality merchandise for a wealthy clientele.

At the same time, there emerged new peripheral centers of commerce. In the last decades of the nineteenth century, retail trade was developing at an especially high rate on the outskirts of Moscow—in Zamoskvoreche ("The Trans-River District") across the river from the Kremlin, and outside Zemlianoi Gorod ("The Earthen-Wall City") (see map 1). Commercial networks both expanded and moved closer to the mass customer, especially to the lower strata of urban population, the majority of whom consisted of villagers who had recently settled mainly in the outlying districts (figure 2.5). The social importance of these changes meant that in the center of Moscow, commerce was concentrated in the hands of affluent traders, mostly from the merchant estate, while on the periphery peasant shopkeepers predominated.[4]

According to the data of the city authorities, there were 1,175 large, 7,000 medium-sized, and 7,000 small commercial enterprises in Moscow in 1910. More than one quarter of these were situated in the central districts, that is, within the bounds of the Boulevard Ring (the old "Belyi Gorod" ring), approximately half of them inside the Garden Ring (the old "Earthen Wall"). The size of a commercial establishment was determined mainly by the number of salesmen it employed. From this point of view, the chief laurels were in the hands of stores located in the center and in Zamoskvoreche. As far as profits were concerned, the center ranked first by far; next came Zamoskvoreche, and the small shops in the suburbs followed.[5]

A heated competition between the luxurious department store emporium and the old-fashioned small shop in the downtown district resulted in the gradual eviction of the latter from the center. A contemporary wrote in 1912:

> The commercial streets of Moscow have greatly changed in recent years thanks to the emergence of new types of shops and stores. In place of the modest small shops, which do not try to attract the customer with luxury and elegance, splendid stores are appearing with entire walls covered with mirrors, with refined displays and stately and decorous arrangements. . . . Stores dominate in the central streets of Moscow: they fill Kuznetsky Most, Tverskaia, Petrovka [streets]. The more remote parts of the city are still the realm of the small shop.[6]

These changes signaled the victory of modern, impersonal commercial organizations over the more traditional personal forms.

The reconstruction of the ancient Trading Rows on Red Square in 1886–93 symbolized the scope of this victory. Medieval Muscovite markets had been organized in long rows of stalls, each dedicated to a specific commodity: Hunter's Row, Cloth Row, Icon Row, Saddle Row, Pot Row, and so on. The corner of Nikolskaia Street and Red Square (figure 2.6) was still a jumble of stores and shops in the mid-nineteenth century. Although these were all swept away by the construction of the largest commercial edifice in the city, the New Upper Trading Rows (figure 2.7; see map 2). This new structure, the "GUM" of Soviet times, retained the linear spirit of those ancient bazaars: the design, executed in the pseudo-Russian style by the architect A. N. Pomerantsev, replicated in architectonic form the ancient lines of stalls of Muscovite times. Yet at the same time the structure mimicked the shape of elegant European arcades (see figure 10.4, in the Brumfield essay). The new complex housed retail shops of prominent Moscow firms including those of the Abrikosov candy company, Prokhorov's Trimont textile firm, the Popov brothers, Brocard, Rallet, Sorokoumovsky, and many others. The building was owned by the joint-stock company Upper Trading Rows, with capital of 9.4 million rubles. In 1913, net profit from the lease of shop premises reached 586,000 rubles, and dividend per share was 4 percent.[7] An adjacent complex, the Middle Trading Rows, was situated opposite Saint Basil's Cathedral on Red Square. Built at the end of the nineteenth century according to the design of the prominent Moscow architect Roman Klein, the Middle Rows were used for wholesale trade in bulk commodities.

Other arcades were also built in the center of Moscow in the 1870s and 1880s on Tverskaia, Lubianka, and Petrovka streets. As early as 1874, the wealthiest merchants moved from the Old Trading Rows on Red Square to the new, more comfortable Warm Rows of A. Porokhovshchikov. This company paid the highest return on investment of all lessors of shop premises in Moscow. In 1878, a splendid set of arcades, including shops, hotels, and apartments, was opened on Petrovka Street; built by the architect Sheltsov, the building belonged to the Petrovka Trading Rows company, under the chairmanship of V. I. Iakunchikov, a well-known and colorful representative of the Moscow merchants.

Construction of new arcades also took place on the most elegant street in Moscow, Kuznetsky Most (Blacksmith's Bridge Street), a short two-block street that boasted the greatest concentration of luxury establishments in Russia (figure 2.8; see map 2). This is how it was remembered by one contemporary: "The broad sidewalks are full of animated crowds scurrying about, splendid shop windows shine with the luxuriance and beauty of their displays, elegant coaches and automobiles rush by."[8] Fashionable foreign stores had been situated here since Pushkin's day, and there they remained until 1918. The Italian firm I. and D. Daziaro traded in works of art, the German company Brothers A. and Ia. Allschwang (figure 2.9) in dry goods and lingerie, while Avanzo and Co. from Italy, immortalized by commercial verse of the young poet Vladimir Maiakovsky, sold paints. In the second half of the nineteenth century, at the urging of Slavophiles who resented the high concentration of foreign stores in the center of the city, Russian merchants also came to Kuznetsky Most. At the end of the century, the Russian entrepreneurs Popov, Solodovnikov, and Aleksandrovsky challenged foreigners by building arcades of their own in this quarter.

The most impressive foreign presence in Moscow was also the largest department store in Russia: Muir and Mirrielees. This fashionable English emporium dated from the middle of the nineteenth century, and through the efforts of its British founders, Archibald Mirrielees and Walter Phillip, it managed to grow into a mighty commercial empire, which included eighty departments, a furniture factory, and a printing house. The stock capital of the company amounted to three million rubles; profits exceeded one million rubles annually, and dividends reached 15 percent. At its inception the store was situated on Kuznetsky Most in the house of Prince Gagarin (figure 2.10), but in 1908, after a fire in the old premises, the architect R. I. Klein completed a superb neo-Gothic edifice for this famous firm at the corner of Theater Square, adjacent to the Bolshoi Theater (see figure 10.9, in the Brumfield essay).[9]

Despite the entrenched position of the foreign tradesmen and their considerable contributions to Moscow commerce, the major role was always played by native Russian merchants. By the end of the nineteenth century, two-thirds of purely commercial enterprises, selling haberdashery and manufactured goods, foodstuffs, and construction materials, were in local hands.[10]

At the turn of the century new commodities exchanges also sprang to life, though their share in wholesale trade remained modest up to the Revolution. This progressive form of trade experienced considerable difficulty in gaining the confidence of the merchants. In spite of the fact that the first decree authorizing the Moscow Exchange was issued by the government as early as 1789, its activity became significant and permanent only after 1837. This exchange functioned as a general clearinghouse for trade in cotton, cotton cloth, and wool. By the end of the nineteenth century, three specialized exchanges— corn, cattle and meat, and foodstuffs and wine—had commenced operations. In the early twentieth century, the Moscow Exchange Society, which regulated commodity trading, was assisted by its in-house textile and cotton committees, the commission on timber industry, and the railroad committee, all of which worked on a permanent basis. These committees played an important role in supplying raw materials to industrial enterprises in Moscow and the Central Industrial Region.

Despite the advent of modern forms of commerce, Moscow managed to preserve its unique traditional appearance into the twentieth century, thanks to several noisy old-fashioned fairs held in city squares. Open-air market trade never lost the flavor of the bazaars of ancient times. According to a contemporary, these markets perpetuated "the intrinsic Russian commercial tradition of enormous overcharging and infinite discounting. The experienced buyer can force the seller to reduce the initial price by two-thirds or three-quarters."[11] Street fairs also preserved the tempo and rhythm of an earlier age in their traditional market days and the seasonal character of their trade. This was the realm of the peasant who came to the city to sell his products and of the buyer of modest means who could find everything he needed at reasonable prices. At the turn of the century, the Moscow open-air markets were still important sites of retail trade (figure 2.11).

The municipal authorities paid particular attention to this form of commerce, for it involved a wide stratum of the population. In 1875, the municipal Duma built a two-story edifice for trade in foodstuffs on Smolensk Square. But the building turned out to be too small for the purpose, and bustling trade soon spilled out into the streets once again.[12]

Two annual fairs were held in the very heart of Moscow from ancient times until the early twentieth century. The Mushroom Market, held on in the first week of Lent, stretched along the walls of the Kremlin to the Moscow River below Red Square. As a rule, housewives from the middle and poor classes shopped there for Lenten food. The Palm Sunday bazaar, with its joyful festivities and imaginative toys with colorful names—"American Devils," "fluttering butterflies," and "mother-in-law's tongues"—filled Red Square itself on the Saturday before Easter (figure 2.12).[13]

Street hawking was another colorful traditional feature of Merchant Moscow. The picturesque figures of venders with metal badges and portable trays shouting their singsong calls "Good oranges and lemons!" or bearing gigantic watermelons on their heads were a ubiquitous sight in the city (figure 2.13). The number of hawkers sometimes surpassed six thousand.[14] At the end of the nineteenth century, the authorities moved to curb this spontaneous but unruly street trade by limiting the number of vendors in various parts of the city. Yet according to one contemporary, this form of commerce persisted because it represented a typical manifestation of the Muscovite character:

> The abundance of various street vendors on each Moscow street also explains a certain recklessness on the part of the Muscovites who cannot plan their housekeeping properly. Lemons, oranges, apples, cigarettes, shoelaces and polish, postcards, glasses, socks, stockings, and handkerchiefs are briskly sold in the streets by lively vendors, though the same goods can be bought with equal ease at the same price in any neighboring shop. "You have to go inside,"—the lazy shopper thinks to himself—"but I can buy the same things here in the street."[15]

Russian shoppers usually carried special bags in their pockets, called an "avoska" ("just-in-case"), for just such serendipitous purchases in the street.

The system of commercial establishments in Moscow as it had emerged by the early twentieth century was adapted to the needs of every stratum of the social hierarchy. It took careful account of the customs and habits of the Orthodox population. Department stores timed their sales for Christmas, and open-air markets followed suit, offering specialty foods for festive meals. Similar ardor was demonstrated by Moscow traders in their preparations for Easter. The shops of the renowned baker D. I. Filippov stocked great quantities of "paskha," Easter cakes, "Warsaw babas," "mazureks," and "Konigsberg marzipans." The company of the Blandov Brothers organized large-scale sales of specialty food products where Muscovites could choose either "Caucasian cheese, cured with a tear" or "sausage from our own factory, made of the best fresh meat." Holiday preparations absorbed everybody without exception. The French company Pathé Brothers company advised its customers to embellish festive celebrations with music, singing, and orations of famous performers, insistently advertising its gramophone records to accomplish this end. After Easter, commerce subsided, and peasants switched to trade in more prosaic edibles: dried and pickled mushrooms, soaked apples, and forest berries. Food shops also adjusted their range of goods to postholiday needs.

To complete the picture of commerce in Merchant Moscow, a few words must be said about the advertisements that dressed the capital in new and fanciful attire. By the turn of the century a multitude of written and painted signs, and display windows decorated with artistic commercial posters adorned (some might say cluttered) the city. The vibrancy of commercial trade at this time is evidenced by this explosive proliferation of signs (figure 2.14). Fixed signs were augmented by the "tableaux vivants," sign-carriers who walked the streets singing original verses imitating familiar popular ditties and doing their best to attract the gullible customer. By the turn of the century the main forms of commercial advertising had become strictly differentiated. Artistically illustrated price lists were issued by all the well-known firms (figure 2.15). Advertising in magazines and newspapers also became commonplace after the 1870s; Moscow dailies often devoted their entire front page, and others inside, to commercial pictures and messages. Advertisements in periodicals reached the largest audience of all prerevolutionary forms of advertising.

Each commercial genre had its own artistic canons and stylistic principles. From this point of view, the commercial poster is particularly interesting (see plates 21–25). Unknown Russian designers of the early twentieth century (practically all posters were anonymous) worked in a wide range of different styles—Art Nouveau, folk art, Chinoiserie and Arabesque forms, and so forth—corresponding either to the origin of the product or whatever exotic association the advertiser wished to conjure up in the buyer's mind. Moscow had dozens of workshops specializing in sign painting and posters of high polygraphic quality.

Newspaper advertising spawned a new industry of its own: the ad agency. The oldest of these was L. and E. Metzl and Co., founded in 1878. Competitors soon proliferated, and by the turn of the century some thirty such agencies operated in Moscow, each vying to place its ads in the most eye-catching places (figure 2.16). This account would not be complete without a word about another interesting phenomenon, the poetic advertisement. The famous Soviet poet Vladimir Maiakovsky got his start in this genre, but many anonymous poets had tried their luck in the same field long before him. They left a whole literature of advertisements-in-verse, often imitating the poetry of Pushkin or Lermontov or popular Russian ballads of the nineteenth century.

Despite a commercial culture rapidly acquiring a European face, Merchant Moscow succeeded in maintaining its innately Russian character, manifested not only in the survival of ancient forms of trade but also in its correspondence to the lifestyle and mentality of the Russians of that day.

NOTES

1. *Istoriia Moskvy*, vol. 4 (Moscow, 1954), pp. 189–90, 200.

2. "Mozhno-li v Moskve torgovat' chestno?" in *Sovremennye zametki* (Moscow, 1896), p. 17; *Istoriia Moskvy*, vol. 4, p. 169.

3. *Istoriia Moskvy*, vol. 4, p. 176.

4. *Torgovo-promyshlennye zavedeniia g. Moskvy v 1885–1890 gg.* (Moscow, 1892), p. 16.

5. *Sovremennoe khoziaistvo g. Moskvy* (Moscow, 1913), pp. 20–21.

6. G. Vasilich, "Ulitsy i liudi sovremennoi Moskvy," in *Moskva v ee proshlom i nastoiashchem*, vol. 10 (Moscow, 1912), p. 6.

7. *Sbornik svedenii o deistvuiushchikh v Rossii aktsionernykh obshchestvakh i tovarishchestvakh na paiakh* (St. Petersburg, 1914), pp. 272–73.

8. *Po Moskve* (reprinted edition of M. and S. Sabashnikov's publication, Moscow, 1991), p. 232.

9. *Sbornik svedenii o deistvuiushchikh v Rossii aktsionernykh obshchestvakh i tovarishchestvakh na paiakh*, pp. 252–53.

10. *Istoriia Moskvy*, vol. 4, p. 170. See also *Torgovo-promyshlennye zavedeniia g. Moskvy v 1885–1890 gg.*, pp. 52.

11. Vasilich, "Ulitsy i liudi sovremennoi Moskvy," p. 8.

12. P. V. Sytin, *Iz istorii moskovskikh ulits. Ochreki* (Moscow, 1958), p. 473.

13. G. Vasilich. "Moskva 1850–1910," in *Moskva v ee proshlom i nastoiashchem*, vol. 11 (Moscow, 1912), p. 21; I. A. Slonov, *Iz zhizni torgovoi Moskvy. Polveka nazad* (Moscow, 1914), p. 191.

14. *Istoriia Moskvy*, vol. 4, p. 184.

15. Vasilich, "Ulitsy i liudi sovremennoi Moskvy," p. 10.

Нижній-Новгородъ.—Nijni-Novgorod. № 67.
Видъ изъ Кремля на торговые ряды и городъ.

Figure 2.1. *Nizhny-Novgorod, view from the Kremlin: rows of shops and the city. The famous fair took place across the Volga, around the large church in the distance.*

Figure 2.2. *Rows of shops of the Nizhny-Novgorod Fair. In the foreground: the fairground outlet of the Moscow textile firm Ivan Konovalov and Son.*

Figure 2.3. *Retail shop of the textile manufacturer Emile Zindel (Tsindel).*

Figure 2.4. *Shop of the tea merchants Perlov on Miasnitskaia Street. The facade and interior were decorated in the pseudo-Chinese style in 1896 by R. I. Klein and K. K. Gippius to commemorate the visit of the Chinese Regent Lu Hung Chang, who attended the coronation ceremonies of Nicholas II.*

Figure 2.5. *Typical Old Moscow commercial architecture. A "beer bar" stands on the corner to slake shoppers' thirst.*

Figure 2.6. *Nikolskaia Street from Red Square. Old Upper Trade Rows (before the reconstruction).*

Figure 2.7. *New Upper Trading Rows. In the foreground: the monument to Minin and Pozharsky (now located in front of St. Basil's Cathedral), the merchant and the prince who raised an army to save Moscow from the Poles during the Time of Troubles.*

Figure 2.8. *The fashionable shopping street of Kuznetsky Most (Blacksmith Bridge Street) in the late nineteenth century.*

Figure 2.9. *Salon of Allschwang Brothers on Petrovka Street.*

Figure 2.10. *Muir and Mirrielees department store (main entrance of the original building).*

Figure 2.11. *The Easter Eve Fair at the Sukharev Tower, April 16, 1905.*

Figure 2.12. *Palm Sunday Bazaar on Red Square, complete with toys and balloons.*

Figure 2.13. *Peddler of toys. His cap is fitted with a special plate for carrying a hawker's tray.*

Figure 2.14. *Shop signs on Okhotny Riad (Hunter's Row) Street.*

Figure 2.15. *Illustration for a price list of the commercial firm of P. Sorokoumovsky, which specialized in furs. The dress and headgear are of ermine. (See figures 1.3 and 1.4, in the Owen essay.)*

Москва - Moscou   Маросейка - Rue Marosseyka.

Figure 2.16. *Streetcar advertisement for Shustov brandy. The exclusive right to place advertisements on streetcars in Moscow belonged to the ad agency Anounce (Announcement).*

CHAPTER 3

"Moscow City": Financial Citadel
of Merchant Moscow

Iurii A. Petrov

There is a street in the Russian capital that was commonly known before the Revolution by an English-sounding name: "Moskva Siti" (Moscow City). During the Soviet period, it bore the name of the Bolshevik Valerian Kuibyshev. Only in 1991 was its authentic name—Ilinka—returned. Stretched between Red Square and New Square, it truly deserved comparison with its namesake, "The City of London," England's financial heart, or with Wall Street in New York (see map 2). The imposing and eminently respectable buildings that still adorn Ilinka were once occupied by large commercial banks, with the Moscow Exchange at the street's beginning just off Red Square (figure 3.1). If St. Petersburg was the window through which foreign capital flowed into Russia, Moscow was the principal financial center of the heartland.

Scores of banks, including both local commercial institutions and branch offices of St. Petersburg firms, societies of mutual credit, mortgage banks, and private banking houses, all operated here. There was enough business to support all these institutions in the sprawling economic network that was Moscow in the early twentieth century. As one turn-of-the-century guidebook testified: "Moscow is the owner of colossal free capital, which feeds banking operations and creates immense financial reserves; it possesses enormous savings invested, with the help of the banks, in stocks and bonds and has extended links with all the provinces. In other words, in the world of banking, commercial and industrial, Moscow plays a role of absolutely exceptional importance."[1]

Modern financial structures typical of the epoch of industrialization emerged later in Moscow than in other European capitals: a network of private banking establishments came into being only in the late 1860s. Upon embarking upon the course of economic modernization after the Crimean War of 1853–56, the state allowed private initiative into the sphere of credit, an area that had previously been dominated by governmental institutions, first among them the State Bank. This centralized financial system could no longer keep up with the burgeoning demand for financial resources fueled by the expanding industrial economy.

In 1864, the first corporate commercial bank, the Petersburg Private Bank, was opened, followed two years later by its counterpart in Moscow, the Merchant Bank established by Vasily Kokorev, a wealthy vodka magnate and Slavophile merchant (figure 3.2). Kokorev managed to attract to his venture a group of cotton textile manufacturers, representatives of the most important branch of Moscow industry, including Timofei S. Morozov, Ivan A. Liamin, and others. These men sought to create "an establishment promoting industry and trade." Ivan K. Babst, a professor of economics, was invited to take the post of chairman of the board.

The example of the Merchant Bank encouraged emulation, and soon competing institutions began to spring up by the dozen. A typical feature of banking in Moscow was the predominance of industrialists on the city's bank boards, as opposed to the professional financiers who peopled the boards of St. Petersburg banks. The profession of banker, associated as it was with usury in the popular mind, was not highly esteemed even in the business circles of Merchant Moscow. Each of the three "Old Moscow" banks founded in this period was headed by a group of businessmen active in trade and industry. The Merchant Bank was controlled by textile families such as the Morozovs, Liamins, Knoops, Krestovnikovs, and others. The Trade Bank belonged to the Naidenov clan, whose head, Nikolai Naidenov, chaired the main organization of Moscow industrialists, the Moscow Exchange Committee, for almost three decades (figure 3.3). The Discount Bank was established by "Moscow Germans," as German-born entrepreneurs in such trading houses as L. Knoop, and Wogau and Co. were known in Russia (figure 3.4). Each of the Old Moscow banks concentrated the authority of their owners in their governing boards, while day-to-day affairs were delegated to hired professional directors who were experienced in the field of finance, but were not independently wealthy.

In the late 1860s, other more speculative financial companies came into being, initiated by "the aristocratic set and rodents from officialdom," as Merchant Moscow disdainfully called representatives of the aristocracy and bureaucracy in its midst. At that time banking was in its formative years in Russia, and these immature enterprises, not yet securely anchored in the textile industry, faced numerous dangers. In 1875, "Moscow City" was stunned by the news of the first major bank failure in Russian history when the Moscow Commercial Loan Bank went bankrupt, going under with reserves of three million rubles, and thirteen million rubles in private deposits. Through the fault of dishonest directors of the board, the bank became entangled with the financial machinations of the German railroad magnate Henry Strussberg, from whom it had received various securities for credits in amounts vastly exceeding deposits. After losses mounted to more than seven million rubles, the bank had to suspend operations. The bankruptcy was accompanied by a well-publicized trial that taught everyone a lesson. The "old" banks became increasingly oriented toward the British system of merchant banks, avoiding risky speculative operations characteristic of the French and German commercial banks (*banques d'affairs*)

A keen observer of the world of Moscow finance, Vladimir Riabushinsky, himself a director of his family's own commercial bank, wrote:

> The native Moscow banks were very specific and differed significantly from Petersburg ones: their major goal was solidity. . . . Moscow traditions implied the rejection of the speculative establishment of new enterprises, in which Petersburg banks were so active. The risk of such a policy was an excessively close dependence of the bank's destiny on that of the establishments patronized by it. Moscow was afraid of this.[2]

Such solidity and caution in business, so typical of traditional Moscow merchants, were interpreted by contemporaries, and later by Soviet historians, as signs of conservatism and backwardness when compared to the more aggressive Petersburg banks, oriented to the model of the German *Grossbanken*.[3] The majority of Moscow banks preferred straightforward financial and commercial operations rather than speculative investments, reflecting the business interests and mores of their owners: big industrialists whose enterprises had been created by the cumulative efforts of several generations. Personally rich, with fortunes of several million rubles each, they had enormous private capital at their disposal, and were in a position to invest large sums of money in the enterprises that interested them. They thus did not need to court outside financial support or resort to the speculative techniques of the Petersburg banks.

Moscow millionaires also needed local financial establishments that could extend regular credit to existing companies. Most Moscow firms had been established by one family whose power had remained intact even when the enterprise was turned into a corporation (see the Owen essay). The working capital of such corporations, known in Russia as share partnerships, was formed from reinvested profits, and the sale of shares was restricted to a narrow circle of relatives. In the early twentieth century, the chairman of the board of Merchant Bank and (after 1905) the head of the Moscow Exchange Committee, Grigory A. Krestovnikov (figure 3.5), wrote about this specific feature of business life in the ancient capital: "In Moscow and Central Russia, the most solid and well-organized establishments are concentrated in the hands of tightly knit circles absolutely uninterested in gambling with their shares on the Exchange."[4] And, in fact, there was practically no trading in shares of the leading Moscow companies on the Stock Exchange.

When it came to securing an important credit for local business operations, however, the Moscow banks were always welcome collaborators. This intimate relationship further cemented the growing alliance between banking and industry in Moscow. The banks functioned as the financial citadels of Merchant Moscow, successfully defending the position of local companies against all outside competitors. Moscow entrepreneurs positioned "their" banks to resist the penetration of Petersburg financial magnates into the cotton textile industry. At the same time, in-house financial institutions helped the Muscovites assure the flow of raw materials, predominately cotton, which came from the American South as well as from Russian Central Asia, where cotton plantations proliferated at the turn of the century.

In the early twentieth century, an aggressive new financial force appeared in Moscow: the Riabushinsky group (figures 3.6 and 3.7; and see the West essay). In 1912 they founded the corporate Moscow Bank with capital of twenty million rubles. As if to announce their modernity, they commissioned their headquarters building to be built on Exchange Square, off Ilinka street, by the architect Fedor Shekhtel in the contemporary style of the German Werkbund (figure 3.8). These energetic representatives of the new generation of entrepreneurs were satisfied neither with the seemingly archaic and conservative banking activity of the Old Moscow banks nor with the speculative tactics of the Petersburg bankers. Under the nationalist slogan "Unification of National Capital," the Riabushinsky bank emerged as an influential force that its owners hoped to use as a "promoter of healthy enterprises."[5] The bank was to play the role of a financial lever by which the Riabushinskys pried open the traditional limits of Moscow business. Their sphere of influence expanded from cotton textiles to include flax production and export, and various industrial companies (lumber, paper, glass, printing, and publishing), as well as a number of financial corporations. During the Great War, the Riabushinskys pioneered the construction in Moscow of the first Russian motor vehicle factory and made plans to construct an aircraft plant as well.

By virtue of their entrepreneurial success and financial sophistication, the Riabushinskys can be justifiably compared with the most prominent Western entrepreneurs of the time. Three generations of Riabushinskys had passed from peasants to magnates of industry and finance of European stature. This activist entrepreneurial family was convinced that only private initiative could propel the Russian economy "to develop its productive forces and take the path to national prosperity and wealth."[6] Claiming leadership of Merchant Moscow both in entrepreneurship and in politics as well, the Riabushinskys urged their fellow businessmen to exert every effort for the larger national interest of Russia. In contrast to the "cosmopolitan" Petersburg bankers, the Riabushinskys viewed the banks not as mere profit-making enterprises but first and foremost as financial instruments in the struggle to secure the economic prosperity of the country as a whole.

There were also bankers in Moscow who showed little interest in mixing Great Russian patriotism with business. Perhaps the most breathtaking career was made by the son of a poor artisan, Lazar Poliakov, who richly deserved his nickname of "the Russian Rothschild" (figure 3.9). "This name became famous among the whole Jewish population of the Pale," said one Moscow rabbi at the banker's funeral on the eve of the First World War, "and blessing their children before their wedding ceremony, our less fortunate brothers say: 'May God make you like Poliakov.'"[7]

This successful financier owned several banks, the largest of which, the Moscow International Trade Bank, occupied an imposing edifice on the elegant shopping street Kuznetsky Most. The secret of Poliakov's success lay in his speculation on the Stock Exchange, for his links with the tight ethnic Russian oligarchy ruling the affairs of Merchant Moscow were understandably rather weak. His string of spectacular financial triumphs came to an end with the economic crisis of the early twentieth century. Poliakov managed to evade formal bankruptcy owing to the timely support of the government, which feared that the collapse of his speculative empire would set off a chain reaction in the world of finance and trade.

In 1909, Poliakov's banks, with the assistance from the Ministry of Finance, were consolidated into the United Bank, headed by the scion of one of the aristocratic families, Count Vladimir S. Tatishchev (figure 3.10). This aristocrat-banker managed to overcome the cultural bias of the Russian nobility against business, and reaped a healthy profit as a result. The Count succeeded in turning his bank into one of the most prosperous financial institutions in Russia. The United Bank boldly entered the European financial arena with the help of its French partner, Banque de l'Union Parisienne, which exhibited great interest in "Russian affairs" in the beginning of the twentieth century. Contacts were established with other French financial groups as well, and on the eve of the Great War, the United Bank opened a branch office in Paris.

This expansion of banks with European partners and the growing integration of Russian banks into the international financial community were exemplified by two corporations founded before the Great War: the commercial bank J. W. Junker and Co., and the Private Bank, reorganized from the Moscow branch of a Petersburg firm. The proprietors of the Junker Bank, like the leaders of the Discount Bank, belonged to the influential group of "Moscow Germans." They kept in close touch with European, mainly German, partners and acted as experts on Russian corporations for German clients. The Deutsche Bank in particular was actively attempting to penetrate the Russian market in the early twentieth century. Its operatives regularly turned to Junker and Co. for information, unofficially referring to its management as "our friends in Moscow." Within the Moscow Private Bank there emerged a block of Petersburg-based founders, headed by the chairman of Petersburg Private Bank, Aleksei A. Davidov, a Moscow group that included the mayor of

Moscow, Nikolai I. Guchkov (figure 3.11), a member of an influential merchant family, as well as representatives of firms owned by ethnic Germans.

The financial establishment of Merchant Moscow was thus an expansive and variegated group on the eve of the First World War. It included representatives of Russian "national" capital, like the Riabushinskys, successful Jewish banking families like the Poliakovs, and businessmen of foreign origin working in Russia, like the "Moscow Germans." The economic power and the level of professionalism of this financial oligarchy compares favorably with Western business elites of that epoch. The interval of time between the emancipation of the serfs in 1861 and the Revolution of 1917 was little more than fifty years. Yet despite the brevity of the historical space granted Russia to develop indigenous capitalist institutions, the country managed to cover an immense distance along the road toward a private and open business culture. This experiment in freedom and modernity was brought to a abrupt end amid the chaos of a disastrous war, when a wave of anticapitalist resentment swept the Bolsheviks to power.

The disruptions of the Revolution and the Civil War doomed the private banking system of Merchant Moscow to ruin and extinction. In December 1917, the Soviet government decreed the nationalization of all banks. Businessmen and directors were arrested and dispersed, operations halted, and funds seized. The bank buildings themselves, being among the most stately edifices in Moscow, were soon occupied by various state and party organizations. The Central Committee of the Communist Party and the Ministry of Finance occupied former bank buildings on Ilinka Street, and the once-vibrant private entrepreneurial and banking culture of Moscow faded from memory for more than seventy years.

NOTES

1. *Putevoditel' po Moskve i ee okrestnostiam* (Moscow, 1913), p. 237.

2. Vladimir P. Riabushinsky, "Kupechestvo moskovskoe," *Den' russkogo rebionka* (April 1951): 179.

3. I. F. Gindin, "Moskovskie banki v period imperializma," *Istoricheskie zapiski* 58 (1956): 38–106.

4. Tsentral'nyi Gosudarstvennyi Istori che-

sky arkhiv g. Moskvy, f. 143, op. 1, d. 261, 1. 44–45.

5. Mikhail P. Riabushinsky, "Tsel' nashei raboty," in *Materialy po istorii SSSR*, vol. 6: *Dokumenty po istorii monopolisticheskogo kapitalizma v Rossii* (Moscow, 1959), pp. 610–11.

6. Ibid., p. 632.

7. Ia. I. Maze, *Slovo u groba L. S. Poliakova* (Moscow, 1914).

Figure 3.1. *The heart of "Moscow City": the financial district on Ilinka Street in the 1880s. At left, the headquarters of the Moscow Trade Bank.*

Figure 3.2. *Vasily Aleksandrovich Kokorev, vodka maker, early advocate of emancipation of the serfs, and ally of the Slavophiles.*

Figure 3.3. *Nikolai Aleksandrovich Naidenov, old-guard chairman of the Moscow Exchange Society from 1877 until his death in 1905. He was a leading investor in and manager of the Moscow Trade Bank.*

Figure 3.4. *Feodor Lvovich Knoop,*
a leading figure among the
"Moscow Germans."

Figure 3.5. *Grigory*
Aleksandrovich Krestovnikov,
chairman of the Moscow
Exchange Society after 1905
and a leading figure in the
Moscow Merchant Bank.

Figure 3.6. *Pavel Pavlovich Riabushinsky, perhaps the most visible figure among the last generation of Merchant Moscow entrepreneurs.*

Figure 3.7. *Mikhail Pavlovich Riabushinsky, the banker of the Riabushinsky clan, most actively engaged in directing the family's Moscow Bank.*

Figure 3.8. *The headquarters of the Riabushinsky Bank on Exchange Square, just off Ilinka street. Designed by the architect Shekhtel.*

Figure 3.9. *Lazar Solomonovich Poliakov, known as the "Russian Rothschild," who founded the ill-fated Moscow International Trade Bank.*

Figure 3.10. *Count Vladimir Sergeevich Tatishchev, the aristocratic banker who assumed control of Poliakov's ailing firm and transformed it into the highly successful United Bank.*

Figure 3.11. *Nikolai Ivanovich Guchkov, mayor of Moscow and investor, along with the "Moscow Germans," in the Moscow Private Bank.*

PART TWO

Icon and Business Card:
Merchant Culture, Ritual,
and Daily Life

CHAPTER 4

Caftan to Business Suit: The Semiotics
of Russian Merchant Dress

Christine Ruane

At the beginning of the eighteenth century, Peter the Great issued a series of imperial orders that were to have a profound impact not just on the Moscow merchantry but on all Russians. In his decrees Peter ordered his subjects, except for the clergy and peasants who worked the land, to dress "in the German style" or face stiff fines.[1] Like so many of Peter's decrees, those dealing with dress had a dual purpose. First, Peter hoped to find another form of tax revenue with which to fill the empty government coffers. Second, and more important, Peter wanted his subjects to become more like Europeans, and one way of accomplishing this goal was to have his subjects dress like their counterparts in Western Europe. Despite Peter's lack of education and sophistication, he understood a fundamental feature of human psychology, namely that clothing is a complex system of symbols whereby human beings weave a pattern of ambiguous messages about who they are and how they see themselves in the larger world. Thus a change in dress can allow individuals to rethink or reflect a change in their social, sexual, or national identities. Clearly Peter understood that he could not force his subjects to transform themselves overnight, but by insisting that they dress like Europeans he hoped that this change in outward appearance would precipitate a profound intellectual and cultural transformation in Russia.[2]

For the Moscow merchants, Peter's decrees represented a direct challenge to their view of what constituted appropriate dress. Invariably described as "semi-Asiatic" in appearance, Moscow merchants wore what scholars have come to think of as "traditional" Muscovite dress. The men donned long coats called caftans. In winter the caftans were made of sheepskins for greater warmth. Under the caftan merchants dressed in trousers and a loosely fitting shirt that buttoned at the neck; the shirts were worn outside of the trousers and belted at the waist. Equally typical of a merchant's appearance was his

long-flowing beard. The full beard was a sign of religious devotion for Orthodox men. Because they imagined God with a beard, they believed that by
wearing beards they were acknowledging that man was made in the image of
God. The women of the merchant estate also dressed according to Muscovite
tradition. They usually put on a garment called a *sarafan*, which was a loose-
fitting, floor-length jumper. Underneath the *sarafan* the women wore a *ru-
bakha*, a long-sleeved blouse frequently decorated with bits of embroidery.[3]
Merchant women also wore a variety of underskirts depending on the season.
Moreover, married women covered their hair completely with various head
scarves and hats. Typically, the quality of the fabrics and materials used in
merchant dress depended upon the wealth of the family.

Peter's decrees demanded a number of important changes in traditional
attire. Merchants were supposed to give up their caftans for waistcoats, vests,
and breeches, shave off their beards, and cut their hair according to the latest
European styles. The women were obliged to uncover themselves. They were
to abandon their heavy shapeless clothes for dresses that bared their arms and
bosoms and emphasized the waist. Women were also to remove their head
coverings and have their hair styled along European models.

Despite the tsar's wishes and the stiff fines, Moscow merchants initially
refused to alter their dress, finding these changes "indecent" (*neprilichnyi*).[4]
This resistance reflected their fundamental conservatism. Poorly educated and
untutored in Western business practices, merchants clung to their traditional
religious, social, and economic beliefs throughout the eighteenth and the first
half of the nineteenth century. This conservatism persisted in large part because Peter the Great, despite his attempt to make Russia more like Western
Europe, had done very little to restructure the relationship between state and
society. Thus Moscow merchants continued to believe that they should look
out for their own interests and leave the role of governing to the autocratic
state.

Underneath merchant conservatism, the seeds of change were beginning to
germinate, however. Beginning in the first half of the nineteenth century subtle changes occurred in merchant attire, and as is frequently the case, the
changes were implemented by the younger members of the merchant estate.
According to one commentator, by the 1840s there were three kinds of merchants in Moscow: those who wore beards, those who were clean-shaven, and
those who trimmed their beards.[5] The clean-shaven men were undoubtedly
members of the merchant aristocracy who dressed according to European
styles. Those men who kept their beards tended to wear Russian dress, but
even these styles had been affected by Western European styles. So-called
Russian merchant dress was frequently made from imported fabrics. The design of the caftan was also "modernized" and made more like European men's
coats. In addition, Russian merchants began to wear leather boots rather than

lapti, which were bast foot coverings that served as traditional footwear for merchants. The only exception to this were the merchants who belonged to the Old Believer religious sect. These men continued to don traditional clothing, footwear, and hairstyles.[6]

The dress of the female members of the merchantry showed an even stronger European influence than men's clothing. According to one observer, "the wife [of a merchant] wears Russian dress and a head scarf when her husband sports a beard, and when the husband is clean-shaven or just trims his beard, she wears a cap or a hat."[7] There were even instances of merchant men decked out in traditional dress while their wives wore the latest Parisian styles,[8] although most cases did not provide such an extreme contrast in conjugal attire. Like the men, the women used imported fabric to make their clothes according to Western fashions, or sometimes even ordered their clothing directly from European dressmakers.

These subtle changes in merchant dress reflected the merchantry's unstable position in Russian society. According to Russian law, it was relatively easy for anyone to become a merchant, and it was equally easy to lose merchant status. As a consequence, there was a great deal of status anxiety among Russian merchants, many of whom had been born into the peasantry but had managed to amass enough money to claim merchant status. Moreover, situated between the nobility and the peasantry, Russian merchants needed to make themselves stand apart from their perceived social inferiors. This was why they tried to use the most expensive material possible to make their clothes; these rich fabrics distinguished them from the peasants.[9] Their desire to separate themselves from the peasant masses also helps to explain their abandonment of *lapti* for boots, as well as trimming their beards and hair.

At the same time, some of the merchants wanted to move up the social ladder by aping the clothing, manners, and lifestyle of the nobility. One anonymous social commentator writing in the early years of the twentieth century lampooned the nineteenth-century merchantry for their social pretensions. The author satirized the merchants' inability to appreciate the opera and ballet, and he mocked their disastrous attempts to educate their sons and daughters. Although these men might dress in European clothing, speak French, and attend cultural events, these changes were perceived as shallow, for beneath this European facade lay the conservative, superstitious, and backward Russian merchant.[10]

The advent of photography in Russia coincided with these changes in merchant dress. The earliest photographs taken in the 1860s give examples of those Moscow merchants who eagerly adopted Western dress, although these individuals were still in the minority in Merchant Moscow. The photograph of Vladimir S. Alekseev (figure 4.1) taken shortly before his death is an example of the type of dress worn by a member of the Moscow merchant elite. The

Alekseev family had made their fortune manufacturing gold braid, and indeed Vladimir Alekseev married three of his daughters to noblemen, in part because of the family's wealth and prestige.[11] Alekseev is clean-shaven and coiffed. His clothing bears all the marks of European design and cut. Even his cane suggests his European manner as well as power and status. The photograph of Bobkova (figure 4.2) also reveals a woman who wants very much to appear as part of the new merchant elite. She is wearing a dress designed according to the latest European style and probably made from imported cloth. Her hairstyle and headdress also suggest close attention to European fashion. Her shawl acts as a sartorial symbol from both systems of dress. Shawls were extremely popular in Europe and were considered an essential element in the dress of respectable women. (They were also useful in providing warmth before central heating!) In Russia virtually every description of merchant wives and daughters mentions the shawl as a fundamental feature of their dress. In this case, Bobkova's shawl serves as a marker of her social rank in Russian society and as a measure of her adoption of Western European fashion.[12]

By the middle of the nineteenth century, this state of affairs had begun to change. In 1855 the Turks, English, and French had allied to defeat the Russians during the Crimean War. This defeat caused the Russian government to initiate a series of reforms which it hoped would improve military capability enough to guarantee Russia world power status. This time the reforms included a modern banking system and plans to begin an industrialization drive. The government recognized that it could not succeed in Russia's industrialization efforts without the support of all social groups, and it called upon the nobility and the merchantry to participate actively in business and local governmental affairs. It was these reforms that energized some Moscow merchants and accelerated the transformation of merchant culture.

As before, there were three basic groups: those who tried to maintain "traditional" merchant dress, those who dressed completely according to European styles, and finally those who combined both traditional Russian and European elements in their attire.[13] Within these general characterizations, there were also important gender differences. Wives and daughters of merchants tended to adopt Western sartorial customs much more quickly than their husbands or brothers. This was due to the growing influence of the fashion industry in Russia, which strongly encouraged women to focus their time and resources on dressing à la mode.[14]

The photographs give some vivid examples of those merchants and their wives who chose to dress according to tradition. The photograph of Silvestr Kononvich Tsarsky (figure 4.3), taken in the 1870s, represents the quintessential portrait of the Russian merchant. His flowing beard and haircut coupled with the rather poor quality of the cut and cloth of his coat suggest traditional merchant dress. The picture of Akimova (figure 4.4), also from the 1870s, gives the same view for women. With her modest dress, shawl, and plain hairstyle, she gives the impression of someone who remains outside of the world of high fashion.

At the same time, a growing number of merchants combined both Western and Russian styles of dress in ways that departed markedly from the traditional norm. The tobacco merchant Mikhail Ivanovich Bostanzhoglo (figure 4.5) was clean-shaven and had given up the traditional Russian bowl haircut for something more stylish. His coat is well cut, and he is holding a cane, which also suggests a man interested in presenting himself in a more modern attitude. Indeed, Mikhail's son was well known in Moscow as someone with fashionable pretensions, but with traditional political views.[15] Mikhail's wife, Elena Iakovlevna (figure 4.6), also combines both European and Russian elements in her attire. Her simple hairstyle is a sign of her social origin. However, her skirt appears to be made from an expensive material that distinguishes her clothing from other merchant wives. In addition, she has abandoned the shawl for what appears to be a jacket, thereby eliminating a central feature of female merchant dress.

Changes in merchant attire accentuated the differences between male and female dress. The Zherebtsov and Bardygin family portraits (figures 4.7 and 4.8) illustrate in different ways the complex social forces at work. Nikifor Bardygin is dressed in a Western suit, but his hair and beard are remnants of sartorial habits from an earlier age. In contrast, Zherebtsov has trimmed his beard and styled his hair, but his clothing appears to be made from less expensive material and is not nearly as well tailored as Bardygin. In both cases, however, their wives are wearing expensive gowns made according to the latest fashions of the time. Even more interesting, both women are wearing watches, that quintessential symbol of progress and modernity throughout Europe. Thus the women's dress has been thoroughly Westernized, while their husbands still wear symbols from both sartorial systems.

For many merchant families, change in dress was a generational issue. In the photograph of Pelageia Mikhailovna Kapustina and her children taken around 1880 (figure 4.9), both she and her son wear traditional merchant clothing. However, her daughters are wearing fashionable gowns probably purchased from a fancy Moscow dress shop. Thus a generation gap could sometimes be observed in merchant clothing. Sons, and especially daughters, would rebel against the fashion dictates of their parents.

The high elite of Merchant Moscow adopted Western fashion entirely and abandoned all traditional markers of their social category. The Tretiakov family (figure 4.10) had made their fortune in linen production, and they were one of the most prominent Moscow merchant families. In this picture there is no generation gap, for both parents and children are dressed in the latest European styles. Even their hairstyles suggest a clear desire to appear European. The photograph of Anna Timofeevna Karpova (figure 4.11) tells a similar story. She was born a Morozova, a merchant family that had amassed their

fortune in textiles. The Morozov family had been Old Believers, the most conservative and traditional of all merchants, but during the nineteenth century
they had Europeanized, adopting Western dress and manners while still retaining their religious beliefs. By the time this photograph had been taken
during the 1870s Anna had dropped all traditional markers of her social origin. Her hair, dress, and jewelry suggest a woman of great wealth and prestige
whose Russian nationality cannot be guessed by her attire.

The photograph of Iakov Ivanovich Babaev (figure 4.12) tells a different
story. His photograph suggests a man who was very interested in appearing
modern and up-to-date. His suit is well tailored, and his hair reflects European
styles of the time. Even more important indicators of his self-identity are the
top hat and watch, which are so prominently displayed in the picture. Despite
all these modern props, there is a certain tentativeness about Babaev that is not
apparent in the photographs of the Tretiakovs and Anna Karpova. Babaev
appears slightly uncomfortable in these modern trappings suggesting that he
himself does not feel entirely at home with his view of himself as a modern
European businessman. Given that this photograph was taken in the 1870s,
Babaev represents that group of Moscow merchants who were just beginning
to take advantage of the opportunities presented to the merchants by the government's new economic policy. Babaev's uncertain gaze reflects the tentativeness of many merchants as they tried to come to terms with the new world that
was growing around them.

By the turn of the century whatever tentativeness existed in Babaev and
other Moscow merchants has vanished. According to most sources, the number of merchants who dressed in traditional merchant dress was a very small
minority by the early 1900s.[16] This new self-confidence as reflected in merchant representation marks a key point in the development of a new class
consciousness on the part of merchantry. And although historians disagree as
to how far this new class identity had evolved before 1917, it is clear from the
photographs that an important change had taken place.

Photographs taken at summer homes or dachas reveal this change in merchant attitudes well. Traditionally only the nobility had been able to afford
summer homes, but the new wealth that accumulated particularly after the
government's industrialization drive of the 1890s allowed merchants to afford
second homes in the countryside. As these pictures reveal, the individuals
who frequented those dachas lived a life of casual elegance reminiscent of a
graceful country life of a leisured class. The relaxed poses of the Peltser family
at the Litvinovo dacha in 1910 (figure 4.13) reveal their attentiveness to Western fashions as well as their desire to enjoy the pleasures of life. Another
interesting feature of these photographs is that they were taken outside the
photographer's studio. This change of setting suggests that merchants no
longer needed the artificial backdrops of the studio but felt comfortable re-

vealing their own surroundings to the camera's eye. And while it is possible to see in these pictures an imitation of the nobility, they also reveal the extent to which noble privilege and status were being eroded by the merchants in the early years of the twentieth century.

The final three photographs reveal quite clearly the new self-confidence and growing importance of the Moscow merchantry. The pictures of the Bardygins (figure 4.14) and Aleksandra Petrovna Baranova (figure 4.15) represent two families who made their fortunes outside of Moscow but came to play an increasingly important roles within the city. Even though these photographs were taken in a studio there is no tentativeness in their gaze. Mikhail Nikiforovich Bardygin was the son of Nikifor Mikhailovich and Mariia Vladimirovna Bardygin (see figure 4.7), and while his father combined both Russian and Western elements in his dress, the son appears in the complete garb of a Western businessman. Baranova, in particular, with her beautiful fur stole and muff, evinces a kind of elegance and sophistication that many less wealthy merchant wives could only try to emulate. The photograph of Nikolai Mikhailovich Krasilshchikov (figure 4.16) represents the male version of this same elegance and sophistication. His studied indifference to the camera reflects a new level of self-confidence among the merchantry. His beautiful suit and well-groomed hair suggest a man of refinement, wealth, and leisure. By the eve of World War I, Moscow merchants like Krasilshchikov had adopted the uniform of the modern business suit and, as a result, could have mingled comfortably with the business elites in any European capital.

It is difficult to say definitively that the sartorial changes in Moscow merchant dress meant an absolute change in values. It is quite possible that for many of these merchants Western clothing served as a disguise that hid their more traditional attitudes. Although they appeared to resemble businessmen in other European countries, the adoption of the business suit did not mean a wholesale rejection of traditional Russian attitudes toward economics and politics. In order to establish this kind of direct link, it would be necessary to know more about the individuals whose images are reproduced here.

What is clear from these photographs is that between 1860 and 1910 Russian business was undergoing a profound transition. In the 1860s and 1870s traditional Russian business methods and manners of dress coexisted with newer, Western European business practices. By 1910, however, the traditional has been almost completely replaced with the modern approach to business. These men were no longer merchants, but businessmen. The new uniform was the suit for men and European fashions for women, and both merchants and their wives needed to dress the part in order to participate fully in that vibrant new world of Russian capitalism. The changes in dress helped Moscow merchants to rethink their social identity and to redefine their position as Russia raced to become a modern industrial nation.

NOTES

1. The text of Peter's decree can be found in *Polnoe sobranie zakonov Rossiiskoi Imperii*, series 1, vol. 4, no. 1887.

2. Evgenii V. Anisimov, *The Reforms of Peter the Great: Progress through Coercion in Russia* (Armonk: M. E. Sharpe, 1993), pp. 218–19.

3. E. V. Kireeva, *Istoriia kostiuma: Evropeiskii kostium ot antichnosti do XX veka* (Moscow: Prosveshchenie, 1976), p. 131.

4. Ibid., p. 131.

5. P. Vistengof, *Ocherki Moskovskoi zhizhni*, as quoted in *Russkii kostium, 1830–1850 godov*, vol. 2 (Moscow: Vserossiiskoe teatral'noe obshchestvo, 1961), pp. 23–24.

6. *Russkii kostium, 1750–1830* (Moscow: Vserossiiskoe teatral'noe obshchestvo, 1961), pp. 24–26; *Russkii kostium, 1830–1850*, p. 25.

7. Vistengof, as quoted in *Russkii kostium, 1830–1850*, p. 25.

8. A. N. Ostrovsky, *Polnoe sobranie socheniniia*, vol. 11 (Moscow: Goslitizdat, 1952), pp. 34–35.

9. Ia. N. Rivosh, *Vremia i veshchi: Ocherki po istorii material'noi kul'tury v Rossii nachala XX veka* (Moscow: Iskusstvo, 1990), p. 207.

10. "Vneshnii vid Moskvy serediny XIX veka," in *Moskva v ee proshlom i nastoiashchem*, vol. 10 (Moscow: Obrazovanie, 1910), pp. 23–27.

11. Jo Ann Ruckman, *The Moscow Business Elite: A Social and Cultural Portrait of Two Generations, 1840–1905* (De Kalb: Northern Illinois University Press, 1984), pp. 42–43, 52.

12. *Russkii kostium, 1850–1870 godov* (Moscow: Vserossiiskoe teatral'noe obshchestvo, 1963), p. 26. For further discussion of shawls, see E. Iu. Moiseenko, *Sharfy i shali russkoi raboty pervoi poloviny XIX v.* (Leningrad: Gosudarstvennyi Ermitazh, 1981).

13. *Russkii kostium, 1850–1870*, p. 25.

14. Christine Ruane, "Clothes Make the Comrade: A History of the Russian Fashion Industry, 1700–1917," *Russian History* 23, nos. 1–4 (1996): 311–44.

15. Thomas C. Owen, *Capitalism and Politics in Russia: A Social History of the Moscow Merchants, 1885–1905* (Cambridge: Cambridge University Press, 1981), pp. 80–81.

16. *Russkii kostium, 1890–1917*, vol. 5, p. 44; and Rivosh, *Vremia i veshchi*, p. 207.

Figure 4.1. *The gold braid merchant Vladimir Semenovich Alekseev, 1860. Alekseev's clothing bears all the marks of European design and cut. Even his cane suggests his European manners and dress.*

Figure 4.2. *Moscow merchant wife Padraga Iakovlevna Bobkova, 1863. She is wearing a dress designed according to the latest European style. Her hairstyle and headdress also suggest close attention to European fashion. The one element in her attire that was typical of female members of the merchant estate is her shawl.*

Figure 4.3. *Silvestr Kononovich Tsarsky, 1870s. His flowing beard and haircut, coupled with the rather poor quality of the cut and cloth of his coat, suggest traditional merchant dress.*

Figure 4.4. *Merchant wife Akimova, 1870s. Her dress is typical of the women of the merchant estate. With her modest dress, shawl, and plain hairstyle, she gives the impression of someone who remains outside of the world of high fashion.*

Figure 4.5. *The tobacco merchant Mikhail Ivanovich Bostanzhoglo, 1870s. Bostanzhoglo is clean-shaven and has given up the traditional bowl haircut for something more stylish. His coat is well cut, and he is holding a cane, which also suggests a man interested in presenting himself in a more modern attitude.*

Figure 4.6. *Elena Ia. Bostanzhoglo, 1870s. Her dress combines both European and Russian elements. Her simple hairstyle and headdress are reminders of her humble social origin. However, her skirt appears to be made from expensive material. She has also abandoned the shawl for a jacket, thereby eliminating a central feature of female merchant dress.*

Figure 4.7. *Nikifor Mikhailovich and Mariia Vladimirovna Bardygin, 1872. Bardygin is dressed in a Western suit, but his hair and beard echo sartorial habits of an earlier age. His wife's dress is completely European, and she is also wearing a watch.*

Figure 4.8. *F. S. Zherebtsov and his wife, 1860s. Zherebtsov has trimmed his beard and styled his hair, but his clothing is made from less expensive material and is not well tailored. His wife, however, is wearing an expensive gown and a watch, that quintessential symbol of progress and modernity.*

Figure 4.9. *Pelageia Mikhailovna Kapustina and her children, 1880. Both Pelageia and her son wear very traditional merchant clothing. However, her daughters are wearing fashionable gowns probably purchased from a fancy Moscow dress shop.*

Figure 4.10. *The Serpukhov branch of the Tretiakov family. In this picture there is no generation gap, as both parents and children are dressed in the latest Western styles. Even their hairstyles suggest a clear desire to appear European.*

Figure 4.11. *Anna Timofeevna Karpova (née Morozova). Although the Morozovs had been Old Believers, the most conservative and traditional of all merchants, by the 1870s Anna had dropped all traditional markers of her social origin. Her hair, dress, and jewelry suggest a woman of great wealth and prestige whose national origin cannot be determined by her attire.*

Figure 4.12. *Iakov Ivanovich Babaev, 1870s. Babaev's photograph suggests a man who was very interested in appearing modern and up-to-date. Important indicators of his self-identity are the top hat and watch. Despite all these modern props, Babaev appears slightly uncomfortable in these trappings, perhaps indicating that he does not feel entirely at home with his view of himself as a modern European businessman.*

Figure 4.13. At the Litvinovo dacha of the Peltser family, 1910. Family portrait with servants. Their clothing clearly indicates the social rank of the individuals depicted. The family members are wearing Western dress appropriate to their leisured existence at the dacha. However, the woman seated second from the right wears the traditional dress of the wet nurse, minus her headdress. The man who is squatting wears clothing that many male servants wore.

Figure 4.14. The Bardygin family, 1900s. Whereas his father (figure 4.7) combined Russian and Western elements in his dress, Mikhail appears in the complete garb of a Western businessman. His wife also wears the latest European fashions.

Figure 4.15. A. P. Baranova, 1900s. With her beautiful fur stole and
muff, Baranova evinces a kind of elegance and sophistication that many
less wealthy merchant wives could only dream of emulating.

Figure 4.16. Nikolai Mihailovich Krasilshchikov, 1900s. His studied indifference to the camera reflects a new level of self-confidence among the merchantry. His beautiful suit and well-groomed hair suggest a man of elegance, refinement, wealth, and leisure.

CHAPTER 5

Old Believers and New Entrepreneurs:
Religious Belief and
Ritual in Merchant Moscow

Galina N. Ulianova

Merchant Moscow was a city of churches; more than five hundred of them adorned the city in the beginning of the twentieth century. The church was the only type of public building that still symbolized in an urban setting the spiritual values surviving in Russian peasant culture. Many of these churches were erected by parishioners of the merchant estate (figure 5.1).

"Moscow merchants are pious," wrote an observer in the mid-nineteenth century; "they fast rigorously, and most of them live modestly with their families."[1] Religion formed the bedrock of the merchants' mental world. N. P. Vishniakov, descendent of an old Moscow family that owned a brocade factory as early as the eighteenth century, recalled that his father and mother donated money to their parish church and regularly attended masses, vespers, and matins on Sundays and holy days. Only those who were seriously ill could stay at home. The family had its own private space in the parish church of Saints Ioakim and Anna on Iakimanka Street. During Lent everybody fasted, and during the first and last weeks of Lent every service was attended without exception.

While private life for the merchants remained secluded from the public sphere until the last third of the nineteenth century, the church was the center of community life. Indeed, the church and the home regularly became one. Not only did the Vishniakovs go to to church regularly; on feast days they invited the clergy of the parish to perform the evening vespers in their home: "In the corner . . . of the sitting room, a table covered with a white tablecloth was set, and the icons, flickering icon lamps, and burning wax candles were put on it. The sitting room was gradually filled with members of the household. The priest and the deacons put on their vestments and began the service."[2] It was the custom among other merchant families as well to invite the clergy of churches where relatives were buried (figure 5.2) to Christmas and Easter dinner. At least once a year, the icon of the Iverian Mother of God, an ancient copy of the eighth-century miracle-working icon in the Iberian monastery on Mt. Athos in Greece, was brought to each merchant house. So venerated was this icon that the event had to be arranged weeks, sometimes months, in advance.

The icons (*obrazy*, or "images") were the most precious possession of the Orthodox merchant family. They were the first object to be rescued from a fire, and family icons were never pawned or sold, even if the owners went bankrupt or became impoverished. St. Nicholas the Miracle Worker (figure 5.3) was among the most popular saints in the merchant culture. One in ten Moscow churches bore his name, and each icon with his likeness was considered miraculous.

Piety, the mainstay of the merchant culture, was passed from generation to generation, even while lifestyles, education, and fashions underwent dramatic changes. A representative of the second generation of the owners of the Trekhgorka ("Trimount") Textile Factory, Konstantin Prokhorov, left Moscow once every few months to go on a pilgrimage to one of the famous monasteries in the region. Yet in the personality of Prokhorov, this exceptional piety was harmoniously combined with broadest Europeanism. In the 1820s, when most merchants still wore peasant clothes, he dressed himself like a nobleman, invited foreign tutors to teach his children, and sent his sons to work in the best enterprises in Germany and Alsace before they entered the family business. In 1851, he took them to the International Exhibition in London.

Prokhorov considered the responsibility of factory management to be "a certain penance imposed from on high," and in this he conformed to the rules of the Orthodox work ethic venerated by his peasant forefathers. Efficiency and capacity for work were combined with reverence for higher things. Timofei Prokhorov, Konstantin's elder brother and the person closest to him spiritually, dedicated to his exemplary brother two essays which he wrote himself: "On Acquisition of Wealth" and "On Poverty." They were written in the style of gospel truth. They particularly emphasized that "wealth is often acquired for vanity, luxury, voluptuousness, etc. This wealth is bad and evil: it leads to the perdition of the soul. . . . if wealth is acquired by work, its loss will preserve the man from downfall; he will resume working and can still acquire more than he had, for he lived in God."[3]

On occasion feelings of piety dictated major business decisions. The father of Konstantin and Timofei, Vasily, abandoned the brewing business, which he came to consider inappropriate for a pious man. His transition to textiles and the founding of his "Trimount" factory marked the beginning of one of Moscow's greatest cotton dynasties. The institutional culture of this and many other factories emphasized the devotion to ritual and piety shared by factory owner and worker alike (figure 5.4).

It is likely that the main psychological motive for the broad programs of patronage and philanthropy sustained by the merchants of Moscow was the effort to purchase absolution for the accumulation of "sinful" wealth, much of it derived from the exploitation of the labor of others. The Bible states unequivocally: "It is easier for a camel to pass through the eye of a needle than for a rich man to enter the Kingdom of God." For this reason family and factory histories often treated philanthropic activities as more central to merchant identity than entrepreneurial ones.

Merchant Moscow provided striking individual examples of intense religious devotion. Vladimir Sapelkin, a merchant in wax candles and winner of a prize at the London Exhibition of 1851, wrote and published books on religious themes. In the 1870s, Ivan Butikov, an Old Believer owner of a textile plant, turned over his factory to his sons and became Ilarii, a hermit-monk at Rogozh Cemetery.

Religious feelings permeated the sensibility of Moscow merchant culture. Vladimir Riabushinsky quoted an ancient Christian poem about St. John the Baptist preserved by the Old Believers: "The Lord hath sent three gifts. Yea, the first gift is the cross and prayer. The second gift is love and charity. The third gift is the night orison. The fourth is a book for reading."[4] The author notes that in the merchant milieu, "the reading of religious books and discussion of religious problems was the only legitimate intellectual outlet and many took advantage of it." It was a recurring situation "in which religiosity provided a stimulus for enlightenment, but enlightenment within a very restricted sphere."[5]

Religious ritual, the external manifestation of Orthodox culture, was the principal focus of public life in Merchant Moscow (figure 5.5). "Church services," contemporaries wrote, "were diligently attended, and religious processions assembled numerous crowds." The religious behavior of the Muscovites was characterized according to one observer by "a hysterical attachment to rituals," "patriarchal and credulous attitude" toward miracles, "love of discussions on religious problems which did not cool off even at *traktirs* [taverns]," stubborn adherence to tradition shared even by the less devout people," and finally "a pious outlook perfectly coexisting with shrewdness in daily life."[6]

Religious processions were most popular because of their exceptional festivity and the intense feeling of devotion to God that participants of all estates and stations seemed to share. Moscow was annually the scene of eight major public services and processions at the initiative of merchants. They were conducted from August until November, either in the Trading Rows or at the offices of merchant organizations. In the course of one such procession marking the successful conclusion of operations at the Nizhny-Novgorod Fair, the participants made stops at the houses of Khludov and Tretiakov, the honorary elders of the Merchant Society of Moscow. Smaller processions on factory premises were a common occurrence (figure 5.6).

Each year beginning in 1875, when the new building of the Moscow Stock Exchange on Ilinka Street was completed, a service was conducted in early November on the premises. In addition to icons from the local church, the Iverian icon and sacred objects from the Kremlin's Cathedral of Assumption were also brought there. Services were dedicated to Christ the Savior, the Most Holy Mother of God, the saints honored on the days of the laying of the cornerstone of the Exchange's building, and finally to the memory of the two churches (Great Martyr Dimitry and the Assumption of the Mother of God) that had previously stood on the site.[7]

Moscow merchants served as wardens in many parish churches of Moscow, and also of some of its major cathedrals, including those in the Kremlin. This tradition existed at least since the early nineteenth century, when the Governor of Moscow was ordered to elect a warden for the Cathedral of the Assumption from either merchants or townspeople. Undoubtedly, the city administration hoped that the church warden elected from well-off citizens would support the cathedral with some of their wealth. Despite all the honor associated with this office, merchants, especially in the first half of the nineteenth century, often declined the offer.[8]

This instinct of evasion arose from the fact that until the Great Reforms of the 1860s the merchantry remained a nonprivileged estate. Merchants endured countless estate obligations and taxes, being required by law to give from their own pockets "voluntary contributions to the public good" in support of state, military, and municipal needs. Because every new public responsibility laid by the state on the merchant saddled him with additional "contributions," it was natural that public service was viewed as a burden to be avoided rather than an honor to be coveted.

In the last third of the nineteenth century, however, when the merchants consciously began to enter the arena of public life, the attitude toward elected service changed. Merchants became eager to gain prominent position in the city administration and other public institutions. The richest businessmen now willingly became church wardens of Moscow cathedrals. At the end of the nineteenth century, the warden of the Kremlin's Cathedral of the Assumption was Michael Abramovich Morozov, the owner of the Tver Manufactory, one of the largest Russian textile enterprises. As a church warden, Morozov, who was in his thirties at the time, demonstrated the two principal features of his character: ambition and love of art. His wife, Margarita K. Morozova, wrote in her memoirs: "He respected and loved this cathedral very much and spent a great deal on its maintenance and interior decoration; apart from this he also studied its history."[9]

In the same period the church warden of the Kremlin's Cathedral of Annunciation was Petr Arsenevich Smirnov, the head of a famous vodka firm. The same post at the Cathedral of the Archangel Michael was held by Dmitry Ivanovich Filippov, a celebrated Russian baker. The big wholesaler of leather goods, Aleksandr Afanasevich Moshkin, served as a warden of St. Basil's Cathedral (the Cathedral of the Intercession) on Red Square, while Petr Petrovich Botkin, a representative of a respected old merchant family and head of a firm trading in tea and sugar, was warden of the mammoth Cathedral of Christ the Redeemer. The church wardens controlled all affairs of their respective churches, which included maintenance of the buildings and their interiors—the iconostasis, icon lamps, and candlesticks—and were responsible for replenishing the sacristy and replacing church objects.

Church holidays played the role of temporal markers in the yearly calendar of commercial and industrial activity. It was customary to schedule the most important undertakings, such as the laying of the cornerstone of a new factory or the creation of a new business, on religious feast days, in the hope that the new enterprise might find "supreme patronage."[10] Factories traditionally hired their work force three times a year, for terms from Easter to the onset of fieldwork (June), from autumn to Christmas, and from Christmas to Easter.

Easter Week marked the end of the old commercial year and the beginning of the new one. Easter canticles praised God, the Holy Virgin, and the saints for their care of the property of the pious. From the village past came the urban tradition of counting money on the morning of Maundy Tuesday. Passion Week, the week before Easter, was the time of lively trade, especially in the Okhotny Riad (Hunters' Row), where ritual foods such as *kulich* (Easter cakes), *paskha* (a sweet cream-cheese dish), decorated eggs, and pink ham were sold.

Great Week and the week after Easter were devoted to commercial accounting. Trade for the new year began on the Monday after the two-week Easter holiday, and it was obligatory not to lose the first customer or client of the year even if the deal was not a profitable one. According to tradition, a good opening day was an omen of business success for the entire year. On St. Thomas's Monday, the merchants unloaded their old stocks, from overripe fruits to outmoded fashions, through special sales. Having disposed of last year's inventory, the satisfied traders left the bazaar with their profits, stopping at the Kremlin's Savior Gates to bow and offer prayers of thanksgiving.

Each year the merchants of Moscow spent approximately three months at the Nizhny-Novgorod Fair. This was the largest fair in Russia, visited annually by 1.5 million people. The fair originated from a medieval bazaar at the walls of the monastery of St. Makary nearby on the Volga. In 1817, the fair was transferred to Nizhny-Novgorod, but St. Makary remained its patron; thus the official opening of the fair took place on this Saint's Day, the 15th of July. Early in the morning before leaving for the fair, the merchants held services at their Moscow homes, asking God for protection and success. On arriving in Nizhny-Novgorod, this ritual was repeated in the cathedral on the fairgrounds, which from the 1860s on onward contained the icon of St. Makary brought from the monastery for the season of trade (about ten weeks).

The fair was opened and closed by a large church service attended by all merchants (figure 5.7). Afterward, there was a religious procession around the grounds of the fair, and only then were the flags raised to signal the opening of trade. At the conclusion of the procession, the owner of each shop invited a priest in, and for these private services the merchants brought their own icons. The whole course of the fair was determined by the Orthodox calendar. Thus every bill had to paid up by August 25, the Day of Judgment.

The civic culture of the fair required charity toward the poor. The fairs were thus crowded with beggars, who knew that there they would be treated better than usual. Merchants had no choice but to give alms either after a successful deal or "in advance," to guarantee success in the future. Charity was especially bountiful at the beginning of trade. "Take this for the sake of Christ," the merchant would say in hopes that "the kopeck would turn into a ruble."

The most generous alms were taken from the merchants by those who collected money for churches, for in Russia it was considered from time immemorial that this kind of charity could atone for the gravest sins, and that such a sacrifice was stronger than prayers of the priest and individual repentance. The peasants even joked maliciously that "the heavier the sin on the merchant's conscience for abusing his countryman, . . . the louder are the bells he casts, and the bigger are the churches he builds."[11] This peasant notion reflected the prevailing negative attitude toward wealth and entrepreneurship. The fact that a few people became wealthy by overcoming the communal constraints woven deeply into the fabric of Russian life was seen as somehow illegitimate. It was said that "nobody can obtain a stone palace by working honestly." But this persistent attitude was clearly at variance with reality. The majority of merchants rose from the peasantry and were simply luckier and more enterprising than others.

Prior to the 1880s, religious tradition and piety still dictated the decorum prevailing among merchants at the fair: upon entering another's shop, for example, they crossed themselves and kissed each other three times. At the same time, the fair was renowned for the wild revels of the merchants who were away from home and thus loose from their family cages. According to A. P. Melnikov, a scholar of the fair, merchant behavior there presented a strange mixture of reckless revelry and pious religiosity: "After a rakish night spent with chorus girls in the restaurants, in the morning one could meet here and there groups of traders praying diligently at the shop's icon, which was decorated with herbs and flowers; the clergymen would sing in unison, the censors tinkle, people bow to the ground, the owners and salesmen cross themselves devoutly, while their faces still bear the traces of the night spent vigorously and merrily."[12]

One group of merchants, however, was never seen among the revelers—the ascetic and frugal Old Believers (see "A Note on Old Belief"). Because these representatives of Russia's most traditionalistic religious subculture constituted the core of the city's business establishment, their influence far out-weighed their numbers. The Nizhny-Novgorod Fair was a traditional gathering place for Old Believers of different sects. After bribing the authorities and the police, they assembled at their secret services not only in the shops of their co-religionists, who were often traders of old printed and manuscript books, but also in the town of Nizhny-Novgorod and the nearby villages of Sormovo and Gordeevka. The Old Believers came together both for prayers and for commercial consultations. They also exchanged news of the faith, information vital for the survival of their underground religion. According to anecdotal accounts, the fair was visited annually by more than seventy thousand Old Believers from all parts of Russia. It is noteworthy that the annual All-Russian Congresses of Old Believers, legalized after the October Manifesto of 1905 and controlled by the Riabushinsky family, continued the tradition of assembling in Nizhny-Novgorod.

Despite, or rather because of, their intense devotion to their dissident faith and ancient traditions, Old Believers were discriminated against and persecuted by the authorities until the early twentieth century. These endless repressions against the Old Belief did not destroy it but, on the contrary, strengthened its resolve and tenacity, producing in many generations of adherents such qualities as persistence, energy, and mutual assistance. "Their enterprise and gumption, steeled by the storms of life, their close cohesion and togetherness, quickly promoted the Old Believers into the ranks of the Moscow Merchants" (figure 5.8).[13] The Morozovs, Guchkovs, Rakhmanovs, Shelaputins, Riabushinskys, Konovalovs, Kuznetsovs, Gorbunovs, and many other rich Moscow merchants belonged to the Schism. From the late eighteenth century onward, Moscow sheltered two All-Russian centers of the Old Belief, one at the Preobrazhensk cemetery (for Bespopovtsy, the Priestless sect) and another at the Rogozh cemetery (for Popovtsy, the Priestly ones). The size and influence of both communes rose sharply after the epidemics of the plague (1771) and cholera (1831), for the Old Believers attracted many converts from among the Muscovites who were cured and saved at their hospices.

At the end of the eighteenth century, the acknowledged head of Preobrazhensk and its predominant Theodosian sect was the Moscow factory owner Ilya Kovylin (figure 5.9), a solid businessman and, despite himself, an early public figure. In 1809 he went to St. Petersburg to defend the rights of the Old Believers and managed to return with a decree authorizing Old Believer burials by special government permission, thus overriding the standing objects of the official clergy with the authority of the police.

During the first half of the nineteenth century, the Preobrazhensk cemetery provided the Theodosian sect all across Russia with spiritual leadership. But the community's fate was sealed by the renewal of repression during the reign of Nicholas I. Beginning in the 1820s, the government began imposing ever more restrictive laws against the "heretical" Old Believers. Some of this punitive legislation (e.g., the Decree of 1826, prescribing the closure of all oratories built ten or more years before the date of the decree) was deflected by Theodosians through the judicious payment of handsome bribes. But later in the same year came the decree "On the Prohibition for the Schismatics to Build Anything like Churches," a measure so unambiguously repressive that it was difficult to evade.

Soon restrictions against the Old Believers in the sphere of civil rights became more refined. The law of 1853 broadened and strengthened the administrative discretion of the police in the localities where the Old Believers lived and provided for the closure of their monasteries. "Schismatics" were banned from holding public office or receiving titles or decorations. But the most onerous of all restrictions for Old Believer entrepreneurs was the clause limiting their admittance into the merchant guilds to temporary status only.[14] Aside from directly threatening their commercial interests, this law made Old Believers liable for military service and subject to corporal punishment. This demoted the "schismatic" merchants to the lowly status of their social inferiors, the peddlers and traders of the petty townspeople (*meshchane*). As was customary with repressive legislation in tsarist jurisprudence, these decrees were never published in the Code of Laws of the Russian Empire. They remained secret, visible only in their zealous application.

As early as the mid-eighteenth century, the Moscow Popovtsy furtively kept their meeting houses at the homes of rich merchants, as well as in two cemeteries, near the Donskoi Monastery and beyond the Tver Gates. During the plague epidemic of 1771, their commune was allotted a piece of land on the eastern outskirts of Moscow, in the village of Novoandronovka, exclusively populated by Old Believers. In place of the two earlier cemeteries, one new graveyard (Rogozh) was established, at first as a temporary quarantine area for those who escaped the plague. The cemetery occupied approximately twenty-four hectares of land and was encircled with a high wall made of logs; its only gates faced the city (figures 5.10 and 5.11). At the turn of the nineteenth century, active construction of chapels and hostels began on its premises. There appeared a hospital, a school, an orphanage, a library rich in rare books, and a cemetery office. Wealthy merchants built a number of small houses nearby for themselves "coming . . . to fast and even to spend the whole of the Lenten period."[15] The Riabushinskys, for example, kept such a house (also known as the *kelya* [cell]) near Rogozh Cemetery (figure 5.12).

The Rogozh community was subject to a lesser degree of official harassment than Preobrazhensk. This can be explained by, among other things, the fact that the rich and renowned merchants faithful to this sect of Old Belief pacified the authorities more successfully through their carefully cultivated connections and "gifts" to officials. In 1825, Rogozh had sixty-eight thousand parishioners, unified not only by the strength of their spirit but also by their collective financial might. Moscow was the supplier of Old Believer priests for the whole of Russia; it was equally profitable to send nuns from local convents to read the sacred books for wealthy Old Believer families. But the real power of the Rogozh Cemetery derived from a steady stream of private donations from the faithful across Russia. Only small sums necessary for day-to-day operations were kept at the cemetery; most of the immense collective wealth of the Rogozh community was entrusted to the care of private individuals who served as elected trustees of the cemetery, such as the merchants Shelaputin, Rakhmanov, and Tsarsky. Soviet historians, and Western scholars following their lead, alleged that this collective wealth passed into private hands when the communities were liquidated by the government in the 1850s, and subsequently formed the nucleus of the fortunes of several Moscow dynasties. Given the strict morals of the Old Believers, however, it is difficult to imagine such machinations on their part, and no evidence exists confirming such behavior.

The pious and acquisitive Old Believer merchants were always eager to buy ancient church utensils and manuscripts from the descendants of old but impoverished aristocratic families. Most attractive to them were the ancient family icons "that once stood in the chambers of the confidants of the first Romanov tsars, but now are removed like some old garbage to the pantries."[16] The Old Believers were thus pioneers of Russian archaeology, and by dint of their efforts many ancient relics of Muscovite piety were preserved and handed down.

For both the Bezpopovtsy and Popovtsy, the 1850s were very difficult years. Police repression was relentless: chapels were sealed or forcibly converted into Orthodox churches, richly decorated garments were confiscated, priceless ancient books and archives were seized and destroyed. For nearly two years no church services were conducted at all, and they resumed only sporadically in 1856. Though strictly prohibited, Old Believer rites were conducted secretly in clandestine home chapels of rich Moscow merchants. These altars were often quite ornate, as illustrated by the home chapel of the Rakhmanovs (figure 5.13).

After the coronation of Alexander II in 1856, the Old Believers became very active in their efforts to recover their churches and property and vociferous in their demands for restitution of their confiscated relics. They implored the government to grant them freedom of worship and permit them once again to acquire trade certificates. By their persistence and tenacity through several generations of resistance, the Old Believers finally began to wrest concessions from the autocracy. Religious emancipation was at last granted in the Manifesto of April 17, 1905, according to which Old Believer communities were legalized, allowed to possess church and communal property, to build churches, to buy real estate, and to open charity and educational establishments. At the Rogozh cemetery, the altars sealed for more than half a century were opened, and the crosses and bells removed during decades of repression were returned to their places (figure 5.14). Soon the construction of Old Believer churches, bell towers, and church hospitals began anew throughout Moscow (figure 5.15).

The Old Believer elite of Merchant Moscow came into its own in the early twentieth century. Combining religious ardor and new impulses toward secular philanthropy, they staged art exhibitions and concerts. One of the major events in the cultural life of this period was the exhibition of Old Russian art from the collections of Stepan P. Riabushinsky, I. S. Ostroukhov, and others, organized by the Moscow Archaeological Institute in 1913. All Russia knew of the Old Believer chorus of Arseny Ivanovich Morozov with P. V. Tsvetkov as conductor (figure 5.16). In 1912, the Old Believer Institute was opened in Moscow as an educational establishment for boys from twelve to eighteen years of age. Its board of trustees was chaired by Stepan Riabushinsky, while Arseny and Timofei Morozov served as members.

Publishing activity among the Old Believers also revived: after 1905, Moscow boasted two specialized newspapers and three magazines devoted to Old Believer affairs. The most prominent and longest-running of these was *Tserkov* (Church), a journal published by the Riabushinskys. Appearing weekly from 1908 to 1914, *Tserkov* became unpopular with the authorities because of its outspoken defense of Old Belief and its barbed criticism of the tsarist government. It was closed down by the censors in 1914, under the pretext of the war emergency. The resourceful and persistent Pavel Riabushinsky promptly reorganized the journal under the name *Slovo Tserkvi* (The Word of the Church) and continued publishing it until 1917. Through their publications the Riabushinskys hoped to appropriate the ancient religious culture of the Old Believers as the ethical core of a new nationalist entrepreneurial ideology (see the West essay).

Thus right up until the Revolution of 1917, religious rites and daily worship in the family circle or in the company of their co-religionists represented the most important sphere of spiritual life for many Moscow merchants and businessmen. The social status of the entrepreneurs in Russian society of the turn of the century remained precarious and contradictory, and they felt compelled to do their best to bolster their fragile social prestige with religious observance. The pangs of conscience caused by moneymaking and the necessity of exploiting the labor of others, on the one hand, and the wish to be "pleasing to God," on the other, could be eased only through strict attention to ritual, constant prayer in business and personal life, and lavish donations to church and charity. Lifestyles and economic circumstances changed, but this religiosity, like a sacred talisman, was passed on undiminished from generation to generation.

This faith and piety was especially strong among the followers of Old Belief, who raised creative labor, fortitude, and persistence to the level of a virtue. It was perhaps paradoxical that the principal basis on which Merchant Moscow lay claim to a new and privileged position in a rapidly modernizing society was rooted in the continued affirmation of a profoundly traditional and conservative religious culture.

NOTES

1. P. F. Vistengof, *Ocherki moskovskoi zhizni* (Moscow, 1842), p. 38.

2. N. Vishniakov, *Svedeniia o kupecheskom rode Vishniakovykh* (Moscow, 1911), chap. 1, p. 43.

3. *Materialy k istorii Prokhorovskoi Trekhgornoi Manufaktury i torgovo-promyshlennoi deiatel'nosti sem'i Prokhorovykh. Gody 1799–1915* (Moscow, n.d.), pp. 108–9, 124–25.

4. Vladimir P. Riabushinsky, *Kupechestvo moskovskoe* (Moscow: Rodina, 1992), nos. 8–9, p. 176.

5. Jo Ann Ruckman, *The Moscow Business Elite: A Social and Cultural Portrait of Two Generations, 1840–1905* (De Kalb: Northern Illinois University Press, 1984), p. 79.

6. G. Vasilich, "Moskva 1850–1910 gg," in *Moskva v ee proshlom i nastoiashchem*, 11th ed. (Moscow, n.d.), pp. 14, 22.

7. *Poriadok soversheniia molebstvii, ezhegodno byvaiushchikh v pomeshchenii Moskovskoi Birzhi* (Moscow, 1893), p. 3.

8. N. A. Naidenov, *Vospominaniia o vidennom, slyshannom i ispytannom*, part 2 (Moscow, 1905), p. 52.

9. M. K. Morozova, "Moi vospominaniia," in *Nashe nasledie*, no. 6 (1991): 97.

10. N. K. Krestovnikov, *Semeinaia khronika Krestovnikovykh*, book 1 (Moscow, 1903), p. 70.

11. S. Maksimov, *Brodiachaia Rus' Khrista radi* (St. Petersburg, 1877), pp. 33, 35.

12. A. P. Mel'nikov, *Ocherki bytovoi istorii Nizhegorodskoi iarmarki* (Nizhny-Novgorod, 1917), p. 3.

13. A. S. Provorikhina, "Moskovskoe staroobriadchestvo," in *Moskva v ee proshlom i nastoiashchem*, 10th ed. (Moscow, 1912), p. 51.

14. *Izvlecheniia iz rasporiazhenii po delam o raskol'nikakh pri imperatorakh Nikolae i Aleksandre, popolnennye zapiskoiu Mel'nikova* (Leipzig, 1882), pp. 14–15, 25.

15. Provorikhina, "Moskovskoe staroobriadchestvo," p. 65.

16. P. I. Mel'nikov-Pechersky, "Ocherki popovshchiny," in *Sobranie sochinenii*, vol. 7 (St. Petersburg, 1910), p. 205.

Figure 5.1. *Ilinka Street. The church of St. Nicholas "The Big Cross," built in 1680–88 through donations of the merchants Filatiev. The name of the church originated from the large cross with relics initially kept in the church. The church was demolished by the Soviet government in 1933. On the right is the building of the Northern Insurance Company. The photograph was taken in the 1910s.*

Figure 5.2. *The graves of Pavel Mikhailovich Riabushinsky and his wife, Alexandra, at the Rogozh cemetery. Demolished during the Soviet period.*

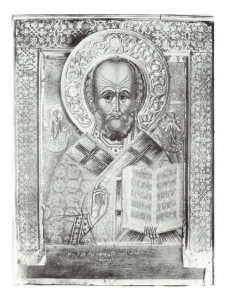

Figure 5.3. *The icon of St. Nicholas the Miracle Worker, 1559.*

Figure 5.4. *A solemn public prayer at the Trimount Textile Factory of the Prokhorovs.*

Figure 5.5. *The funeral of a rich merchant.*

Figure 5.6. *A religious procession at a factory.*

Figure 5.7. *The religious procession at the opening of the Nizhny-Novgorod Fair. The flag-raising signaled the fair's beginning.*

Figure 5.8. *The council of the community of the Rogozh cemetery in the early twentieth century. Bottom row: the priests (center, the Metropolitan Makarii). Top row: the merchants, Old Believer activists (center, I. A. Pugovkin, M. S. Kuznetsov, I. P. Tregubov).*

Figure 5.9. *Ilya Kovylin, the head of the Preobrazhensk community in the late eighteenth–early nineteenth centuries. The inclusion of a written document in the portrait reflected the Old Believers' veneration of text and love of reading.*

Figure 5.10. *Rogozh cemetery in the 1850s.*

Figure 5.11. *Rogozh cemetery in the early twentieth century.*

Figure 5.12. *The "cell" of the Riabushinskys at the Rogozh cemetery.*

Figure 5.13. *The interior of the home chapel of the Rakhmanovs.*

Figure 5.14. *The great bell of the Rogozh cemetery just before its installation, early twentieth century.*

Figure 5.15. *The newly built Priestless Old Believer church on Tokmakov Lane, 1908.*

Figure 5.16. *The Old Believer chorus at one of Moscow's textile factories.*

CHAPTER 6

Daily Life among the Morozovs

===

Karen Pennar

My grandmother, Vera Ivanovna Morozova, was born in 1900 in Moscow, the fourth child of the wealthy prerevolutionary industrialist Ivan Vikulovich Morozov and his wife, Varvara Aleksandrovna. Her youth, like that of all children born in Russia at that time, was rocked by war and revolution. But for my grandmother and her siblings—as for many of their contemporaries in the nascent merchant class—the contrasts that marked their lives as they approached adulthood were especially stark. Over a period of a few years, the Morozov children watched their privileged daily life disintegrate, and in its place an existence marked by loss, imprisonment, terror, and death took hold.

Little wonder that the memories of that former life remained crystalline for them and for so many other Russians, and that the photographs that captured that life were preserved with such devotion for so long. In 1991, when I met my grandmother's older sister, Olga Ivanovna (see plate 4), in Moscow, she was ninety-four years old, sharing a two-room flat on the outskirts of the city with her daughter and grandson. We settled into a creaky, century-old divan, and she sent her grandson to retrieve a cardboard box from a cupboard in the tiny room she shared with him. Her gnarled hands working eagerly, my great-aunt pulled out of the box packet after packet of photographs. As we viewed the photographs, we were transported—away from the dingy surroundings of cinder-block Soviet-style apartment life, away from the trials of daily living in a harsh and unstable society—to another, sunnier world, where the good life prevailed for a few fortunate Russians nearly a century earlier.

My grandmother and her siblings grew up at no. 10 Leontievsky Street, in the center of Moscow (figure 6.1). (Today the street is known as Stanislavsky Street, and the building houses the headquarters of a large private bank, Credobank.) Their father, Ivan (figure 6.2), had commissioned the construction of the house in 1905, and the family moved in the following year after returning from a self-imposed six-month exile in France to avoid the violence in Moscow (figure 6.3). The new residence put Ivan in the center of town, not far from the offices of textile manufacturers Vikula Morozov and Sons, of which he was the managing director, and closer to Petrovsky Park (figure 6.4), where he regularly rode his beloved horses. It also suited his wife, Varvara, a former student at the Bolshoi, to live in the more fashionable part of Moscow.

Prior to taking up residence on Leontievsky, the family lived in a wing of the rambling townhouse built by Vikula Eliseivich Morozov in the eastern part of the city, on Podsosensky Street. Ivan's older brother, Aleksei Vikulovich (figure 6.5), a bon vivant, bachelor, and avid collector of porcelain and engravings, remained at Podsosensky, as did another brother, Sergei Vikulovich, and his wife. A fourth brother, Elisei Vikulovich, also an unmarried and devoutly religious man, moved in with his brother Ivan's family.

Like many members of the Russian merchant estate, the Morozovs were Old Believers, or followers of the austere and fundamentalist sect that broke away from the Russian Orthodox church in the seventeenth century (See "A Note on Old Belief"). The Old Believer faith was popular among the peasantry in the 1700s, and there were many adherents in the Vladimir region where the serf Savva Morozov, the progenitor of the Morozov dynasty, was born in 1770. The faith remained so important to the Morozovs that Savva's first son, Elisei, in his later years preferred religious study to the textile business. He wrote a long treatise on the Antichrist, and took less and less interest in the firm that he formed in 1830. It was left to his son Vikula (figure 6.6) and grandson Ivan to expand the business, bringing in English looms to boost both the quality and the quantity of the output of cotton cloth.

By the time Ivan was courting Varvara in the early 1890s, many members of the merchant estate had, at least outwardly, shed their Old Believer faith and converted to Russian Orthodoxy in order to gain social acceptance. But the Morozovs were slow to do this. While Vikula had the business drive his father lacked, he nonetheless was a devoted Old Believer, and he disapproved of his son's courtship of Varvara, both because she was Orthodox and because she was an artist.

Ivan was twenty-nine, handsome yet of a serious demeanor, and had just recently become a jurist, when he met Varvara backstage at the Bolshoi after a performance. He was swept away by the vivacious and beautiful young woman, then just eighteen (figure 6.7). They married in 1895 after Vikula's death, and Ivan converted to official Orthodoxy before the marriage. Still, because their pairing was considered out of the ordinary, they were married in a quiet ceremony at a small church outside Moscow. Their four children were all brought up Russian Orthodox, and my grandmother remembers special services at her home: "Every Christmas and every Easter a choir of about thirty or forty young men came to sing in our house, to glorify God. They sang in our children's hall, and the noise of their steps in high, black boots still resounds in my ears. Lovely boys, clean and well-outfitted in their long, black caftans, tight at the waist, and young men, who looked like their elder brothers. I loved it."[1]

Ivan Morozov was, according to his daughters' description, a somber but gentle man who took his work very seriously. Every day, Vera Ivanovna recalled,[2] her father would follow a set regimen. He would leave his second-floor bedroom at about 8:00, pass the winter-garden gallery with its huge palm trees, walk down the corridor past the billiard room, and descend the red-carpeted, double-winged marble staircase. Passing through his study and the large, tapestry-bedecked formal dining room, he would settle down in the smaller, pear wood–paneled family dining room. There he would take his morning tea in a silver glass-holder, munch on some fresh rolls with butter, and review the daily newspapers. At 9:30, his troika, driven by a heavyset coachman fitted out in a bottle-green caftan with silver filigree buttons, pulled up outside the main entrance. Ivan was helped into the carriage by his man-servant, Eustache, and then he was off to the Varvarka, the street in the financial district of Moscow where many manufacturing businesses, including Vikula Morozov and Sons, had their administrative offices. Directors of the factory held their office hours and meetings in Moscow, and less frequently traveled the ninety kilometers east to Orekhovo-Zuevo to check on conditions at the factory.

At 1:00, Ivan would return from the office for lunch in the family dining room, served by Eustache and Nastya, the chambermaid. Anka, the Latvian housekeeper who was with the Morozovs for many years, supervised the meal preparation in the pantry. Lunch consisted of an appetizer, a main dish, fruit, and coffee, as well as a glass of red wine and a bottle of Narsan mineral water. After lunch, Ivan would retire to his study for a consultation with his intendant, Tarasov, who looked after his employer's personal affairs. Tarasov resided in a small house on the grounds of Petrovsky Park in northwest Moscow, where Ivan maintained stables for his racing horses as well as his riding horses. Then Ivan would remain in his study for an hour, reviewing papers. That room, on the main floor just above street level, had three large windows facing the street and one facing the garden. Heavy, dark green draperies framed the windows of the room, which was decorated with landscape paintings by Shishkin, small bronze sculptures, glass cabinets lined with silver cups won by Morozov's racehorses, and sofas covered in a rich red brocade. Ivan would return to the Varvarka offices at three o'clock in the afternoon and remain there until about five.

Although work occupied his attention during the day, Ivan was devoted to his wife and children in the evenings. Every day on returning home, my great-aunt Olga remembered, her father would head immediately toward the children's wing, through a special pass-through room from the main house that he had the architects design. "Father wanted to speak with us and play with us," Olga said. Her mother, who had borne Fedya, Olga, Kirill, and Vera in quick succession, was cooler toward her children. "She liked order, and she came to our rooms to see that everything was in order. . . . She didn't like very much to play with us. . . . Perhaps she didn't know how; perhaps it tired her," Olga recalled.[3]

After visiting with the children, Ivan would generally sit down to dinner with his wife and his brother Elisei at about 7:00. The children, who were served dinner in their own wing of the house at about 6:00, were brought around by their nannies to say goodnight to their parents. Many evenings were capped off by a visit to the theater or the ballet. The Morozovs regularly attended the Moscow Art Theater, to which Ivan's cousin, the legendary Savva Timofeyevich Morozov, was a major financial contributor. And the Morozovs regularly booked box no. 3 at the Bolshoi for Wednesday-night performances.

For Varvara, daily life was comfortable, decidedly slower-paced than her husband's routine. Varvara studied music and took French lessons, but she spent most of her days supervising the activities of the household staff, which at any one time numbered about a dozen people, including a cook, housekeeper, nannies, governesses, and assorted footmen and manservants. Then, too, Varvara looked after her bachelor brother-in-law, Elisei, and also entertained her other brothers-in-law, Aleksei and Sergei.

Ivan's siblings dubbed her the *koroleva* (queen), and Varvara certainly seemed to enjoy being the center of attention, the beautiful lady of the Morozov household. A photo of her when she was nearly thirty years old shows her posing coquettishly, her waistline pencil-thin, a diaphanous scarf twirled around her arms and her hair swept up, Gibson girl–like, with a few wispy tendrils teasing her neckline (figure 6.8). In group photographs, she typically appears a bit more radiant than the other woman in the picture (figure 6.9).

Varvara was always beautifully turned out. She had dresses from the French designers Worth and Patou, as well as the Moscow dressmaker Lamonova, who charged five hundred gold rubles for her creations. She powdered her shoulders white, and the French hairdresser André came to Leontievsky to arrange her hair. Vera remembers two of her mother's evenings gowns, one of red and gold and the other of white and gold, both made of plisse fabric. She wore parures of emeralds and diamonds or sapphires, turquoises and diamonds, many that she designed herself and ordered executed by the jewelry houses Klebnikov, Bolin, or Fabergé in Moscow. When she swept through the children's wing in the evenings to bid her children goodnight before setting out for the theater or the ballet, she was, Vera wrote, "like a vision from a fairy tale, leaving an exquisite scent behind her."[4]

Varvara frequently showed off her beauty and her figure at the theater and the ballet, and also entertained at Leontievsky. There were lavish dinner parties for which members of the Hotel Metropole staff would be hired to help. And she maintained a tradition of having two *jours-fixes*, Tuesdays and Fridays, when she received guests at the townhouse and served cakes, candy, and coffee. Still, she was less of a social butterfly than many of her peers in Merchant Moscow, and her guests were most often relatives—her mother, her siblings, and, invariably, her brother-in-law Aleksei.

As the eldest of four brothers (a fifth had died at a young age), Aleksei took on the top director's job at Vikula Morozov and Sons when his parents died, within a few months of each other, in 1894. But it was a job he hated. "In my character, I have always leaned toward scientific and artistic interests, especially toward collecting, and I always found business affairs to be a terrible burden for which, by the way, I had not received any preparation," he recollected. "Throughout my father's life, it was a secret dream of mine to be liberated from the heavy yoke of business. After my father's death this dream became an obsession."[5] So Aleksei soon ceded management of the firm to his younger brother, Ivan, and remained as a largely passive shareholder, along with his other brothers.

Aleksei had long loved to travel and to collect beautiful things, from porcelain figurines to portrait engravings. He developed a fine sense of Russian culture. Indeed, he was always urging his nephews and nieces to study Russian literature and not to be overawed by European culture. And because he was well traveled, his tastes were keenly developed and widely admired. The socialite and patron Margarita Kirillovna Morozova, who married his cousin Mikhail Morozov, was a good friend and a guest at dinner parties on Podsosensky Street many times. "He was a person with a refined mind, very witty, and he loved the company of women, even though he was unmarried. . . . His dinners were always the best of all the ones that we were invited to. A huge table was placed in the middle of a small dining room, covered with a snow-white tablecloth, which was crammed with hors d'oeuvres and decanters with different-colored vodkas and wines. In the middle of the table on a long silver dish lay pink fishes, salmon and smoked salmon, and on the side, a sparkling crystal bowl with fresh caviar. At the other end of the table there was a huge side of ham and red langoustines. The rest of the table was crammed with bowls and plates filled with every possible sausage, cheese, smoked fish, salads, nothing was forgotten!"[6]

The most frequent guests at Aleksei's rambling house were his siblings and nieces and nephews. My grandmother loved the grand entrance to the townhouse on Podsosensky, which boasted Egyptian-style columns and sphinxes painted in bold colors. On the ground floor, to the left, was a library and study designed by the artist Mikhail Vrubel, called the "Doctor Faust" study because of its elaborate wooden staircase, carved with demonic figures based on characters from the legend (figure 6.10). Vera's "Uncle Lenya," as she called her Uncle Aleksei, would climb the stairs to the mezzanine level, where a richly cushioned bench allowed him to survey the room, or he could gaze up the staircase to the fine tapestry that hung just below the ceiling. In the room beyond the library was the intimate study, with a pale pink stained-glass ceiling.[7] Upstairs was his porcelain collection, displayed in specially designed vitrines. Pavel A. Buryshkin, the biographer of Moscow merchant families, says that Aleksei's collections were little known in Moscow,[8] but my grandmother remembered that he often invited visitors expressly to see the collection.

It was appropriate that Aleksei lavished so much attention on his study, because to him, learning was critical to the cultured life, and he tried to instill the importance of reading and a wide-ranging education in his nephews and nieces. Books were his most frequent presents to them, and he was always encouraging them to read Russian prose and poetry, the better to understand their own culture and surroundings. Among the merchant estate, it was usually European works and art that had the greatest cachet.

Aleksei's nephews and nieces received extensive education, first at home then at Moscow schools: the boys' gymnasium Medvediakov for Fedya and Kirill, and the girls' gymnasium Arseniev for Olga and Vera. Their education, much like their upbringing, was both privileged and lonely. As very young children they spent most of their days in their own wing of the house, looked after by nannies. Later, governesses from Europe instructed them. True to Uncle Lenya's wishes, the governesses saw to it that the children read in their native language. By the age of eleven, my grandmother wrote, she had read all the Russian classics save those by Dostoevsky, an author deemed too complicated for a young girl to understand.

The children grew close to the governesses with whom they spent so much time. The two elder children, Fedya and Olga, were instructed by Mlle Julie, a Swiss woman, while the two younger children were taught by Mlle Fevrier, a French woman whom the children adored. A photo taken in about 1913, when Vera was thirteen years old, shows the two of them swimming in the Moscow River, just down the embankment from the summer estate Isslavskoe. Young girl and governess are hugging each other, laughing conspiratorially (figure 6.11).

In the days when the Morozov children were growing up, Moscow was newly vibrant, exciting and worldly. Bankers and businessmen were energizing Moscow, which had traditionally played second fiddle to St. Petersburg. The merchants' money was financing a building boom, and shops, theaters, libraries, exhibition halls, and, of course, fine townhouses dotted the streets. "Our books were mostly bought at Wolf and Co., on Kuznetsky Most," my grandmother wrote. "Very elegant, it was the most fashionable street in Moscow, like Nevsky Prospekt in St. Petersburg. It was the place of rendezvous, flirtations, and escapades. A show of uniforms and pretty, well-dressed women. The best shops were on Kuznetsky Most." Fabergé, Einem, Cadet, Noeff, she began, reeling off the names of the renowned jewelers, the excellent candy and patisserie houses, and Moscow's finest florist. There were others, too, branches of the best shops in Vienna, Paris, and London. "Mlle Fevrier loved to walk down Stoleshnikov Street, then Petrovka and finally Kuznetsky Most. Several times, having my sister Olga and me, clutched on either side of her. We spoke French, keeping our heads up, as she told us to. It was like the first debut in society."

For the Morozov children, such excursions were enjoyable ventures into the world at large. But because of their station in Moscow society, the children could not go out often, and they were always chaperoned. The only place where the children could achieve a sense of freedom and independence was in the countryside, where they would play and wander on lazy summer after-noons. For many years, the Morozovs spent long stretches of time during the summer at Odintsovo-Arkhangelskoe, the one hundred–room estate Aleksei inherited from Vikula (figure 6.12). The huge house, designed by the Swedish architect Ericson, was both Gothic and whimsical in its style, with towers, secret passages, rooftop spires, red and gray bricks, and endless galleries. There, and on the expansive ground with its lime trees, orchards, sweeping lawns, and elaborately maintained gardens, the young Morozov children would play with their cousins, and the adults would gather for al fresco lunches and relaxation.

In addition to family members, the painter Nikolai Ivanovich Chechelov would tag along, eager to please. He would paint portraits on the spur of the moment—a photograph captures him painting my great-aunt Olga when she was about ten years old (figure 6.13). And he would commandeer the children for afternoon activites such as blowing up balloons, with the adults gazing on approvingly. When Ivan and Varvara and their children stayed at Odintsovo-Arkhangelskoe, a fireworks show was usually given in their honor. On the evening of the show, the streams of water that gurgled up from the fountains were illuminated in different colors, swans and boats with various fairy-tale figures floated on the river beyond the estate's grounds, and the entire family and their guests would gather amid the weeping willows to watch the fire-works display.[9]

Three large parks surrounded the estate house, and the parks had long alleys set in a crisscross fashion, with strawberries planted between the alleys. From the drawing room windows, my grandmother would look out on the grounds, and often saw peasant girls watering the gardens. At the time, there were no pipes to carry the water, so local girls would haul large watering cans, lifting their skirts as they trudged in their bare feet. Sometimes, they would climb planks protecting the flower arrangements, and they would sing as they transported the water.[10]

Isslavskoe, the estate on the banks of the Moscow river that Ivan had built in 1913, was very different (figure 6.14). It didn't have the familiar and com-fortable quality of Aleksei's estate. Instead, it had a grand aura, and at first my grandmother found it forbidding. In family photographs, the estate seems unfinished, its grounds just planted and its rooms only sparsely furnished (figure 6.15). The house was built in the Russian Empire style by the Russian architects Adamovich and Mayat, with an array of columns and arches, an elegant Palladian-style dome, and an interior with parade rooms and columns echoing the exterior style. It sat at a commanding height above a bend in the river about fifty kilometers west of Moscow, and the lawns and gardens were terraced down to the river. The children could amble down to the bathhouse on the river for summer swims, and a motorboat was ready for family outings. At that point the river was very narrow, so little or no traffic moved along its banks.

The estate covered one thousand hectares, with parkland on both sides of the house, and wilderness extending beyond the park. Ivan had stables built for his horses, complete with electricity, and the horses could gallop in the nearby fields. There was also a small working farm, where cows, fowl, and Varvara's English sheep were kept. There was a great deal for the family to do at Isslavskoe.

Still, Vera's memories of Isslavskoe were colored by the First World War and the Russian Revolution. The summers of 1915 and 1916, my grandmother recalled, she and her sister helped their governesses to sew clothes and dressings for Russian soldiers who were wounded and home from the front. As the Morozov children grew older, their visits to the countryside seemed less carefree. And in 1916, after Olga married, Vera was increasingly left to fend for herself. She read French novels, kept a notebook, and wandered the grounds of Isslavskoe picking mushrooms.

Vera's last visit to Isslavskoe was in the autumn of 1917, with her mother and her mother's maid, Arisha, just before the October revolution. It was already too dangerous for Ivan to make such a trip. The house was dark and the electricity was shut off. Candles were lit in the white marble hall, and a modest dinner was prepared and served. Vera and her mother climbed the winding stairs to the belvedere, where Varvara kept some of her jewels and other possessions in some closets. They gathered the most valuable things together and returned quickly to Moscow.

Three-quarters of a century later, the estate is off limits, beyond a Russian government militia post and behind a cement-block wall. Locally it is known as "Gorky's Dacha," after the writer Maxim Gorky, who lived there for many years as a guest of the Bolshevik government. Viewed from the town of Nikolnaya Gora on the opposite side of the river, the embankment is heavily overgrown, and there is no sign of the house. Like so much of merchant Russia, Isslavskoe has been hidden from view and unknown. In the Morozov family photographs, Isslavskoe is a monument to a way of life cut short, and a bittersweet reminder of what might have been, had the families of Merchant Moscow survived to help make Russia in the twentieth century a very different place from what it turned out to be.

NOTES

1. Vera Ivanovna Morozova Pennar, unpublished memoirs written in the 1970s.

2. Ibid.

3. Olga Ivanovna Morozova, interview with Karen Pennar, June 1991.

4. Pennar, unpublished memoirs.

5. Alexei Vikulovich Morozov, unpublished memoirs written in 1933, trans. Karen Pennar.

6. Margareta Kirillovna Morozova, "My Recollections," *Nashe Naslediye* 6 (1991): 100, trans. Karen Pennar.

7. Pennar, unpublished memoirs.

8. Pavel A. Buryshkin, *Merchant Moscow* (New York: Chekhov Publishing, 1954), p. 119.

9. Pennar, unpublished memoirs.

10. Ibid.

Figure 6.1. *The Morozov house on Leontievsky Street, commissioned by Ivan V. Morozov in 1905. The family moved here the following year. (Photo by Karen Pennar, 1991.)*

Figure 6.2. *Ivan Vikulovich Morozov as a young jurist. (Photo by permission of the family of V. Morozov.)*

Figure 6.3. *Ivan Morozov in Nice, 1905. (Photo by permission of the family of V. Morozov.)*

Призовыя конюшни И. В. Морозова,
Петровскій паркъ.

Figure 6.4. *Ivan Morozov's stables in Petrovsky Park. (Photo by permission of the family of V. Morozov.)*

Figure 6.5. *Aleksei Vikulovich Morozov in Nice, 1905. (Photo by permission of the family of V. Morozov.)*

Figure 6.6. *Vikula Morozov and his daughter, Liudmila, who married into the Zimin family, 1880s. (Photo by permission of the family of V. Morozov.)*

Figure 6.7. *Varvara Aleksandrovna Morozova as a student at the Bolshoi Theater. (Photo by permission of the family of V. Morozov.)*

Figure 6.9. *The Morozov family at the country estate of Odintsovo-Arkhangelskoe, c. 1908. Ivan is standing at the far left, Aleksei is seated at the far right next to Varvara, and Elisei is seated on the left. (Photo by permission of the family of V. Morozov.)*

Figure 6.8. *Varvara Morozova at Odintsovo-Arkhangelskoe, c. 1908. (Photo by permission of the family of V. Morozov.)*

Figure 6.10. The "Doctor Faust" study in Aleksei's home on Podsosensky Street, house designed by architect Fedor Shekhtel. (Photo by permission of the family of V. Morozov.)

Figure 6.11. Vera and her governess, Mlle Fevrier, swimming near Isslavskoe, c. 1913. (Photo by permission of the family of V. Morozov.)

Figure 6.12. *The Morozov estate at Odintsovo-Arkhangelskoe. Olga is in the foreground. (Photo by permission of the family of V. Morozov.)*

Figure 6.13. *Varvara Morozova and Olga with the artist Nikolai Chechelov at Odintsovo-Arkhangelskoe, c. 1908. (Photo by permission of the family of V. Morozov.)*

Figure 6.14. *The new estate, Isslavskoe, c. 1913. (Photo by permission of the family of V. Morozov.)*

Figure 6.15. *The dining room at Isslavskoe, c. 1913. (Photo by permission of the family of V. Morozov.)*

PART THREE

Beyond the Boardroom:
Social Hierarchies—Gender,
Class, and Education

CHAPTER 7

Peasant Entrepreneurs and Worker Peasants: Labor Relations in Merchant Moscow

Mikhail K. Shatsillo

The topic of social relations between employers and their workers in Merchant Moscow evokes associations with the old two-story houses of Moscow, some of which still survive. Sunk deep into the earth, they preserve the basements of ancestral boyar palaces of the seventeenth century. But above, they are over-built by more recent stories featuring nineteenth-century neoclassical facades. And behind these walls, modernist Art Nouveau interior styles predominate. Labor relations in the Moscow region were long shaped exclusively by custom and tradition, and these archaic patriarchal attitudes gave way only slowly, intermingling with newer forms of industrial partnership and conflict typical of developed countries. Merchant Moscow was a complex and often paradoxical social entity.

Unfortunately, the surviving photographic documents do not permit us to illustrate the full complexity of relations between master and worker in Russia. The reason is not limited to the obvious fact that at the time of the birth of the merchant factory, photography was still in its infancy. The problem resides more in the issue of who controlled the camera; the obedient lens, at the command of the merchant patron, focused most often on idyllic factory scenes. Visual signs of social conflict and exploitation were left to be documented by a later generation of Soviet propagandists in no way beholden to merchants.

Early patterns of patriarchal organization in merchant enterprises were shaped by the common social origin and status shared by masters and workers alike. In the factories of the Moscow region, in contrast to industries run by the state and the nobility-owned factories of the Urals, both the proprietors and the workers of merchant enterprises were of the same social provenance: all were descended from the peasantry of the Russian heartland. In the nineteenth century, the peasant workers often viewed temporary factory labor as an opportunity to earn supplemental income, after which they could return to the village. Even permanent industrial workers, as a rule, retained their juridical links with agriculture, remaining members of rural commune and paying corresponding taxes.

The peasant nature of the Russian factory work force persisted into the twentieth century and actually intensified after the 1890s as the rapid pace of industrialization stimulated a renewed influx of raw peasants from the village to the factory. Professional workers, who may have been linked with the enterprise for generations and were skilled in the most complex industrial operations, were always in the minority, perpetually dissolved in the mass of peasant newcomers. Existing photographs suggest that on the factory grounds one would only rarely encounter a worker in European clothes, for the majority still wore village garb: men were in long shirts, blouses with collars fastening at the side, peaked caps, and cotton trousers tucked into high boots, while women came to work wearing their ubiquitous white calico kerchiefs (figures 7.1 and 7.2). The most highly qualified workers and shop foremen who wore modern clothes were usually lost in a sea of peasantness that permeated the factory environment (figure 7.3).

This connection with the village was long maintained not only among the workers but also by the factory owners. Though among the elites of Merchant Moscow there were occasional descendants from other social strata, the majority of the most prominent entrepreneurial families claimed peasant ancestors. The founders of future merchant dynasties resembled the peasants in every detail: their dress, lifestyle, and vernacular speech. They were distinguished only by their enterprise, their energy, and sometimes their luck. These humble origins remained a defining element in the social self-identity and group psychology of later generations of entrepreneurs. During the emancipation debate in the 1850s, Vasily Kokorev, the son of a peasant trader of modest wealth who became one of the richest entrepreneurs in Russia, reminded his fellow merchants of their ties to the people. In a speech at a banquet in 1857, he voiced the notion that the merchant estate had a special responsibility to support the emancipation of the serfs. "We will be ashamed even to look at the peasants," he said, "because many of us have only recently descended from [them], and I myself have relatives in the peasant estate."[1] Kokorev's veneration of his rustic origins permeated his private life. He drank champagne, but only mixed with kvas, the Russian peasant brew. His most prized possession, the object of numerous jokes from radical publicists of the day, was a gold-plated bast shoe demonstratively exhibited in his study. More sympathetic contemporaries used to say that this curiosity, along with his magnificent collection of peasant handicrafts, represented the origin of a pattern of patronage of indigenous folk arts among the merchant elite that flourished later in the century.

The genetic link with the popular masses was still the object of pride of some renowned merchant politicians of the early twentieth century. Aleksandr Guchkov, scion of a Moscow merchant dynasty and the leader of the Octobrist Party after 1905, when accused of being a "merchant patriot," replied with proud defiance from the Duma podium: "I am not only the son of a merchant but also the grandson of a peasant, a peasant who had made his way in the world starting as a serf by his diligence and persistence."[2]

Some businessmen of the second generation insisted on ostentatious display of their relations with the peasantry. There was a category of entrepreneurs who demonstratively remained within the peasant estate and did not join the merchant one, being content with the legal status of the so called "temporary merchants." The case of such contrived behavior was captured by the writer Anton Chekhov, who was himself the grandson of a serf and the son of a merchant: "X, rich and intelligent, a peasant by origin, implores his son: 'Misha, do not change your status! Be a peasant until death, do not become a nobleman, nor a merchant, nor a townsman. If they say that the land captains have the right to punish the peasants, let it be so that he will have the right to punish you as well.' He was proud of his peasant status and was even arrogant."[3] Thus the masters and the workers, the two groups that evolved toward opposite social poles, originated from the same timeless agrarian culture.

Despite their emotional and rhetorical ties to the peasantry, the factory owners were soon subject to a radical process of social differentiation, which gained momentum during the late nineteenth century. Whatever his origins or conceits, the peasant-entrepreneur owned the means of production, the factory, of which he grew to be immensely proud. The family enterprise, Vladimir P. Riabushinsky recalled, represented for the entrepreneur the same emotional center that the ancestral castle was to a medieval knight. And indeed, not only did the factory guarantee the well-being of its owners and his clan, it also was also literally the citadel of his dynasty. It was not accidental that even the architectural design of the factory buildings often emphasized the heraldry and motifs of hereditary ownership (figure 7.4). The origin of the merchant "castle" dates back to the early nineteenth century, when the cotton industry, previously nonexistent in Russia, took root and began its rapid development. This branch of private industry managed to survive without any direct assistance from the state, which supported instead the noble-owned linen cloth mills and iron foundries that served the needs of its army and navy.

The guarantee of success of the new branch of industry was its orientation toward the vast but undeveloped consumer market. Cotton production was extremely simple from a technical point of view, and initially it relied on manual labor alone. Many peasants engaged in this kind of hand production, and the most successful of them managed in the course of time to save enough money to open their own artisanal workshops. An additional impulse to the development of peasant-owned industry was provided by the Great Moscow

Fire during the War of 1812, when nearly all the older merchant-owned factories of the city were destroyed. It was after that time that new factories began to be built by the former peasant artisans and craftsmen. As these newcomers began to amass great personal fortunes, the social anomaly of the serf millionaire arose.

In the early nineteenth century, the village of Ivanovo, a city that is still today the largest center of the Russian textile industry, exemplified this paradox. The richest factory owners there, all of whom employed more than one thousand workers each, were juridically as much without rights and privileges as the poorest of their workers. All of them together were serfs of Count Sheremetev. These serf entrepreneurs amassed extensive property and real estate, and even owned their own serfs. Thus, for example, the serf Ivan Garelin owned the entire village of Spasskoe with all the peasants who lived there. Another Ivanovo capitalist, Grachev, also possessed serfs. Naturally, all legal rights to these serfs, and in theory all property and profits, belonged to the seigneur of Ivanovo, Count Sheremetev. But the estate office of Sheremetev acknowledged and sanctioned the property transactions of the entrepreneur-serfs who were within its jurisdiction, for as long as the Count received his share of the profits, the serf capitalists were permitted to operate freely under the protection of the seigneur.

Despite this advantageous symbiotic relationship, it goes without saying that such serf entrepreneurs sought to purchase their freedom at the first opportunity. The lord of Ivanovo agreed to this kind of self-purchased manumission very reluctantly, and very rarely; prior to the Peasant Emancipation of 1861, only about fifty peasant families were emancipated in this way, and the average ransom for a family was exceedingly high for that time, reaching twenty thousand rubles. The newly freed factory owners quickly registered themselves as merchants.[4]

This convoluted path of social mobility left its mark on the entrepreneurial culture of the textile industry. A prototypic example was the Alekseev enterprise. Its founder started an artisanal enterprise of gold thread production not far from Moscow. Alekseev, who enjoyed the confidence not only of his fellow villagers but of the people of the whole district, soon became a traveling salesman of his own goods. When he had amassed enough money, he bought a plot of land in Moscow and founded the Alekseevs' gold thread factory, which is still in existence. At the outset the only people he employed were his relatives, but soon the enterprise expanded, and peasant artisans also started to work at the factory. The owners not only knew all the workers by name but called the most experienced and qualified among them by patronymic as well to show the respect due them by virtue of their skill. Life at the factory was patriarchal until the mid-nineteenth century: the owner fed the workers, all the employees lived in his house, and it was not infrequent that scores of factory hands gathered at the Alekseevs' table. The patriarch closely controlled their behavior of his charges: each night the gates were locked at ten o'clock, and anyone who was late or absent faced a reprimand in the morning.[5]

The feeling of community between the merchant and the worker was also promoted by the fact that despite growing differences in wealth, both shared the same civil and juridical deprivations perpetuated by the nobility's monopoly of power. The workers often labored in factories to earn the money to pay their rent to the landlord, and in summer they returned to the village to work in the fields. For their part, the merchants tried to tie the workers closer to the factory, sometimes even helping them pay the redemption fee necessary to gain freedom. Some factory owners did not hesitate to employ fugitive serfs. This was especially typical of Old Believer merchants such as the Guchkovs, who could register illegal workers with the connivance of their dissident religious community.[6]

Such shared hardships strengthened the merchants in their perception of certain moral obligations toward the worker, who in selling his hands to the capitalist also looked to him for protection. According to Pavel Buryshkin, Merchant Moscow considered entrepreneurship not merely as a source of profit but as the fulfillment of a certain mission prescribed by God. It was said that God bestowed wealth and would eventually demand an account of it.[7] Displays of concern for the "lesser ones" was a conspicuous trait among the early entrepreneurs. Such initiatives as those taken by the Prokhorovs in building factory schools, hospitals, barracks for workers, and almshouses for the elderly, were accompanied with showy ceremonies and church services to set an example for other factory owners to follow. Many followed this lead (figures 7.5–9).

Patriarchal relations between the masters and the workers could not survive forever, for life itself drove these two groups in opposite directions. The social distance between them became especially noticeable after the mid-nineteenth century, when manual labor began to be replaced by machinery. Experience and skill began to matter less than other qualities, such as endurance, discipline, and submissiveness. The search for maximum efficiency in the use of equipment prompted the entrepreneurs to prolong the working day and to introduce round-the-clock schedules. Expanding production required the influx of new workers, and child labor became common. At the same time, living conditions in the factory deteriorated. Newcomers, if they were not residents of nearby villages, were lodged in overcrowded barracks, or in the worst cases passed the night under their machines in the factory.

These transformations in methods and conditions gradually outstripped the psychology of the factory owners, who in large measure continued to see themselves as benefactors to their workers. Because they saw their relationship with their workers as a personal and traditional one, they resisted at every turn the attempts of the state to regulate labor relations. Merchant Moscow fought tenacious rear-guard battles to delay official attempts to prohibit child labor, to limit the length of working day, and to outlaw night shifts. The government's proposals to introduce a system of state factory inspectors in the 1880s elicited the following reaction from the Moscow factory owners: "The introduction of inspection, instead of the expected benefits, will produce harm by destroying all ties between the owners and the workers, will give cause for abuse and will increase the number of complaints."[8]

The "Golden Age" of the Russian factory occurred in the 1880s, when productive techniques underwent a real technological revolution. These improvements, however, widened still further the distance between master and worker. This change occurred across a succession of generations. In place of the simple and straightforward mentality of the patriarchal founder of the enterprise came his educated and refined descendant, whose appearance retained nothing of the peasant his father once was (figure 7.10). He would buy the house of some impoverished landlord near the factory, where the local notables, district doctors, country lawyers, and marshals of nobility would assemble for an evening party with cards and champagne. The enormity of the contrast between the lifestyle of the new master and that of the worker is suggested by the description left by one obviously unsympathetic factory inspector who had spent fifteen years on the job, and therefore knew the situation very well:

> My reader, have you ever been to a large factory village of Central Russia? The picture caught by your eye is joyless: naked and barren terrain, untilled and unsown naked fields covered with weeds; a stinking river slowly flowing between flat banks without a single bush or willow. It is an ordinary landscape in the middle of which you notice the high smokestacks and enormous blocks of factory buildings. If you are going on a visit to the factory owner, driven there by his precious trotters, the horses will quickly rush you past a cluster of squalid shacks at the outskirts, then along the paved main street, and you will hardly have time to bat an eye before you find yourself at the doorstep of the magnificent palace of the factory owner. The soft carpets, marble, bronze, stuffed bears at the bottom of the wide staircase, and the flunky in dress coat gives you the impression of being in the most fashionable quarters of St. Petersburg or Moscow. But if you were to venture into the middle of the village turning onto other streets and lanes, you would see the long rows of tiny huts without any sign of household structure and deep in murderous mud and foulness; you would see half-naked children rummaging in the heaps of litter, the motley rags drying on ropes and poles, the clothes of those who dwell in these shacks. You would notice a lot of suspicious teahouses with characters drinking near them, empty tents waiting for the array of attractive goods, and mountains of blue coffins near every small shop. If you come here in summer when the weather is warm but humid, you will be assaulted by the eternal stench of latrines and human sweat. The smell of sweat that permeates the air inside the factory building, dominating the terrain, would come out at

this time and spread far around. There is no escape from it, nor from the smell of the stinking river and latrines, not even for the factory owner in his opulent palace, no matter how tightly the windows are closed at that time. Close to the factory buildings you would notice long, barracklike structures: the factory dwellings for workers, the so-called sleeping rooms.[9]

The German economist Schulze-Gävernitz, who personally visited and inspected many Russian factories at the end of the nineteenth century, distinguished three specific features of Russian enterprises that differentiated them from factories in the West: low wages, an overextended workday, and the "muteness" of the workers.[10] If the first two distinctions survived into the twentieth century, the last one did not. In the winter of 1885, the Morozovs' Nikolskaia textile mill became the scene of the first large-scale industrial strike in the Central Industrial Region. The strike was caused by wage cuts and the severe system of fines imposed on the workers for all kinds of offenses. This unrest was put down through the use of military force and several score of the most active instigators were taken to court. Russian public opinion did not support the Morozovs; the jury acquitted all of the accused, and in the summer of 1886 the government was forced to decree a limitation on penalties assessed against workers, stipulating that fines should not exceed 5 percent of the worker's wage.

The success of the Morozov strike, which had first demonstrated the efficacy of organized struggle against the factory owners, gave impetus to a mass labor movement in Russia and paved the way for the confrontation between the rich and the poor that was to take such dramatic form in the early twentieth century. To quote Vladimir Riabushinsky:

> In the '80s and '90s of the last century, the relationship between the masters and the workers reached the turning point. The patriarchal period, with its good and evil, with its simplemindedness and sin, with its caring, help, cheating, and grievance was over. . . . At that time, some elder factory owner could say in full certainty of his righteousness: "I've committed a lot of sins, but I can take credit for one thing: founding this factory and promoting it; now I can feed ten thousand people." And the old workers who had played *babki* ['knucklebones'] with their master when they had been children also considered it to be a merit. But the years passed, and the same master who grew very old by now could occasionally hear a crowd of youngsters at the time of some strike [grumble]—"We are ten thousand, and we all feed you, the fat one."[11]

Patriarchal relations, previously sanctified by tradition, now showed signs of cracking to release the germ of future social conflict. This change was recognized both by radical intellectuals, who began active agitation among the workers in support of socialist ideas, and by the factory owners themselves. From the 1890s until World War I, there was a steady rise in wages paid at

Russian factories. But raises alone could not ease growing social tension. The common arguments of the agitators in favor of active and continuous struggle against capitalism took root in the widening gulf that yawned between the financial position of the masters and that of the workers. It was endlessly repeated that the proletarians in the developed countries like the United States, Great Britain, and Germany were paid two to three times more than their Russian counterparts.

The generalized political crisis rising in Russia at the beginning of the twentieth century prompted some Moscow entrepreneurs to join the movement for reform. Especially after many factories became battlegrounds in the great Moscow Insurrection of December 1905, leading figures like the Guchkovs and the members of the Riabushinsky Circle became active in forming liberal and centrist political parties (see the West essay). This liberal vanguard of Merchant Moscow stood for the realization of democratic changes in the country, which they saw as the only means of easing labor tensions and precluding another revolutionary explosion over the labor problem. These progressive industrialists did not limit themselves to political declarations alone, but actively tried to change the social climate in their "family castles" and factories through concrete and real reforms. Some measures undertaken by enlightened factory owners to improve the life of the workers corresponded to the highest Western standards of the time. Members of the Riabushinsky Circle were particularly assertive in this regard. Aleksandr Konovalov built whole workers' settlements around his cotton factory in Vichuga (figure 7.11), complete with schools, nurseries, a palatial theater rivaling the Bolshoi, and a hospital that is still in operation today. Sergei Chetverikov, who had limited the length of the working day at his linen enterprise even before the introduction of factory legislation and had spent a great deal of money on improving the living conditions of his workers, in 1907 made them shareholders in his business (in Russian, "co-partnership").

In the years before the Bolshevik Revolution, many Moscow industrialists attempted to defuse radical socialist appeals to the laboring masses by pinning their hopes on cultural and educational work at the factories. Various societies, centers organizing public lectures, educational courses, popular theaters, and sport clubs came into being one after another (figures 7.12 and 7.13). These tactics were denounced by most intellectuals; the radicals did their best to "unmask" the "exploitive" motivation of such actions. In 1905, the Bolshevik leader Vladimir I. Lenin wrote with obvious irritation: "The intelligent bourgeois around Russia are doing . . . everything in their power in thousands of methods and ways—books, lectures, speeches, discussions, and so on—to inspire the workers with the ideas of (bourgeois) sobriety, (liberal) practicality, (opportunistic) realism."[12] One is tempted to wonder what Russia would have been like had the "intelligent bourgeois" succeeded in inculcating these values into the population.

The search for new forms of social partnership pursued by some enlightened entrepreneurs was overwhelmed by accelerating changes in the nature of the work force. The Stolypin Land Reforms after 1907 forced ever more peasants off the land and into the cities. They brought with them into the industrial landscape age-old rural resentments that festered in the regimented atmosphere of the factory. As the war approached, Russian labor was becoming more restive, more prone to violent outbursts, more receptive to radical appeals. Military defeats and civilian hardships during the Great War, of course, further radicalized this already explosive situation.

The hegemony of the factory owners over the workers was abruptly terminated by the Russian Revolution. In 1917, the Bolsheviks claimed that by destroying the idea of private property, they could magically solve the problem of master and worker forever. But subsequent events soon demonstrated that the problem was not at all solved, but made infinitely worse. The replacement of the private owner by the state, which concentrated in its hands all economic, political, and judicial power, resulted in modes and degrees of exploitation of labor unimagined in prerevolutionary Russia, and the wage differential between Russian and West European workers, far from decreasing during the Soviet period, in fact sharply widened. Russia's blind leap "from the realm of necessity to the realm of freedom" (Trotsky) transformed the stern factory patriarch of Merchant Moscow into a distant, and perhaps even fond, memory.

NOTES

1. K. S. Kuibysheva, *Krupnaia moskovskaia burzhuaziia v period revoliutsionnoi situatsii*, in *Revoliutsionnaia situatsiia v Rossii v 1859–1861* (Moscow, 1965), p. 331.

2. See A. N. Bokhanov, "A. I. Guchkov," in *Istoricheskie siluety* (Moscow, 1991), p. 331.

3. A. P. Chekhov, *Sochineniia*, vol. 17 (Moscow, 1987), p. 70.

4. M. I. Tugan-Baranovskii, *Russkaia fabrika* (Moscow, 1934), p. 80.

5. S. I. Chetverikov, *Bezvozvratno ushedshaia Rossiia* (Berlin, 1920s), p. 112.

6. Kuibysheva, *Krupnaia moskovskaia burzhuaziia v period revoliutsionnoi situatsii*, p. 329.

7. P. A. Burshkin, *Moskva kupecheskaia* (Moscow, 1991), p. 113.

8. Tugan-Baranovskii, *Russkaia fabrika*, p. 30.

9. S. Gvozdev, *Zapiski fabrichnogo inspektora* (Moscow, 1911), p. 149.

10. G. Schulze-Gävernitz, *Ocherki obshchestvennogo khoziaistva i ekonomicheskogo polozheniia Rossii* (St. Petersburg, 1901), p. 127.

11. V. P. Riabushinskii, "Kupechestvo moskovskoe," *Byloe*, no. 3 (1991): 12.

12. V. I. Lenin, *Polnoe sobranie sochinenii*, vol. 2, p. 110.

Figure 7.1. *Workers of the Ivan Konovalov and Son Company in the factory yard during a change of shift (early twentieth century).*

Figure 7.2. *Workers of the Konovalov factory at dinner (mid-1890s).*

Figure 7.3. *Group of foremen of the Elagin factory (founded in 1812), Bogorodsk, Moscow Province (late nineteenth century).*

Figure 7.4. *The main gate of the Konovalov cotton mill in Vichuga, Kostroma Province.*

Figure 7.5. *Factory school of the Maliutin and Sons Company, founded in 1828 (1890s).*

Figure 7.6. *Lesson at the Maliutin school (1890s).*

Figure 7.7. *Construction of the maternity home of the Morozovs' Bogorodsko-Glukhovskaia factory in Moscow Province (1907).*

Figure 7.8. *Room of a worker's family in factory housing of Maliutin and Sons Company (late 1890s).*

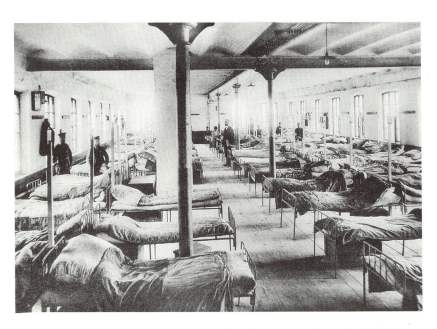

Figure 7.9. *The interior of a workers' barrack at the Konovalov factory (mid-1880s).*

Figure 7.10. *Factory owner Aleksandr Ivanovich Elagin (second from left) surrounded by employees in the process of installing new steam engines.*

Figure 7.11. *Workers' settlement of Sashino at the Konovalov factory, named for the owner's son, Sasha (1910s). The bourgeois impulse to impose order on the unruly Russian countryside is clearly in evidence.*

Figure 7.12. *Meeting of the temperance society of the A. Ia. Balin and Sons Company.*

Figure 7.13. *Library at the factory of the A. Ia. Balin and Sons Company.*

CHAPTER 8

Daughters, Wives, and Partners: Women of the Moscow Merchant Elite

Muriel Joffe and Adele Lindenmeyr

Few social groups in Russian history were as invisible as the wives, mothers, and daughters of the merchant estate in the nineteenth century. Merchant women left few published writings about themselves. They are seldom mentioned in the rare histories of factories or merchant dynasties written in the nineteenth and early twentieth centuries. In the absence of other information, literary representations of merchant wives and daughters exerted significant influence on public opinion and colored later historians' perceptions as well.

The most influential creator of the merchant stereotype was Aleksandr Ostrovsky, whose plays achieved great popularity in the middle decades of the nineteenth century. Ostrovsky often depicted merchant wives as comically pathetic victims of their tyrannical, boorish husbands. His merchant daughters, preoccupied solely with marriage, seek either to climb into the nobility or to avoid a repulsive suitor arranged by their fathers for financial advantage. In a widely cited article entitled "The Kingdom of Darkness," published in 1859, literary critic Nicholas Dobroliubov elevated Ostrovsky's fictional, often comic, representations of merchant life to the level of sociological truth. In Dobroliubov's condemnation of the merchant estate, wives and daughters are more than ignorant, oppressed victims of merchant greed and patriarchal despotism. They also helped perpetuate the social-climbing ambitions, dishonesty, and cultural backwardness that, in Dobroliubov's view, afflicted the merchant estate.

Although nonliterary sources are limited, they nevertheless make it possible to test the historical accuracy of these tenacious literary stereotypes. To what extent did fathers or husbands really dominate merchant women's lives? Were they as ill-educated as Ostrovsky's merchant daughters, who massacre the French language and can barely pick out a tune on the piano? If arranged marriages were the norm, were their motives as base or their consequences for brides as grim as the literary images suggest? Did women really "do nothing all day," as August Haxthausen remarked in the 1840s,[1] confined by tradition and patriarchy to the four walls of their homes; or could they play significant roles in the family business or public life?

Evidence to answer these questions is most available about the private and public lives of women who belonged to the Moscow merchant elite, those two dozen or so families who achieved preeminence in the second half of the nineteenth and early twentieth centuries because of their business success, public service, and patronage of the arts. Using examples from the lives of these women, this essay follows them from childhood through adulthood, reconstructing as far as possible their upbringing, education, marriages, and public activities. It compares the experiences of women born in the 1840s or 1850s, the last decades of serf Russia's old regime, to those of their daughters and granddaughters, who came of age amid the accelerating social and economic transformations of the late imperial period, in order to assess the degree of change and continuity in merchant women's lives.

Girls born into the Moscow merchantry before or around the mid-nineteenth century usually grew up in very large families (figure 8.1). Houses in the city's merchant districts were filled with numerous children; families of seven or more children seem to have been the rule. Vera N. Tretiakova (figure 8.2), born in 1844 to Nikolai F. Mamontov, founder of a lacquer and varnish factory, was one of seventeen, for example. Married in 1849, Ivan V. Shchukin and his wife, Ekaterina, a daughter of the eminent Botkin family, had five daughters and six sons. Pavel M. Riabushinsky had a total of twenty children by two wives: six daughters with the first, whom he divorced, and fourteen more children with Aleksandra S. Ovsiannikova, whom he married in 1870.

In some cases, as when the patriarch commanded his sons to remain under his roof, families were further enlarged by retaining multiple generations. Born to a particularly old-fashioned family in 1847, Anna I. Volkova (*née* Vishniakova) (figure 8.3) lived in Zamoskvoreche in her grandfather's twenty-room house. The family included not only Anna, her parents and brother, and her grandfather and his second wife but also her five uncles and their wives. By stipulating in his will that this arrangement last for six years after he died, Anna's grandfather sought to rule his family even after death.

It is useful to speculate about the causes and effects of the very large family size that prevailed in the merchant generation born around midcentury. One contributing factor may have been the early age at which merchant women tended to marry; impressionistic evidence suggests that they were usually married by age eighteen. High rates of infant and child mortality, even in this privileged milieu, also encouraged couples to have many children. Of the seventeen Mamontov children, for example, six did not survive to adulthood. In Russian merchant families, as in Western European ones, children were a valuable asset. Sons would run and expand the business, and daughters would extend or solidify contacts with other merchant families through marriage. Yet numerous children could sometimes contribute to a decline in the family fortunes in succeeding generations, since prevailing inheritance patterns gave shares of the family wealth and business to all sons and daughters.

An attempt to forestall such a decline may help to explain why women born into large merchant families tended themselves to have fewer children. The evidence suggests that for merchant women raising families in the later decades of the century, six children was a maximum. Though one of seventeen herself, Vera Tretiakova (figure 8.4) had four daughters and two sons with her husband, the collector and museum founder Pavel Mikhailovich (born 1832), himself one of eleven children. Vera's cousin Savva I. Mamontov and his wife Elizaveta (born 1847), founders of the Abramtsevo art colony, raised five children after their marriage in 1865. Pavel A. Buryshkin's parents, married in 1882, had only Pavel and his two sisters.

One important factor behind the noticeable trend toward fewer children is that women in the later generation enjoyed far greater opportunities for education and public activity than their mothers did. As will be seen presently, in the late nineteenth and early twentieth centuries many women in the merchant elite became accomplished in the arts, involved in public service, or committed to various intellectual and cultural endeavors that ranged from liberal journalism to spiritualism. Fragmentary evidence also suggests that more children were surviving to adulthood than before. In addition, as small family businesses grew into large, well-established enterprises, numerous children may have seemed less necessary.

What was childhood like for the girls who grew up in the large families of Merchant Moscow? For Anna Volkova, who left a detailed memoir of her childhood, growing up in Zamoskvoreche fit Ostrovsky's and Dobroliubov's description of the "dark kingdom." The dim, narrow nursery that she shared with her brother was seldom brightened by any demonstrations of affection. Both parents were strict and occasionally used corporal punishment. Her lonely life became even more dreary after the slow, wasting death of her young mother.

But the childhood so poignantly depicted in Volkova's memoirs was far from universal. Her contemporary, Vera Tretiakova, grew up happily in the 1840s and 1850s with her inseparable companion, her sister Zinaida. The first girls to be born after six boys, they were showered with attention and tenderness by their parents and brothers. According to theater pioneer Konstantin Stanislavsky, born in 1863 into the prominent Alekseev family, his parents were devoted to each other and their children; "in order to keep us children nearer to the home hearth, our parents listened willingly to all our demands."[2] The childhood experiences he describes—excursions to the theater and circus, family parties and theatricals, and long summer vacations at estates outside of Moscow—were fairly typical for the second half of the nineteenth century. Even childhoods touched by tragedy or loss could be happy ones.

Margarita K. Morozova's father (Vera Tretiakova's brother) abandoned his family, leaving her young mother to support two daughters by establishing her own dressmaking business. Although she felt "deprived of a father's protection" and pity for her hardworking mother, Margarita Morozova (figure 8.5) recalled a childhood of comfort and love in Moscow of the 1870s and 1880s.[3]

Similarly, the literary stereotype of uneducated merchant mothers and daughters oversimplifies a complex reality. To be sure, merchant wives born in the early nineteenth century often came from peasant or petty bourgeois families and seldom received much formal education; some were probably illiterate. In this regard they differed little from their husbands; the founders of Moscow's merchant dynasties, also rising from humble origins, were sometimes barely literate themselves. Their often-noted reluctance to educate their children beyond the three Rs and memorization of Proverbs and Psalms was directed especially at their sons, who after all were expected to join the family firm, not the intelligentsia. If their daughters' education was neglected, it was probably as much from indifference as from opposition to female education.

Even during the first half of the nineteenth century, however, some women, if not highly educated themselves, believed in the intrinsic importance of education. One such woman was Anna S. Vishniakova, born in 1808, whom her well-educated son credits with bringing "a certain degree of culture" into the home.[4] Merchant families could vary widely at this time in their interest in education and culture; while many resisted European manners and education in favor of a more old-fashioned upbringing based on religion, others, like the Botkins and Mamontovs, created a highly cultivated atmosphere for their children. Such differences among families in attitudes toward education sometimes resulted in unequal and unhappy marriages. Both Anna Volkova and her mother, for example, were avid readers married to men completely indifferent to intellectual pursuits. Varvara A. Morozova (figure 8.6), born in 1850, was an educated woman who could hold her own in the intellectual circles in which she traveled, while her uneducated husband never learned to spell Russian correctly.

Educational and cultural disparities within or among merchant families were becoming less common in the second half of the nineteenth century, however. Growing interest on the part of merchant parents in educating all their children paralleled the steady expansion of educational opportunities, especially for Russian girls. Memoirs of merchant sons and daughters reveal a pattern of upbringing and education common to families of the Moscow merchant elite and, probably, to the Russian upper class generally. Both boys and girls began their education at home, with governesses and tutors. "My sisters had Russian, French and German teachers," writes Stanislavsky, "who taught us boys also."[5] Margarita Morozova recalled, "We began to study somehow ourselves, very early. Then a Russian teacher came to us every day. Mama spoke French with us, and when I turned eight, a French teacher began to come to us."[6] Sometime between the age of nine and thirteen many girls, like boys, began to attend school—either a private *pension* or, increasingly, a more academically challenging girls' gymnasium.

Upon finishing the gymnasium, some merchant girls entered the "higher women's courses," which offered young women a university-level education, though not an official diploma, for women were not allowed to receive higher educational degrees until the early twentieth century. The Guerrier Higher Women's Courses, which opened in Moscow in 1872, for example, enrolled significant numbers of women of the merchant estate; some of the less wealthy were able to attend, no doubt, only because the Moscow Merchants' Society provided five hundred rubles annually for stipends.[7] By the time Alexandra and Nadezhda Buryshkina (figure 8.7), born in the 1880s, were old enough to attend the courses, higher education for women had largely overcome the financial constraints and government mistrust that had plagued its first years. Nadezhda Buryshkina became "a very good surgeon," in her brother's opinion; when the family turned their house into a hospital in World War I, she served as its senior physician.[8]

The domestic environment in which daughters of the second- and third-generation merchant elite grew up also bore little resemblance to the insular, culturally barren world depicted by Dobroliubov. Thanks to their parents' love and patronage of the arts, many of Moscow's leading artists, musicians, playwrights, actors, and directors visited their homes regularly. Margarita Morozova and her cousins freely roamed her uncle Pavel Tretiakov's gallery of contemporary Russian paintings on days when it was closed to the public. This cultured milieu encouraged many girls to perfect their musical or artistic talents or to develop a lifelong devotion to the opera or theater. Merchant parents tended to be quite protective of their children, however, and often sought to limit especially their daughters' contacts with the outside world. Despite the urging of Peter Tchaikovsky, for example, Tretiakov refused to allow his gifted daughter Vera to study at the Moscow Conservatory because it was a co-educational institution.

However educated and talented, daughters of the Moscow merchantry were destined for marriage, the most important step in their lives. Virtually all merchant daughters married, and most marriages were arranged. The selection of marriage partners was equally important for sons as for daughters, and parental authority was exercised in both cases. Existing genealogies reveal a high degree of intermarriage among the families of the Moscow merchant elite. Although there are some notable exceptions, such as Ivan V. Shchukin's five daughters, all of whom married outside the Moscow merchantry, most merchant sons and daughters married distant cousins, friends of the family, or the children of their fathers' business associates. The marriage of Varvara to Abram

Morozov, for example, strengthened existing ties between two preeminent merchant dynasties of the Moscow region, the Khludovs and Morozovs. In Old Believer families, religious considerations sometimes also dictated the choice of appropriate mates. Pavel M. Riabushinsky chose the daughter of an Old Believer grain millionaire in St. Petersburg as wife for his younger brother; but he fell in love with her himself, and married her instead!

As social critics like Dobroliubov predicted, arranged marriages sometimes proved disastrous. Varvara Morozova's life with the uneducated and mentally unbalanced Abram could hardly have been happy. Even after he died in an insane asylum, he continued to control her life by the terms of his will, which deprived her of her share of his fortune if she remarried. Varvara obeyed the letter of his posthumous conditions, though she subsequently established a long-term relationship with Vasily M. Sobolevsky, a liberal journalist. The experience of Grafina I. Abrikosova, of the same older generation of merchant women, fits Ostrovsky's stereotype of daughters sacrificed by greedy or social-climbing parents, and demonstrates the legal prison that marriage could become. Fearing that her daughter would become an old maid, Grafina's mother forced her at age seventeen to wed a nobleman fifteen years her senior. When Grafina discovered that he already had a mistress at his dilapidated estate, she ran away. Although her mother and husband enlisted the police to try to force her to return, Grafina refused and received asylum in her brother's home. Assisted by her brother and his influential friends in St. Petersburg, she eventually received a divorce directly from Alexander III. During the more than ten years it took to gain her freedom, Grafina Abrikosova completed medical studies in Paris—a plot twist not anticipated by Ostrovsky!

Such disastrous outcomes were relatively rare, however. An arranged marriage in itself did not preclude matches based on mutual affection. By the late nineteenth century, children grew up in a wider social environment than the one described by N. P. Vishniakov for the earlier part of the century, when visitors to his parents' home were limited to a small number of close relatives. Memoirs reveal that the children of leading merchant families socialized together at plays, concerts, and dances, and spent the summers together at their families' dachas in Kuntsevo, outside of Moscow. In the 1890s, for example, Aleksei A. Bakhrushin courted Vera V. Nosova at her father's box at the theater, proposed to her at the skating rink, and received her acceptance at a Merchants' Club ball. Thus normal social life brought suitable marriage partners together and reinforced marriages within the group.

Underlying the merchantry's strong preference for arranged marriages within the estate was the very real fact that membership in the merchant guilds and, until 1898, the right to engage in certain types of trade and industry depended on ownership of a specific amount of capital. A reversal of the family fortunes could mean rapid downward social mobility. The marriages of merchant daughters, especially if there were no male heirs, could be critical to the survival of the family firm and therefore the family itself; merchant sons-in-law brought in both managerial skills and new capital.

Parents' protectiveness and concern for their daughters' well-being reinforced their economic reasons for preferring marriage within the merchantry. When Mikhail Z. Tretiakov, founder of the family linen enterprise, was dying, he asked his favorite daughter, fifteen-year-old Lizaveta, to promise to marry his employee Vladimir Konshin. But the context of this match bears little resemblance to the swindle that motivated the marriage of Ostrovsky's odious clerk Podkhalyuzin to his employer's daughter in the play *It's a Family Affair, We'll Settle It Ourselves*. The sisters Vera Ziloti and Aleksandra Botkina, the daughters of Pavel Tretiakov, attributed their grandfather's decision to both his concern for the "sickly" Lizaveta and his desire to bring the well-loved Konshin, his trusted confidant, into the family.

Many merchants especially feared that alliances with nobles, whom they considered to be nonproductive members of society, would bring financial harm to their daughters and undermine the security of the entire family. Such concerns became particularly important in the latter part of the century, when merchant daughters began to play a more active role in the selection of their partners. The memoir of Vera P. Ziloti, born in 1866 to Vera and Pavel Tretiakov, describes a number of cases, including her own, of daughters who overcame formidable parental resistance to marry the man of their choice. Vera suffered a number of serious nervous disorders before her father agreed to her marriage to Aleksandr Ziloti, who was both a nobleman and a musician. When Tretiakov finally acquiesced, he apologized for causing her suffering, but stated that he had wanted her "carefully to think it over and know her true feelings."[9] Concern over his daughter's future emotional and economic well-being accounted for Tretiakov's hostility to Ziloti. Despite assurances from Ziloti's mentor that his protégé was not after Vera's money, Tretiakov structured his daughter's wedding settlement to prevent her funds from being eaten up by people he found "distasteful," most likely the young couple's artist friends.[10]

At the end of the nineteenth century an additional factor emerged to reinforce merchants' antipathy to marriages with the nobility and preference for intermarriage: a new merchant consciousness and self-respect. Pride in their merchant status helps to explain the opposition of Vera Nosova's father to her sister's marriage to a prince, for example, and Vladimir Konshin's objection to his daughter's marriage to Anatoly Tchaikovsky, brother of the composer and a high-ranking prosecutor at a circuit court. (In both cases the daughters prevailed against their fathers, after many tears and the intervention of friends.) In the words of Vladimir P. Riabushinsky, it was considered "better to be first among the merchants than last among the nobility."[11]

Marriage represented the transfer of merchant daughters from the authority of fathers to that of husbands. Russian family law declared men the heads of families, obligated women to obey and live with their husbands, and made divorce almost impossible. Thus marriage potentially subjected women to the tyranny of their husbands; and patriarchal authority unquestionably prevailed in merchant families into the twentieth century. Yet in some ways marriage offered women opportunities beyond home and family. It served as the focal point for merchant women's productive as well as reproductive lives.

One can find numerous cases of marriages in which wives played an active and valued role as their husbands' partners and advisers. The parents of Nikolai P. Vishniakov, married in 1824, illustrate the complex interplay between patriarchal domination and cooperation that could occur between marital partners even in the early nineteenth century. To be sure, the elder Vishniakov exercised authority in even the smallest of household decisions. While he addressed his wife as "thou" (*na ty*), as one would a child or a dependent, she always addressed him with the more respectful "you" (*vy*). According to their son, however, Anna Vishniakova was still her husband's "first adviser," whose opinions he invariably consulted and respected. In instances when she held strong views, she did not hesitate to stand up to him.[12]

Later in the nineteenth century companionate marriages seemed fairly common. Pavel Tretiakov, for example, encouraged his wife Vera to pursue her musical studies and participate with him in various cultural and philanthropic activities. Elizaveta Mamontova was her husband Savva's active partner in the extensive activities of the Abramtsevo art colony, some aspects of which she initiated or directed herself. Aleksei Bakhrushin "was proud of his wife—of her beauty, tact, her talents and skills."[13] Vera Bakhrushina was as passionately interested in the theater as her husband. As they jointly built the collection of theater memorabilia that became the Moscow Theater Museum, her typing, bookbinding, and photography skills proved invaluable.

Partnerships between husbands and wives also extended to the family business. The pattern of merchant women's involvement in the direct operation of Russian businesses resembles that of their counterparts in France or Great Britain in the early stages of industrial development. When family enterprises were small and new, wives often worked alongside husbands to assure their survival. In the Russian case, this cooperative stage frequently paralleled the family's upward climb from serfdom into the merchant estate, or from a lower to a higher guild. One example is the Vikula Morozov and Sons Manufacturing Company. This firm, one of the four major enterprises that developed from the pioneering activities of the serf entrepreneur Savva V. Morozov, originated in 1837. At that time Savva's son Elisei established his own small dyeworks. Since Elisei, a devout Old Believer, dedicated most of his time to religious activities, his wife, Evdokiia, ran the business. When their son Vikula took over and modernized the family firm, his wife also worked alongside him, and became a founding partner in the company that he established in 1882. Similarly, Tatiana I. Smirnova (d. 1913) spent almost her entire life at her husband's cotton manufacturing firm, and oversaw many aspects of the factory, including construction of housing, baths, and schools for workers.

In contrast to American or West European law, which until the mid-nineteenth century or later surrendered the economic identity of married women to their husbands, Russian law allowed women to maintain control over their own property, including their dowries. Consequently, merchant wives and daughters who owned the required amount of capital were registered in the merchant guilds, owned stock in family corporations, and attended meetings of corporate shareholders.

Yet Russian property law was not sufficient in itself to stimulate active female participation in business. Women shareholders appeared less often on corporations' boards of directors than as members of the less important audit commissions, for example. In some cases husbands either assumed complete control of their wives' property or represented their interests. When Gerasim I. Khludov died without a male heir, for example, his daughters inherited the family company and sat on its board of directors. But the actual management of the company passed to their husbands, members of the Naidenov and Prokhorov families, who were already deeply involved in Moscow's cotton manufacturing and banking worlds. When Buryshkin's mother (figure 8.8) became sole heir to her father's business, she willingly passed all authority to her husband. If any single factor enhanced the possibility for female involvement, it was not female rights of ownership but the persistence of the family firm or family corporation as the dominant element in the industrial life of the Moscow region, especially in its textile and light industries. Property law opened corporate life to women as individuals, but their role as wives and daughters provided the impetus for their genuine participation.

Also consistent with patterns found in Western Europe, widowhood created the greatest opportunity for merchant women to participate in family businesses. In many cases merchant widows ran family firms until their male children came of age. Left with three minor sons when her husband died in 1883, Varvara Morozova took over as head of the board of the directors of the Tver Cotton Goods Manufacturing Company, and ran the business alone until 1892, when her son Ivan joined her. During this time she did much to improve the material conditions and education of her workers. She also appointed the first Russian engineer in the company's history as technical director of the factory.

Unlike Morozova, Anna M. Krasilshchikova (figure 8.9) established her reputation as a shrewd businesswoman while her husband was still living. A major history of Russian cotton manufacturing published in 1915 attributes the survival of her family's textile firm during the crisis of the 1860s in large part to her energy and business skills. She also played a major role in the introduction of mechanical weaving to the factory. When Krasilshchikov died in 1875, leaving her with minor children, Anna Krasilshchikova transferred the entire business to her name. With her brother's help she expanded the firm's credit. In contrast to Varvara Morozova, Anna Krasilshchikova did little to improve the condition of her work force, however. Between 1888, when her youngest son, Nikolai, took over the factory, and her death in 1902, she steadfastly if unsuccessfully opposed her son's attempts to educate their workers. In this respect she had much in common with many male factory owners of her generation, who opposed modifications in the patriarchal order that traditionally prevailed in Russian factories (see the Shatsillo essay).

In the case of Maria F. Morozova, a strong personality reinforced her position as majority shareholder in the family firm after her husband Timofei's death in 1889. Although their son Savva actually ran the family's giant Nikolsk Manufacturing Company, she headed the board of directors. In 1905 she forced her son Savva's removal from management of the company after he proposed a profit-sharing scheme for the firm's workers. A few months thereafter, her son committed suicide.

Despite the striking examples of these powerful widows, merchant women in general exercised little authority as business leaders. They were notably absent from the chief representative organizations of the city's commercial industrial community, dominated by the *khoziaevy* (male "bosses") of Moscow's family firms. Moreover, women's direct involvement in the management of established businesses probably diminished in the late imperial period. In part, this decline may be explained by changes in these firms. As they grew larger and their administration increasingly required specialized training, direct female participation became less likely, with the exception, perhaps, of involvement in the philanthropic institutions for workers attached to some factories. At the same time, members of the later generation of merchant families, male and female, developed other interests. Vera Ziloti, for example, visited her father's factory only once; her life centered on art and music, with little interest in the economic basis for the refined milieu in which she grew up.

In addition, by the late nineteenth century women of the Moscow merchant elite were engaged in a wide variety of public activities unknown to their mothers or grandmothers. To be sure, many women, like Buryshkin's mother, continued to devote themselves to their homes and children; others, like the red-haired beauty Evfimiia Nosova (one of Pavel M. Riabushinsky's daughters), used their fortunes to support Parisian fashion and conspicuous consumption. But a great many women used their wealth, leisure time, and connections to contribute significantly to their city and to Russian culture. While the philanthropy, cultural patronage, and public service of the Moscow merchants are well known, the activities of their wives and daughters, sometimes with their husbands and sometimes independently, have received relatively little attention.

Sanctioned by Orthodox religious traditions and deeply rooted merchant customs, charity was one of the most accessible and acceptable forms of public involvement for merchant women. For women as for men, charitable work often revolved around church or factory. While some made donations or bequests to churches or monasteries, others dedicated themselves to supporting the housing, hospitals, and other services that many paternalistic Russian employers traditionally provided to their workers.

Women of the merchant elite also contributed to the many innovative secular charities that helped make Moscow Russia's most progressive city in the late imperial period. A few examples can only suggest the diversity of the causes they supported. Although Varvara Morozova's name could be found on the donors' lists of many of Moscow's most important charitable and cultural organizations, she was especially committed to workers' education. Her highly popular Prechistenskie Courses for Workers offered Moscow's lower classes a unique opportunity to further their education. Critical assistance from Morozova's daughter-in-law Margarita enabled Stanislav Shatsky, a pioneer in the rehabilitation of juvenile delinquents, to build his experimental children's colony. Aleksandra G. Naidenova (*née* Khludova) (figures 8.10–12), a director in her family's firm, was a major supporter of Moscow's reorganized municipal relief system, the district guardianships of the poor. Women such as these three, who inherited fortunes from fathers or husbands or directed successful businesses themselves, enjoyed both the means and the independence to initiate and support large, innovative projects.

Other merchant wives and daughters, perhaps more limited in the funds they controlled, volunteered their time and effort to smaller-scale projects. Along with numerous other ladies of Moscow's upper classes, Vera Tretiakova adopted one of the city's elementary schools for girls. Serving as its patroness for more than twenty-five years, she visited the school two or three times a week to provide both advice and financial assistance, including scholarships for accomplished graduates. She and her husband also donated much time and money as principal patrons of the Moscow School for the Deaf. One indication of the depth of Vera Tretiakova's commitment to these schools is her daughter's recollection of her own involvement as a child: "We attended all the examinations, every Christmas party, played with the children, knew them all by name, knew the fate of every girl."[14]

Merchant women also undertook charity work beyond the boundaries of factory or city in response to such national crises as famines and wars. Maria F. Iakunchikova (*née* Mamontova) was not even twenty years old when she opened a soup kitchen for famine victims in Tambov Province in 1881; out of this experience she started a successful enterprise that supported and marketed peasant women's embroidery. Ekaterina I. Beklemisheva (*née* Pro-khorova) caught typhus at the rural hospital she opened during the 1892 famine and epidemic. During the Russo-Japanese and First World Wars, nu-merous women opened hospitals for the wounded, sometimes in their own mansions.

Women from the merchant elite can also be found supporting the richly diverse intellectual life of late imperial Moscow. Varvara and Margarita Moro-zova, Nadezhda N. Abrikosova (*née* Khludova), and others held regular salons attended by Russia's leading writers, philosophers, artists, and scholars. Others pursued interests that may have raised a few eyebrows: Nadezhda Buryshkina, for example, used income from her share of the family business to support the popular spiritualist movements of theosophy and anthroposo-phy, followers of which met regularly at her apartment. Several merchant women also became involved in journalism. Varvara Morozova subsidized the leading journal *Russkoe bogatstvo* (Russian Wealth) and the preeminent liberal newspaper *Russkie vedomosti* (Russian News), whose editor was also her com-mon-law husband. Anna Volkova edited one of Russia's first feminist journals and published hundreds of articles on education and women's issues.

Finally, women of the Moscow merchantry shared their fathers' and hus-bands' singular love of the arts. While some supported artists as patronesses and collectors, a number of merchant daughters made careers as artists them-selves. Two who became famous in the twentieth century are Aleksandra S. Khokhlova, granddaughter of Vera and Pavel Tretiakov and a Soviet film star in the 1920s and 1930s, and the Constructivist painter and designer Liubov Popova, born into a Moscow merchant family in 1889. The domestic environ-ment and upbringing described earlier provided excellent preparation for these women and other merchant daughters who became actresses, singers, painters, and sculptors. Khokhlova's parents, for example, were close friends of Diaghilev, Bakst, Rakhmaninov, Benois, and other members of the artistic avant-garde at the turn of the century. Liubov Popova, from a wealthy but less elite family, benefited from the expanding educational opportunities for mer-chant girls; in addition to early art lessons at home, she received a thorough education in the humanities at a gymnasium and the Alferov Higher Women's Courses.

To be sure, negative stereotypes of merchant women persisted. Ostrovsky's plays became a staple in the repertoire of both professional theaters and amateur groups in the second half of the nineteenth century. Unfortunately, there is no evidence of Varvara Morozova's own feelings when she played one of Ostrovsky's female leads in a charity performance in the 1870s. But surely few in the audience missed the irony behind the participation of this cultured representative of two powerful merchant dynasties in the play titled *Stick to Your Own Kind* (*Ne v svoi sani ne sadis'*), whose plot concerns the elopement of a lovesick merchant's daughter and a faithless, money-seeking nobleman.

Dramatist Vladimir Nemirovich-Danchenko expressed similar sentiments about merchant women who tried to move out of their milieu when he caricatured Margarita Morozova's philosophical pursuits in his play *The Value of Life*.

Yet even literary representations of merchant women reflected some of the important social and economic changes taking place in the Moscow merchant elite during the second half of the nineteenth century. One example is the 1882 novel about merchant Moscow *Kitai-gorod*, by the "Russian Zola," Peter D. Boborykin—a now-forgotten novelist whose meticulously detailed novels of contemporary life attracted a wide following. Anna Stanitsyna, the principal female character, is the diametric opposite of Ostrovsky's typical merchant wife or daughter. Modeled after Varvara Morozova herself, Anna Stanitsyna is an independent, highly capable businesswoman who takes direct control of the factories belonging to herself and her dissipated husband. In spite of her ability, beauty, and character, however, Boborykin's heroine is acutely self-conscious of her merchant origins.

Stanitsyna's ambivalence was not unique to fiction. When women addressed prevailing merchant stereotypes directly, they tended both to accept and reject them. Anna Volkova, for example, alternately defended her merchant origins and blamed them for her narrow education, unsatisfying marriage, and social and intellectual inferiority. Although Vera Ziloti's family diverged in significant ways from Ostrovsky's "typical" merchantry, she sometimes used the stereotype to describe relations and acquaintances. "There were many petty tyrants [*samodurov*] in our city of white stone," she remarks, "but the most famous of them, by hearsay, were the Mamontovs and Khludovs."[15] Elsewhere, she refers to the wife of her father's bookkeeper as "a type straight out of Ostrovsky."[16] Clearly, some women in the Moscow business elite apparently shared at least some of the intelligentsia's criticisms of their estate; yet their own lives belied the petty tyranny, greed, and cultural backwardness attributed to the merchantry.

A number of factors help to explain the persistence of the merchant stereotype. Many members of the nobility and intelligentsia, especially radicals like Dobroliubov, scorned the capitalist origins of this new elite's wealth and resented its claims to public service and political leadership. Another reason is the rapidity and unevenness of the changes that took place within the merchant estate. Many of Moscow's elite families rose to prominence from humble or obscure origins in the course of one or two generations. Yet a sizable social distance separated them from merchant men and women on the lower rungs of the social ladder. The great majority of merchants lived not in Moscow but in provincial towns, where business, educational, and cultural opportunities could be quite limited and traditional customs and attitudes probably ran deep. Elizaveta Diakonova, daughter of merchants from the provincial town of Kostroma, complained in her diary in 1894, "In our merchant circle one encounters the kind of scenes that show how close we still are to Ostrovsky's times."[17] Yet even she eventually overcame pressure from her family to marry, and attended higher women's courses in St. Petersburg!

While the stereotype of unproductive merchant women imprisoned in a "kingdom of darkness" may have applied to some aspects of merchant life in the early nineteenth century, it is misleading even for this era and anachronistic for the second half of the century. Women were an integral part of the productive and creative life of merchant Moscow throughout the nineteenth century. They ensured the perpetuation of the family, the economic and social foundation of Moscow businesses, and the merchant estate. As wives, mothers, and daughters they strengthened ties between families and firms, raised the next generation of entrepreneurs, and channeled new capital resources and personnel into businesses. As investors, partners, and directors, they participated in the management and growth of Russian enterprises.

Women growing up in the Moscow merchantry during the second half of the nineteenth century enjoyed significantly broader opportunities and more choices than their mothers and grandmothers (figure 8.13). Taking advantage of their growing autonomy and educational opportunities, they increasingly married whom they wished, developed their own philanthropies, pursued intellectual interests, or carved out artistic careers. These broad social and cultural changes, coupled with the economic success of the merchant elite, made it possible for both the women as well as the men of second- and third-generation Moscow merchants to contribute actively to the transformation of Russian society in the late imperial period.

NOTES

1. August von Haxthausen, *Studies on the Interior of Russia*, ed. S. Frederick Starr (Chicago: University of Chicago Press, 1972), p. 22.

2. Constantine Stanislavski, *My Life in Art*, trans. J. J. Robbins (n.p., 1948), p. 24.

3. M. K. Morozova, "Moi vospominaniia," *Nashe nasledie*, no. 6 (1991): 91.

4. Nikolai Petrovich Vishniakov, *Svedeniia o kupecheskom rode Vishniakovykh*, 3 vols. (Moscow: Tip. G. Lissner i D. Sobko, 1903–11), vol. 2, p. 52.

5. Stanislavsky, *My Life in Art*, p. 55.

6. Morozova, "Moi vospominaniia," p. 91.

7. Christine Johanson, *Women's Struggle for Higher Education in Russia, 1855–1900* (Kingston and Montreal: McGill-Queen's University Press, 1987), pp. 49–50.

8. P. A. Buryshkin, *Moskva kupecheskaia* (Moscow: Vysshaia shkola, 1991), p. 216.

9. V. P. Ziloti, *V dome Tretiakova* (Moscow: Vysshaia shkola, 1992), p. 227.

10. A. P. Botkina, *Pavel Mikhailovich Tretiakov v zhizni i iskusstve* (Moscow: Izdatel'stvo Gosudarstvennoi Tretiakovskoi galerei, 1951), p. 239.

11. Vladimir P. Riabushinsky, "Kupechestvo Moskovskoe," *Den' russkogo rebenka*, April 1951, p. 186.

12. Vishniakov, *Svedeniia o kupecheskom rode Vishniakovykh*, vol. 2, p. 148.

13. Natal'ia Dumova, *Moskovskie metsenaty* (Moscow: Molodaia gvardiia, 1992), p. 310.

14. Ziloti, *V dome Tretiakova*, p. 88.

15. Ibid., p. 55.

16. Ibid., p. 32

17. Quoted in B. B. Kafengauz, "Kupecheskie memuary," in *Moskovsky krai v ego proshlom: ocherki po sotsial'noi i ekonomoicheskoi istorii XVI–XX vekov*, ed. S. V. Bakhrushin (Moscow, 1928), p. 127.

Figure 8.1. *Evpraksiia Gregorievna Olovianshinikova with her children who worked in the family business: casting of bells, production of paints and church utensils (1901).*

Figure 8.2. *The Tretiakovs: Pavel Mikhailovich and Vera Nikolaevna.*

Figure 8.3. *Anna Ivanovna Volkova (née Vishniakova), late nineteenth century.*

Figure 8.4. *Vera Nikolaevna Tretiakova with relatives: standing on the left, daughter Aleksandra Pavlovna (Botkina); sitting third from left, daughter Vera Pavlovna (Ziloti).*

Figure 8.5. *Margarita Kirillovna Morozova* (née *Mamontova*).

Figure 8.6. *Varvara Alekseevna Morozova* (née *Khludova*).

Figure 8.7. *Pavel A. Buryshkin and his sisters, Nadezhna (standing) and Aleksandra (sitting).*

Figure 8.8. *Four generations of Buryshkin women. Left to right: Olga Fedorovna Buryshkina (née Shiriaevna), mother of Pavel; her daughter Alekhsandra Afanas'evna Luzhina (née Buryshkina); her granddaughter Vera Sergeevna Luzhina (who eventually married a Sidorov); and her mother-in-law Natalia Dmitrievna Buryshkina (mother of Afanasii Vasilevich Buryshkin).*

Figure 8.9. *Anna Mikhailovna Krasilshchikova, director of the textile firm Anna Krasilshchikova and Sons after the death of her husband in 1875.*

Figure 8.10. *Aleksandra Gerasimovna Naidenova (seated in center), her husband, A. N. Naidenov (standing in center), and their children (six daughters and two sons), at home on Pokrovsky Boulevard.*

Figure 8.11. *Aleksandra Naidenova, granddaughter of the founder of the A. and G. Khludov Company (established in the early nineteenth century), takes part in the ceremonial laying of the first bricks at the building site of a new factory block, 1906.*

Figure 8.12. *Aleksandra G. Naidenova with her children who remained in Soviet Russia, 1924. Aleksandra's somber expression perhaps suggests the stresses of life under Bolshevik rule.*

Figure 8.13. *Anna Nikolaevna Buryshkina* (née *Organova*), *c. 1912 (see plate 14).*

CHAPTER 9

Commercial Education and the Cultural Crisis
of the Moscow Merchant Elite

Sergei V. Kalmykov

Pavel A. Buryshkin, the author of the classic memoir on Moscow merchants, points out that although the roots of the most prominent families of traders and industrialists were often crudely rustic, it took only one or two generations before the merchants began to take an interest in things beyond selling calico: "[Kant's] Categorical Imperative, Hegelianism, Steiner's anthroposophy, and the art of Matisse, Van Gogh, and Picasso."[1] What we see here is the fundamental shift in the mentality of the Russian bourgeoisie, particularly that of Moscow, which occurred when its cultural maturity and the degree of "Westernization" coincided with the quest for a new social identity.

This shift in self-perception manifested itself first in the continued erosion of the rigid structure of the old estate system. By the early twentieth century, the representatives of the most prominent merchant families in Moscow gradually discontinued their annual membership payments to the merchant guilds in favor of more informal acquisition of certificates (*promyslovye svidetel'stva*) that authorized them to engage in industrial and commercial activity. Others became obsessed with the pursuit of social status and official recognition and attempted to secure noble status with the corresponding title "Excellency." Still others preferred to break with family tradition altogether and to become doctors, lawyers, and actors. The result of all these processes of social transformation, starting at some undefinable moment late in the nineteenth century, was the gradual disappearance from Merchant Moscow of the really colorful characters of the old merchant type.

With the passing of the old patriarchs, something was lost. Among their children it was often the case that some did not have an obvious talent for entrepreneurship. This was particularly true of the Shchukins and the Morozovs. It appears that much of the passion for business was spent by the generation of the so-called "founding fathers." Many members of the succeeding generation either demonstrated modest abilities and contented themselves with the formal position of junior partner in the family firm, indulging in "la dolce vita" and dissipating their inherited wealth, or retired completely from business and moved on toward social or artistic activities.

Some representatives of the young merchant generation who did not lack a talent for commerce, such as the members of the Riabushinsky Circle (P. P. and V. P. Riabushinsky, A. I. Konovalov, S. I. Chetverikov, etc.) began to take a keen interest in politics (see the West essay). This proliferation of interests and pursuits can be interpreted in a positive manner as American scholars such as Alfred Rieber and Thomas Owen have, but they can also be seen as an ominous sign of the coming "eclipse" of the old Moscow bourgeoisie, which increasingly lost ground to the newer rising financial oligarchy of St. Petersburg and, to a certain extent, that of the provinces.

Of course, Moscow always occupied a prominent place in the commercial and industrial life of Russia. As one author from the last century put it:

> All the necessary conditions for the success of industry and commerce, both material and mental, have been concentrated in Moscow from time immemorial, for it has been inhabited by the affluent people gifted according the degree of enlightenment of our Fatherland. . . . Despite the long distance between this capital and Western Europe, all the improvements, all the innovations in the field of mechanics and chemistry manifest themselves there ahead of all Russia, even ahead of St. Petersburg.[2]

The textile industry, Merchant Moscow's mainstay, was always on the technological cutting edge. It was in the textile factories of Moscow that many new production technologies from the West (the Jacquard loom, cylindrical printing machines, *ban-au-broche*, and mule-jenny spinning machines) were introduced for the first time in Russia. The same is true of technological developments such as sulfuric acid production through the continuous burning of sulfur and the first production of stearine and stearine candles by a Russian factory.

These innovations resulted in part from government educational policy, which sought to foster the spread of technological knowledge. As early as 1836 Moscow University offered lectures to industrialists devoted primarily to technical chemistry. The number of factory owners, foremen, and amateurs who attended the lectures during the first year was just over fifty; by 1844, attendance had risen to four hundred.

The first educational institutions aimed at training future traders and manufacturers were also founded in Moscow. The earliest of these, the so-called Educational Commercial School for Merchant Children, a boarding school with free tuition, was founded at the behest of a descendent of the Demidovs, the famous mining industrialists from the Urals. The project was completed under the supervision of I. I. Betskoi in the year 1772. At the time, no school with such a specialization existed in the West, although various elements of commercial education were already well developed there by that date. By 1799, 239 students had been admitted to the school, though for various reasons only 46 of them had graduated.[3] Later the location of the school was deemed unsatisfactory by the government, and in 1799 it was transferred to St. Petersburg.

When Alexander I donated the former monastery of St. Andrei to the Moscow Merchant Society in 1803, the society decided to establish a commercial school there to board and educate up to fifty pupils from the merchant and other urban strata. Its curriculum for 1804 was approved by the emperor personally. Thus the Imperial Commercial School (figures 9.1 and 9.2), equal by decree to the St. Petersburg school, came into being. The distinguished graduates who completed the eight-year course were awarded the degree "Candidate of Commerce" and received the rank of "Personal Honorary Citizen."

In addition, another commercial school opened in Moscow in 1804. Charles Arnold, an immigrant from Prussia, founded a commercial boarding school with the aim of "educating youth willing to enter the commercial calling." He appealed to Moscow merchants for assistance, receiving in response a number of donations and subsidies. Among the principal enthusiastic supporters of this enterprise was the first guild merchant, A. A. Kumanin, who in 1806 authored a petition to rename Arnold's school the Practical Commercial Academy (figure 9.3). He donated two thousand rubles to be held by the institution "in perpetuity." From 1810, the Academy was under the supervision of the "Society to Promote Commercial Education" organized by the Moscow merchants (see the Bradley essay).

The first five years of the eight-year course of study at the Academy were general gymnasium courses, and the last three focused on two specialized areas: commercial and technical sciences. The Practical Commercial Academy offered essentially the same curriculum: religion and the history of religion, foreign languages (German, English, and French), penmanship, general and commercial arithmetic, algebra and geometry, statistics, geography, and product research and natural sciences, including natural history, mechanics, and chemistry. Graduates were entitled to the same rights and distinctions as those of the Commercial School. From 1806 to 1910, only 1,251 students completed the course of study at the Academy; similarly, only 1,588 students graduated from the Demidov Commercial School between 1804 and 1904.[4] Both of these were boarding schools. The Demidov School was financed from the annual donations of the Moscow Merchant Society combined with tuition paid by the students. Numerous private donations from Moscow merchants and industrialists also supported the school. The amount of these (including gifts of books, pictures, icons, and utensils) escapes calculation. For a long time, the Academy existed on only tuition fees and charges for boarding; budget deficits were therefore endemic, and the problem of finances was a constant concern for the board (figure 9.4). This situation lasted until 1869, when the Moscow Merchant Mutual Credit Society was established; 5 percent of its profits were allocated to the Academy.

Until the mid-nineteenth century, the commercial schools in Moscow and St. Petersburg were the only ones in Russia that offered broad professional training to their students. In 1835, another commercial education institution, the School for Petty Townspeople (Meshchanskoe Uchilishche) (figure 9.5), was opened in Moscow and offered courses in accounting and bookkeeping in simplified form. It was famous for its high standards in penmanship and abacus counting.

The demand for commercially educated specialists only increased with time, which prompted in the opening of still more commercial schools. In 1880, merchants financed the opening of Petrov Commercial School in St. Petersburg, followed by the Aleksandr Commercial School in Moscow five years later (figure 9.6).

The Russian government undertook extensive revision of the university statutes in the 1890s, and commercial education was also revamped. "The Statute of Commercial Educational Establishments" (1896) made critical changes to the entire system of commercial education in Russia. Prior to its enactment, each school lived by its own rules. The new statute represented the first all-Russian legislative act of its kind, and it endowed the boards of these institutions with expanded rights, even as it curtailed the autonomy of state educational establishments and universities. The result of this favorable legislation was rapid growth in the number of commercial schools. In 1906 there were 238 such schools in Russia; this number increased to 394 by 1911. The number of students in attendance also increased, rising to 46,800 in 1910–11, of which 8,800 were women.

At the same time, it became increasingly clear that a higher educational system capable of training instructors for commercial schools was also needed. The statute for the Moscow Commercial Institute (figure 9.7), founded by Moscow merchant Alexei S. Vishniakov (figure 9.8), was signed by the emperor in 1902. This new higher educational institution had two principle faculties: the Department of Economics and the Department of Commerce and Technology. Both admitted students with high school diplomas already in hand, the former selecting alumni of humanities majors, while the latter admitted only science majors. Graduates of these higher institutes received the degree of Candidate of Economic Sciences or Candidate of Commercial Engineering, respectively.

The curriculum of the Department of Economics encompassed a number of general education disciplines. The senior semesters offered the following four programs: commerce and finances, industry, administration, and finance. The first was intended for those who wanted preparation in the field of banking and insurance. Specialization in industry was chosen by those who anticipated extensive activity in either factory production or factory inspection. The curriculum included a number of special disciplines: labor legislation, industrial statistics, and more narrow technical areas such as technology, mechanical engineering, and so on. Finally, there was an administrative-financial department for those preparing for a career in local government, the zemstvos, or the new field of agricultural cooperatives. Natural science and engineering disciplines were dominant in the curriculum of the Department of Commerce. Various engineering specialties were taught in conjunction with the basic focus of the department: the production, transportation, and storage of commodities.[5]

Tuition for these courses was twice as much as that for secondary schools. These private commercial institutes differed from the state educational establishments in the fact that they were controlled by boards of trustees, composed of persons well known in the business world, and the quality of the teaching staff employed by them was very high. The board of trustees of the Moscow Commercial Institute included the most prominent representatives of the commercial and industrial sectors of the city: V. S. and P. A. Vishniakov, S. I. Chetverikov, M. N. Bardygin, P. A. Morozov, A. N. Naidenov, Baron A. L. Knoop, I. K. and A. I. Konovalov, and P. P. and V. P. Riabushinsky. For many years, the board was chaired by A. S. Vishniakov, the man whose name was most closely associated with the institute from its birth.

The Commercial School and the Practical Academy (and later the Commercial Institute) were often staffed by the same people. Among the professors and tutors were a number of prominent academic figures (figure 9.9). Mechanics, for example, was taught by Professor N. E. Zhukovsky, a world-famous scholar. P. P. Melgunov, who taught the course on Russian history and the history of trade, was especially popular; he was a disciple of the great Russian historian S. M. Soloviev. Also known for their outstanding instruction, the courses in commodity research (figure 9.10) and chemistry were taught by Ia. Ia. Nikitinsky and A. N. Reformatsky, respectively. Some of the best intellects in Russia were concentrated in Moscow Commercial Institute. These included the historian A. A. Kizevetter; Professor of Law and the Institute's rector P. I. Novgorodtsev (figure 9.11); the economist S. A. Kotliarevsky; S. N. Bulgakov, the future luminary of Russian religious philosophy; M. Ia. Gertsenstein; A. A. Manuilov; I. Kh. Ozerov (figure 9.12); the statistician A. F. Fortunatov; and many others. Several of these professors and intellectuals were well-known activists in the liberal movement and leaders of the Constitutional Democratic (Kadet) Party. Some of these same people contributed to the famous essay collections *Problems of Idealism* and *Vekhi* ("Signposts"): Novgorodtsev, Bulgakov, and Kistiakovsky, as well as the future minister of the Provisional Government, Manuilov.[6] Interaction with individuals of this prominence and stature no doubt left a lasting imprint on the students' worldview.

The system of commercial education in Russia clearly met world standards and sometimes even surpassed them.[7] The founders of the Moscow Commercial Institute tried to transform it into an academy to train a future managerial elite. In this respect it can be considered the predecessor of the Harvard Business School or the French École Nationale d'Administration.

Given the advanced state of commercial education in Russia, it is somewhat surprising that contemporaries came to the conclusion that the influence of professional education on businessmen was relatively slight. This assessment was based on the observed fact that few graduates of these institutions found their way into business in Merchant Moscow. The low demand for the alumni of commercial schools was explained by Pavel Buryshkin, himself a graduate of the Moscow Commercial Institute, as a consequence of a lingering distrust of abstraction and theory among Moscow's businessmen: "The world of trade and commercial organizations treated the young men who graduate from the institutes with a certain mistrust, apparently assuming that in Russian conditions, knowledge of a lengthy of series of theoretical disciplines was less important than elementary practical training in bookkeeping or even simply the ability to calculate on an abacus."[8] Because of these views, graduates from primary commercial schools found employment at commercial and industrial enterprises with greater ease than those who possessed the diploma of "Candidate of Economic Sciences." The data actually suggest that the graduates of these higher institutes did enter upon careers in business: 637 out of the 859 graduates for whom information is preserved took up business careers. But their career patterns did not exhibit the kind of mobility that might be expected for such an educational elite. Prominent positions in Moscow firms (e.g., member of the board, vice-president, factory or branch manager) were attained by no more than thirty persons during the whole history of the higher schools. The majority were not able to rise higher than the post of clerk or bookkeeper. Out of the 127 alumni who constituted the first graduating class of the Commercial Institute (figure 9.13), only 21 managed to pursue careers in commerce and industry or become librarians relatively soon after graduation. The majority became teachers and officials in the rural zemstvos. These career patterns raise troubling questions about the relative effectiveness of investments in education and professional training. How was the future of Russian capitalism to be secured if professional training gave new cadres no advantage in their careers, but actually impeded promotion and hindered upward mobility in the world of Russian business?

Another negative phenomenon was equally symptomatic: while the Moscow business elite generously sponsored educational institutions and served on their boards of trustees, they generally refrained from sending their own children to Russian schools, choosing instead to educate them in Europe. For example, a list of the first graduating class of the Moscow Commercial Institute includes not a single name of a prominent Moscow business family. Moscow merchants, according to contemporaries, were indifferent to formal education at home,[9] preferring instead to educate their children in ways that promised enhanced social status rather than professional competence.

Commercial education assured only a very specialized training that also was extremely utilitarian. In fact, the special educational establishments were geared only to the production of qualified employees, middle managers at best. They were not able to prepare their students for the management of large-scale business, which the elite achieved instead through training within the family firm. Likewise, commercial education did not offer young men the social prestige coveted by the Moscow business elite, and which was traditionally associated in the public mind, and clearly in the merchant mind as well, with university education and experience abroad.

Over the course of time, the representatives of Merchant Moscow were increasingly inclined to relinquish business activity altogether and migrate toward a variety of distinctly nonbusiness professions, such as art patronage and acting (see the Clowes essay). The co-founder of the Moscow Art Theater, Konstantin Stanislavsky; the founders of the St. Petersburg and Moscow Conservatories, brothers Anton and Nicholas Rubinstein; the brilliant physician S. P. Botkin; the poet Valery Briusov; the famous barrister F. N. Plevako—all were of merchant families.

Such social mobility undoubtedly increased the charm of the splendid and fascinating culture of Merchant Moscow in the early twentieth century. But with the same eloquence such trends suggest a growing crisis within both business elites and the system of commercial education that was intended to serve its interests. This proliferation of social, cultural, and political diversions suggests a generalized turning away from entrepreneurial pursuits. Such dispersal of energies points toward a conscious abandonment by the Moscow business elite of its leading role in designing, constructing, and managing a modern industrial economy in Russia. Thus the very cultural flowering of Merchant Moscow might also be seen as a symptom of the impending erosion of its status as the citadel of native Russian capitalism.

NOTES

1. P. A. Buryshkin, *Moskva kupecheskaia* (New York: Chekhov Publishing, 1954).

2. *Atlas promyshlennosti Moskovskoi gubernii*, ed. L. M. Samoilovym (Moscow, 1845), pp. 5–6.

3. Ia. Ia. Nikitskii, "Kommercheskoe obrazovanie," in *Entsiklopedicheskii slovar'*, vol. 24 (Granat), p. 613.

4. *Stoletie Moskovskoi kommercheskoi akademii* (Moscow, 1910), pp. 774–75.

5. D. S. Margolin, *Spravochnik po vyshemu obrazovaniiu*, 3d ed. (Kiev, 1915), pp. 394–96.

6. *Ezhegodnye obzory prepodavaniia Moskovskogo kommercheskogo instituta na 1908–1915 gody* (Moscow, 1908–15); and Moskovskii Kommercheskii institut, *Al'bom fotografii* (Moscow, 1910).

7. See K. Zakharchenko, *Kommercheskoe i technicheskoe obrazovanie v Avstrii, Frantsii, Germanii i Rossii* (St. Petersburg, 1901).

8. Buryshkin, *Moskva kupecheskaia*, pp. 89, 92–93.

9. In the 1860s Prince V. P. Meshcherskii wrote about the merchants that "to learn at high school or commercial school was out of the question." See V. P. Meshcherskii, *Ocherki nyneshnei obshchestvennoi zhizni v Rossii: Pis'ma iz srednikh velikorusskihk gubernii*, vol. 2 (St. Petersburg, 1868), p. 57.

Figure 9.1. *The Imperial Moscow Commercial Institute.*

Figure 9.2. *Accounting class at the Commercial School.*

Figure 9.3. *The Moscow Practical Commercial Academy.*

Figure 9.4. *The Board of Trustees of the Moscow Practical Commercial Academy.*

Figure 9.5. *The chapel of the School for Petty Townspeople (Meshchansky School).*

Figure 9.6. *The Aleksandr Commercial School.*

Figure 9.7. *The Moscow Commercial School, founded in 1902 by A. S. Vishniakov.*

Figure 9.8. *Aleksei Semenovich Vishniakov.*

Figure 9.9. *Faculty gathering at the Moscow Commercial Institute.*

Figure 9.10. *A product laboratory at the Moscow Commercial Institute.*

Figure 9.11. *Professor Petr Ivanovich Novgorodtsev.*

Figure 9.12. *Professor of Economics Ivan Khristoforovich Ozerov.*

Figure 9.13. *Sergei Vasilevich Shchenkov, student at the Moscow Commercial Institute.*

PART FOUR

A City of One's Own:
Reshaping Culture
and Space

CHAPTER 10

Aesthetics and Commerce: The Architecture of Merchant Moscow, 1890–1917

William Craft Brumfield

The general direction of Moscow architecture now [1904] differs little from that of four centuries ago: the spirit of the people has remained the same. In new buildings as in earlier ones, there resounds the same melody, in which the accustomed ear can hear the motifs of different epochs, of different peoples united most primitively into one colorful whole. The motifs are just as naive, just as unexpected now as then, and they still amaze us with their contrasts, combining prayers to heaven with bows to mammon.[1]

Thus concludes a survey of Moscow's latest architecture, published in four issues of the journal *Zodchii* (Architect) in 1904. The pseudonymous author— presumably a prominent Petersburg critic—adopted a lightly ironic, bemused tone in describing the city's architectural exuberance; yet this generally positive appraisal accurately noted not only the mixture of cultures and periods in Moscow's buildings but also the economic force that gave rise to them.

Moscow, with its position at the crossroads of a vast trading network, had long been renowned for its merchants. But at the turn of the twentieth century, the merchant community gained power and wealth unprecedented in the city's history. And architecture was an essential part of this process: it provided buildings for the expansion of trade, houses and apartments for those who benefited from the expansion, as well as institutions that signaled the social and cultural responsibilities of the entrepreneurial elite: museums, theaters, hospitals, churches, and schools. Through architecture this elite created an urban space adapted to the needs of commerce and to an image of a new culture.

There is no clear point of origin for the stylistic and technical innovations that occurred in Russian architecture at the turn of the century; and the "new style" (Art Nouveau)—also known as the *style moderne*—assumed a protean character reflecting its varied sources of inspiration, from Art Nouveau to

Vienna Secession to Glasgow Arts and Crafts.[2] It was in Moscow, however, that the *style moderne* achieved, under merchant auspices, its most distinctive expression during the building boom at the turn of the century. Moscow's geography, with its relative availability of land and a varied, hilly relief that delineated neighborhood enclaves, enabled architects to display their interpretation of the *style moderne* to dramatic effect for their entrepreneurial patrons. In addition, the city's medieval history defined a concentric and radial pattern of development that would further determine the positioning of new buildings as a part of urban expansion in the 1900s (see map 1).[3]

The development of the new style was most evident in the citadel of Merchant Moscow, the Kitai Gorod (Stockade City), the ancient trading district located adjacent to the Kremlin. In the 1870s and 1880s, the area around Red Square had seen the construction of several large buildings in the Russian Revival style, inspired by the Kremlin and other medieval Muscovite monuments. The search for an authentic form of expressing the national identity in the arts in the second half of the nineteenth century was reflected in the designs of buildings such as the Historical Museum by Vladimir Shervud (figure 10.1) and the Moscow City Hall or Duma by Dmitry Chichagov (figure 10.2).[4]

The culmination of the Russian Revival style was the design of the new building for the Upper Trading Rows, facing the long east wall of the Kremlin across Red Square and located on Moscow's main site for trading activity since the twelfth century. The project was supported by stocks issued through a private company of entrepreneurs formed to rebuild a chaotic warren of shops that had evolved over several decades. Designed by the Petersburg architect Alexander Pomerantsev, the Upper Trading Rows (1889–93) can be seen as a turning point in Russian architecture, both because the project represented the apogee in the search for a national style (figure 10.3) and because it demanded advanced, functional technology on a scale unprecedented in Russian civil architecture. The basic concept of Pomerantsev's plan derived not only from the "passage," which had been used in Russia since the 1830s, but also from the example of the Milan Galleria.[5] Yet nothing in Russia equaled the size of this complex which included 1,000 to 1,200 shops for both retail and discount trade.

The general plan consisted of three parallel arcades along the length of the structure (242 meters), connected by three passages across its width.[6] Each arcade contained three levels, with shops fronting the passageway on the first and second levels. Walkways of reinforced concrete (possibly the first use of this material in Russia) spanned the opposing galleries of shops on the second level, as well as the offices on the third level. The entire three-story space ascended in a set-back toward the iron and glass arched skylights extending the length of the passage and providing the main source of natural illumination for the interior (figure 10.4).

The fact that this enormous edifice functioned is a tribute to the engineering genius of Vladimir Shukhov, who specialized in the design of large metal-frame structures, and to the high level of technical proficiency achieved in Russian construction at the turn of the century.[7] The use of reinforced concrete for the interior walls and vaulting eliminated the need for thick masonry support walls and provided space for circulation and light. In addition, the complex was serviced by a complete network of basement corridors, beneath which was a subbasement with heating boilers and an electrical generating station.

Despite these impressive resources, the Upper Trading Rows revealed a disjunction between the insistence on a "national" style and the functional demands of modern commercial architecture. Pomerantsev's design of the facades provided an appropriate complement to the other structures on Red Square and reaffirmed the historical geography of the site as a trading center. Yet the draping of a large retail center with motifs of historical reminiscence showed little promise from either a contemporary aesthetic or commercial point of view. It could also be argued that the growth patterns and modernization of the city infrastructure were leading away, in a physical sense, from such a centralized concept of retail marketing. Indeed, many prospective tenants saw little advantage in moving to the small, tightly segmented shops of the new building, which yielded only a modest return to the investors who had bought five million rubles' worth of stock in the Upper Trading Rows Company.

The transition to the new style and the extent of the change it entailed first appeared on a large scale in Moscow's Hotel Metropole (1899–1905) (figure 10.5), the planning for which began at the end of the nineteenth century. Commissioned by the Petersburg Insurance Society to provide Moscow with a hotel that would meet international standards of design and luxury, the Metropole had a complicated construction history. Even the winning design of William Walcot was substantially modified—in certain respects almost beyond recognition—before work began in 1899.[8] During the five years of construction, other architects were involved in the project, most notably Lev Kekushev, who supervised construction and added a number of elements of his own.

Many aspects of the Metropole classify it as a landmark of the *style moderne*; although it has elements of horizontal and vertical emphasis, and a large arched panel at the center of the main facade, the facade itself contains virtually no reference to the classical system of orders. Texture and material acquired the dominant expressive role, exemplified in the progression from an arcade with stone facing on the ground floor to the upper floors in plaster over brick. The central two stories are contained within two horizontal strips formed by wrought-iron balconies, while vertical accents—both functional and decorative—are provided by glass bays in the center and at the corners of the main facade. The patterned brick surface of the uppermost floor completes the contrast of texture and material, in which the decorative arts and structural form are combined.

This new relation between structure and material at the Metropole enabled the architect to use the facade as a ground upon which other art forms could be displayed, such as the plaster frieze by Nikolai Andreev on the theme "The Four Seasons" along the fourth floor, and seven ceramic panels designed by Aleksandr Golovin above the fifth story. Most prominently, the great arch at the center of the main facade contains the ceramic panel "The Princess of Dreams" (from the play *La Princesse lointaine* by Edmond Rostand), designed by Mikhail Vrubel, Russia's great forerunner of modernism in painting. It is significant that both Vrubel and Golovin had been active in the arts and crafts movement at the Abramtsevo estate of railroad magnate Savva Mamontov, and the influence of the arts and crafts revival is evident in the design of the Metropole. From the modest experiments at Abramtsevo to the unprecedented scale of a modern "first-class hotel," a new aestheticism had asserted its presence in a deluxe building financed by an insurance company. (Comandeered by the new Soviet government for office space in 1918, the Metropole endured many turns of fortune that defaced much of its interior decoration. After a recent, complicated restoration, it is again the premier grand hotel of Moscow.)

The new functional aestheticism in commercial architecture appeared in several other buildings within or adjacent to Kitai Gorod, including several designed by Fedor Shekhtel, the most distinguished architect to work for the merchant elite at the turn of the century (see plate 15). Shekhtel was the architect of choice for many merchants in the construction of their private homes (see plates 16–19). Among the largest of his public buildings was one for the Moscow Insurance Society on Old Square (1901) (figure 10.6), which represents a shift from the Renaissance detail and arched facades of the preceding buildings to an orthogonal, grid framework of brick and reinforced concrete.[9] Although the Insurance Society building—more commonly known as "Boyars' Court," after the hotel situated in the building—retains a number of stucco decorative devices familiar from earlier buildings, the rationalism of its design signaled the beginning of the modern era in Moscow's financial district.

Shekhtel's efforts in the creating a modern business environment culminated in the building for the Moscow Merchant Society, located on New Square two blocks above his much larger Boyars' Court building. Like his other commercial structures, the Moscow Merchant Society building (figure 10.7) consisted of load-bearing brick walls and iron columns for interior support, with a reinforced concrete and plate glass grid for the front and north side facades. Whatever the building may have lacked in comparison with contemporary towers in Chicago and New York, it proved entirely functional as a merchandise showroom and office space. And even with the virtual lack of architectural ornament on the rectangular grid, the building revealed Shekhtel's thorough understanding of proportions and of the aesthetic properties of building materials, such as yellow pressed brick over the vertical structural members and tinted plate glass. In this union of form and function Shekhtel suggested the practical spirit of a new economic order in Moscow—and in Russia.

Subsequent office buildings in the Kitai Gorod district adopted a more austere form, exemplified by Ivan Kuznetsov's Business Court (Delovoi dvor, 1912–13), a hotel and office complex located on New Square. The initiator of the project was Nikolai Vtorov, one of the most enterprising of Moscow's capitalists and, in the words of a contemporary observer, "the first to break the age-old traditions in favor of a rational and intelligent organization of commercial business."[10] Vtorov located his project just beyond the Kitai Gorod wall (a block from Shekhtel's "Boyars' Court") and stipulated a modern construction design. The plan included an elongated hotel in three attached segments and a trapezoidal office building for wholesale trade, each five to six stories in height.

Kuznetsov focused on his client's business requirements in the ferroconcrete structure, but he also provided a neoclassical "cover" to mitigate the rigorous application of the grid design on the exterior and to provide a suitably imposing frame for the main entrances. The corner wedge of the hotel entrance on New Square is marked by the familiar neoclassical rotunda with Corinthian columns and dome. Likewise, the main point of entry to the office block displays a Corinthian portico and pediment hovering over the entrance arch (figure 10.8). This neoclassical window dressing stands in contrast to the side facades of the building, which are altogether without ornamentation and display the clean lines and sense of proportion characteristic of a new rationalist aesthetic.

For the retail trade in the area surrounding Kitai Gorod, the largest modern development was Roman Klein's department store for the British firm of Muir and Mirrielees (1906–8). Klein's earlier emporium for the wholesale trade at the Middle Trading Rows (next to the Upper Trading Rows) had attempted to fuse historicism with serviceable commercial space. Over a decade later, the requirements for a modern, unified retail center led to a radically different design. As with the Hotel Metropole, the primary goal lay in creating a convenient setting that would attract a prosperous clientele and at the same time rationalize the operation of retail merchandising from small shops to one universal store.

With Klein's design of a reinforced concrete frame to support the structure, the Muir and Mirrielees store was probably the first in Moscow to use a system of suspended exterior walls, whose strips of plate glass provided natural illumination for the interior (figure 10.9). Klein chose to emphasize the lines of the facade grid, but he stopped at creating a streamlined modernist frame.

Like certain American contemporaries, he gave the building a Gothic decorative overlay. In addition to pinnacles, lancet windows, and crockets, a large rose window dominates one corner of the south facade; yet these elements do not alter in any substantial way a perception of the building's grid. Even the ornament was based upon the innovative use of materials such as zinc (with an overlay of copper to simulate bronze) and marble aggregate.[11]

Along the radial thoroughfares extending from Moscow's financial core, the *style moderne* was applied in structures that exemplify the diversity of the city's economic and cultural development. Between Petrovka and Tverskaia streets, both leading from the center to the northwest, Shekhtel created one of his most brilliant *style moderne* interiors for the Moscow Art Theater (figure 10.10), a project financed in part by the textile magnate Savva Morozov. Because the theater's limited funds were spent almost entirely on the interior—not in lavish decoration but in advanced lighting and stage design—Shekhtel was unable to realize his *style moderne* facade design in its entirety. Thus the facade retains the eclectic character peculiar to much of central Moscow's architecture. The Petrovka also had a number of modern apartment buildings (known as *dokhodnye doma*, or "income houses"), with space for shops and offices on the ground floor.

On nearby Tverskaia Street, Adolf Erikhson, another of Moscow's prominent modern architects, constructed headquarters for publishing magnate Ivan Sytin, who published not only the newspaper *Russkoe slovo* (The Russian Word) but also popular mass editions of both Russian and foreign literature. Sytin required a multipurpose structure with commercial and production areas, in addition to living space. Erikhson's design of the Sytin Publishing House (1905–7) used ferroconcrete for an open, unobstructed interior work space, illuminated by large windows (figure 10.11). Shekhtel had already explored this approach, but Erikhson pushed its decorative possibilities further with a variety of windows, including circular and modified Venetian openings with the curved ornamental mullions common in the early *moderne*. The frame of the main facade is sheathed in lightly glazed brick, with *moderne* details (including a female mask) sparingly applied in stucco under the cornice and at the corners of the building.[12] Whereas the decorative details resemble those of contemporary Viennese design, the grid pattern is typical of Moscow commercial architecture in the new style.

If Moscow's modern commercial architecture often resembled European styles of the same period, there were other contemporary structures that drew upon Russian motifs for design inspiration. It is telling that one of the first and best examples of the neo-Russian style was built in the traditional merchant district to the south of the city center and beyond the Moscow River (*Zamoskvoreche*). In his design for the expansion of the Tretiakov Art Gallery, devoted to the public display of Russian art, the artist and architect Viktor Vasnetsov blended modernity with the arts and crafts movement. Vasnetsov did not, in fact, build the entire gallery. Although the precise dates are not clear, he was commissioned around 1900 to create a new main entrance and facade for the gallery, which had been open to the public since 1892, when the merchant Pavel Tretiakov donated his collection to the city of Moscow.[13]

The building that housed the collection formed part of an earlier complex of structures typical of the Zamoskvoreche district, including the Tretiakov home, initially expanded in 1873 to accommodate a private art collection. In providing a focal point for the assortment of structures around a central yard, Vasnetsov created an entrance structure for the long building that held most of the paintings. Work on the facade decoration can be firmly dated to 1903 and was probably completed in 1905.[14]

Vasnetsov's design of the entrance consisted of a brick facade, lightly stuccoed and painted, that provided a clear spatial outline as well as a base for the decorative bands along the upper part of the facade (figure 10.12). The strips include a ceramic frieze resembling fin de siècle symbolist painting, a large inscription (announcing the Tretiakov donation) on a white background in a medieval Russian stylization, and a decorative brick border. The superb quality of architectural ceramic work in Moscow, much of which was provided by the Abramtsevo ceramic workshop (now relocated to Moscow), did much to encourage the use of traditional decorative elements within a new architectural aesthetic.[15]

The most noticeable impact of the *style moderne* on the architecture of Moscow occurred in the construction of housing, where its emphasis on the decorative arts and a more rational arrangement of interior space formed an integral part of the design of both the private house and the apartment building. Indeed, it can be said that in Moscow the large apartment building is essentially a product of the new style, whose standards of efficiency, comfort, and technological progress were suited to accommodate the growth of an increasingly prosperous and professional middle class living in the central area of Moscow, the limits of which were expanding with the tram network.[16] Despite a severe housing shortage for the lower classes, large parts of the city were still underbuilt; therefore the construction of large apartment complexes were usually designed to attract a sufficiently prosperous clientele.

An impressive example of this trend appeared in N. M. Proskurin's two large apartment blocks built on Sretensky Boulevard—one of the northeastern segments of the Boulevard Ring—during 1899–1902 for the Rossiia Insurance Company (figure 10.13). Like many apartments of the 1890s, the complex contains elements from the Italian Renaissance, combined with Gothic pinnacles on the dominant corner tower in imitation of the Kremlin Spassky Tower. Yet the scale and quality of the apartment complex exceeded anything that had been produced in Moscow, perhaps also in Petersburg in the 1890s. The primitive services offered by Moscow at the time made it essential that such a large project provide its own source of water, heat, and electricity.[17] The substantial investment required for a building and services on this scale was generally available only from insurance companies as with the Hotel Metropole, and the Rossiia firm had already undertaken another apartment complex the preceding year (1898) on Lubianka Square. Although these two projects show little evidence of the stylistic traits of the *moderne*, they depended on the same economic climate essential for the development of the new style.

The 1900s in Moscow witnessed an increase in apartment complexes the design of which reflected the need to provide living space for a clientele with more modest income in the central city. One of the earliest examples of middle-level housing on a large scale was L. Shishkovsky's eight-story apartment house for F. I. Afremov, built in 1904 (figure 10.14). Located to the northeast on Sadovaia-Spasskaia Street near its intersection with Miasnitskaia Street, the building resulted from the boom in apartment construction along the Garden Ring, a circular thoroughfare composed of several tree-lined segments. The extension of a tram network in 1904 brought such previously outlying districts within convenient reach of the center, while the larger sites available in areas around the Ring permitted new configurations in apartment blocks. In the Afremov building, for example, perpendicular wings extended from the back facade, thus increasing the amount of space while providing additional light and ventilation. Despite its austere functionalism, the facade of the building, particularly along the cornice, contains a number of decorative elements typical of the *style moderne*.

Structural fantasy and the Jugendstil influence appear more obtrusively in Georgy Makaev's apartment house of 1905 on Vvedensky (now Podsosensky) Lane, beyond the Boulevard Ring to the east of the central city. At the corner tower, with its floral plasticity and three-storied tulips, the two main facades intersect (figure 10.15). Although architects in the nineteenth century frequently exploited a corner location with a projecting tower, none surpassed Makaev's flamboyant design, with its asymmetrical decoration on each of the facades. The windows of the building are plain rectangles cut into a wall of roughcast, the undecorated background of which highlights the plaster strips on the facade, the window surrounds on the first floor, and the projecting bays. The contrasts in material, from the various stuccos and reinforced concrete cornice to the ironwork of the balconies, emphasize the interplay between structure and texture.

Whatever the stylistic emphasis, all the apartment houses surveyed here show a resemblance to some continental source such as Paris or Vienna. Yet the possibilities of using traditional motifs in a modern context, demonstrated by Viktor Vasnetsov in his design for the Tretiakov Gallery, also appeared in the construction of apartment buildings. The prominence of the crafts revival and the use of folk motifs demonstrate a confluence of purpose among artists, set designers, and architects at the turn of the century.[18] The close relation between material and structure in the medieval or folk traditions of pre-

Petrine Russian architecture acquired a renewed aesthetic interpretation in the "neo-Russian" variant of the *style moderne*, which strove for an aesthetic transformation of the urban milieu rather than a programmatic commentary on the nation's history, as on the facade of the Historical Museum.

No one in Moscow proclaimed these possibilities more dramatically than the artist Sergei Maliutin in his design for the apartment house of N. P. Pertsov at Prechistenka Quay (1905–7), located in the same southwestern area as the Isakov apartment house, but closer to the center and overlooking the Moscow River. Maliutin had already achieved a reputation for his work in the arts and crafts community at Talashkino, the estate of Princess Maria Tenisheva.[19]

In his design for the Pertsov building, Maliutin made more extensive use of ceramic panels and other ornamentation based on representations of folk art (figure 10.16). The staginess of his sketch for the building—reproduced in the 1907 issue of the *Annual of the Society of Architect-Artists*—masked the basic structure with a panoply of steeply pitched roofs, towers, elaborately decorated balconies, doors, and window surrounds. Maliutin intended to reproduce the asymmetry of the medieval *teremok* (a word that includes the concepts of "tower" and "chambers"); but his imagination exceeded practicality, and the original design was considerably modified by Nikolai Zhukov, the architect responsible for construction of the building.

Virtually all of Moscow's radial thoroughfares, from the south (Zamoskvoreche) to the northeast, witnessed the construction of modern apartment houses during the two decades before the First World War. The density of multistoried apartment construction varied greatly: streets such as Arbat (extending to the west) achieved a distinctly urban density, yet radial arteries such as Prechistenka, Volkhonka, and Ostozhenka (on the southwest) and Pokrovka on the northeast had large apartment buildings interspersed with low-density construction, often consisting of single-story houses built several decades earlier. This feature was still more noticeable on the Garden Ring thoroughfare, which displayed some of the most advanced and most primitive examples of Moscow's urban housing.

While apartment buildings were primarily located on main arteries, the modern private houses of the newly rich merchants and industrialists were typically sequestered on side streets in the same areas. Significant examples include the Derozhinskaia house (see plate 17), designed by Shekhtel in 1901 and located on quiet Prechistenka Lane, just off bustling Prechistenka Street near the site of Kekushev's apartment house for Isakov. These mansions deserve a separate study as the most revealing and brilliant cultural artifacts created by Moscow's capitalist elite.[20]

As new commercial buildings, cultural institutions (particularly theaters and museums), and apartment houses arose throughout the central districts of the city, the area beyond the Garden Ring was marked at main intersections by stations for the rail lines that served Moscow, Russia's transportation hub.

Most of these nine stations had taken shape during the latter part of the nineteenth century in various eclectic, utilitarian styles. At the beginning of the twentieth century, with the expansion and consolidation of railroads, some of the most important of these stations were rebuilt.

Indeed, the most dramatic example of the *style moderne* for a large, functional public structure was Shekhtel's rebuilding of the Iaroslavl Railroad Station, main terminus for a northern railroad network managed by Savva Mamontov and leading from Moscow through Iaroslavl to Arkhangelsk (figure 10.17). Like his mentor, Vasnetsov, Shekhtel was capable of fluently reinterpreting traditional Russian decorative elements in a modern idiom related to the "neo-Russian" style. The same characteristics are immediately obvious in the entrance facade of the station, with towers on each corner modeled on the brick fortresses and monastery walls that exist in rich profusion in Moscow and Iaroslavl.[21]

As at the Hotel Metropole, the Russian arts and crafts movement provided the means for incorporating the applied arts into the aesthetic system of the new architecture. The ceramic tiles referred to earlier form a green and brown frieze along the main facade of gray pressed brick, which merges into the exuberantly molded main entrance. At this central point, the decorative effects of ceramic, stucco, and iron are combined with attention to both texture and symbolism, as in the gargantuan representation of wild strawberries of the northern forests in ceramic tile on turrets flanking the entrance.

In the next decade, references to traditional Muscovite design took a very different shape in a historicist architectural movement exemplified by the design of the Kazan Railroad Station (serving cities to the east and south), located opposite the Iaroslavl Station on Kanchalevsky Square. The neo-Russian style, which had formed part of the modern aesthetic movement at the beginning of the century, was replaced by a more insistent, retrospective form of architectural fantasy, as demonstrated in Shchusev's winning design for the Kazan Railroad Station (1913–26)—an elaborate seventeenth-century stylization based on fortress towers in Moscow and Kazan.[22]

The city's crucial rail network to the west and southwest also required a new, much expanded terminal. For this purpose, Moscow received its grandest monument in modernized classicism before the revolution in Ivan Rerberg's design for the Kiev (Briansk) Railroad Station, across the Moscow River via Roman Klein's newly rebuilt Borodino Bridge (1912–13). Rerberg, who graduated from the Petersburg Institute of Military Engineering in 1896, was a major architect in the design of the business complex for the Northern Insurance Company in Kitai Gorod and thus was no stranger to the uses of classical elements on a large scale. Work on the station began in 1914; by 1917 the basic structure was complete, although the final details were not finished until 1920.

In the design of the main terminal building, Rerberg adopted the Moscow Empire model of the early nineteenth century, with attached Ionic columns on the main facade and end blocks containing arched entrances and surmounted with domed rotundas (figure 10.18). A clock tower on the right corner provides the visual dominant to the entire ensemble. In contrast to the classicizing detail of the main terminal, however, the great platform shed, projected and built by Shukhov, represents the epitome of functionalism in the articulation of its curved ferrovitreous vault (47 meters in width, 30 in height, and 231 in length).[23] Here is striking evidence of a continuity extending through the three decades of modern architectural engineering in prerevolutionary Moscow, from Shukhov's participation in the design of the Upper Trading Rows, to his soaring arch over the platforms of the city's rail link to the west.

This look at the new architecture in Merchant Moscow demonstrates a diversity created by the energy of a developing capitalist economy. Little consensus existed among architects concerning the proper relation between style and structure or the social role of architecture in creating a livable, ordered urban setting. These problems were particularly acute for the mass of workers moving into the city and its fringes. Yet with the support provided by public-spirited merchants, Moscow's architects created a remarkable variety of buildings that served commerce as well as culture and were at once cosmopolitan and Russian in design. Although lacking a comprehensive vision, the *style moderne* and related movements filled the cityscape in ways that accommodated both tradition and topography. To this day architecture remains the clearest testimony to the vitality of Merchant Moscow from the time of the Great Reforms to the Bolshevik Revolution.

NOTES

1. Ivonne d'Axe (pseudonym), "Sovremennaia Moskva," *Zodchii*, no. 18 (1904): 215. On the identity of "Ivonne d'Axe," see William Craft Brumfield, *The Origins of Modernism in Russian Architecture* (Berkeley and Los Angeles: University of California Press, 1991), p. 304, n. 48.

2. On the development of the new style in Russian architecture at the turn of the century, see ibid., pp. 47–62.

3. E. A. Kirichenko provides an informative survey of this process of urban transformation in *Moskva na rubezhe dvukh stoletii* (Moscow: Stroiizdat,, 1977).

4. Moscow's historicist architecture during the latter third of the nineteenth century is discussed in Brumfield, *The Origins of Modernism in Russian Architecture*, pp. 9–14.

5. On the development of trading arcades and galleries in Russia, see William Craft Brumfield, "Dai bassifondi all'edificio superiore dei Torgovye Rjady; il *design* delle gallerie commerciali di Mosca," *Ricerche de Storia dell'arte* 39 (1989): 7–16.

6. Detailed photographs of the old trading rows, as well as the construction of the new building for the Upper Trading Rows, appeared in the album *Torgovye riady na Krasnoi ploshchadi v Moskve* (Kiev, 1893). See also I. P. Mashkov, ed., *Putevoditel' po Moskve* (Moscow: Moskovskoe arkhitekturnoe obshchestvo, 1913), pp. 259–62.

7. Shukhov's life and work are surveyed in G. M. Kovelman, *Tvorchestvo pochetnogo akademika inzhenera Vladimir Grigorevicha Shukhova* (Moscow: Stroiizdat, 1961).

8. For details of the construction history of the Hotel Metropole, see V. M. Chekmarev, "Obnovlenie gostinitsy 'Metropol,'" *Arkhitektura i stroitel'stvo Moskvy*, no. 6 (1987): 22–25.

9. The building's structural system is analyzed in Kozlovskaia, "Konstruktivnye struktury," in Iu. S. Lebedev, ed., *Konstruktsii i arkhitekturnaia forma v russkom zodchestve XIX-nachala XX vv.* (Moscow: Stroiizdat, 1977), pp. 155.

10. Pavel A. Buryshkin, *Moskva kupecheskaia* (New York, 1954), p. 198. Information on the financing of the project appeared in "Novaia Moskva," *Moskovskii arkhitkturnyi mir* 3 (1914): 62–63, with accompanying photographs.

11. On structural innovations in Klein's building for the department store, see Kozlovskaia, "Konstruktivnye struktury," pp. 155–56.

12. For a history of the Sytin Printing Works and the subsequent fate of the building, see R. E. Krupnova and V. A. Rezvin, *Ulitsa Gor'kogo, 18* (Moscow: Moskovskii rabochii, 1984), pp. 14–17. In the 1930s the brick facing was removed from the first floor and replaced with rusticated stucco. During the same period the original interior underwent a complete modification.

13. An authoritative account of the Tretiakov Gallery is D. Ia. Bezrukova, *Tretiakov i istoriia sozdaniia ego galerei* (Moscow, 1970).

14. Vasnetsov's work on the facade in 1903 is mentioned in the journal *Zodchii*, no. 36 (1903): 427, and photographs of the completed building appeared in architectural publications by 1906.

15. On the Abramtsevo workshop's role in the development of architectural ceramics in Moscow, see E. R. Arenzon, "'Abramtsevo' v Moskve: K istorii khudozhestvenno-keramicheskogo predpriiatiia S. I. Mamontova," in *Muzei 10* (Moscow, 1989), pp. 95–102.

16. In Russian scholarship the disparity between housing levels in Moscow at the beginning of the century has been examined by P. and B. Gol'denberg, in *Planirovka zhilogo kvartala Moskvy* (Moscow: Stroitelnaia literatura, 1935), pp. 126–78. See also E. I. Kirichenko, "O nekotorykh osobennostiakh evoliutsii gorodskikh mnogokvartirnykh domov vtoroi poloviny XIX-nachala XX vv.," *Arkhitekturnoe nasledstvo* 15 (1963): 158–61. Attempts to provide cheap housing subsidized by the bequest of the merchant G. G. Solodovnikov catered almost entirely to a growing "white-collar" service population. See Brumfield, *The Origins of Modernism in Russian Architecture*, p. 77; and Robert Thurston, *Liberal City, Conservative State: Moscow and Russia's Urban Crisis, 1906–1914* (Oxford, 1987), pp. 143–44. Plans for the Moscow Ring Railroad and the designs of some of its stations were presented in "Sooruzhenie Moskovskoi zhelٍeznoi dorogi," *Zodchii*, no. 10 (1909), pp. 105–9.

17. The Proskurin design is analyzed in detail in Elena Vokhovitskaia and Aleksei Tarkhanov, "Dom 'Rossiia,'" *Dekorativnoe iskusstvo*, no. 7 (1986): 34–38.

18. E. A. Borisova discusses the neo-Russian variant of the *style moderne* and its theatrical quality in "Neorusskii stil' v russkoi arkhitekture predrevoliutsionnykh let," in *Iz istorii russkogo iskusstva vtoroi poloviny XIX-nachala XX veka* (Moscow, 1978), pp. 59–71. A contemporary defense of theatricality in the design of apartment houses appeared in P. Sokolov, "Krasota arkhitekturnykh form," *Zodchii*, no. 49 (1912): 490.

19. See Sergei Diagilev, "Neskol'ko slov o S. V. Maliutine," *Mir iskusstva*, no. 4 (1903): 157–60. In Diagilev's view, Maliutin and the Finnish painter Gallen-Kalela had established in the north of Europe the basis for a "second rinascimento" that would eventually lead to a "new aesthetic, a new Florence" (ibid., pp. 159–60). The Pertsov building was the subject of a laudatory, illustrated essay (unsigned) on the neo-Russian style: "Mastera russkogo stilia," *Moskovskii arkhitekturnyi mir*, no. 2 (1912): 43–49.

20. A similar observation could be made in regard to the influence of the new style on Moscow's churches. Built primarily for Old Believer merchant patrons in modernized re-creations of early medieval church architectures, these modest but beautifully designed churches were located in quiet lanes and defined secluded, semi-urban enclaves of the city. On their de-

sign, see William Craft Brumfield, "The 'New Style' and the Revival of Orthodox Church Architecture, 1900–1914," in William Craft Brumfield and Milos M. Velimirovic, eds., *Christianity and the Arts in Russia* (New York, 1991), pp. 105–23. On *style moderne* mansions, see Brumfield, *The Origins of Modernism in Russian Architecture*.

21. On decorative symbolism in the design of the Iaroslavl Station, see Brumfield, *The Origins of Modernism in Russian Architecture*, pp. 153–57.

22. Shchusev's winning proposal for the Kazan Railroad Station was the subject of detailed reports in *Arkhitekturno- khudozhestvennyi ezhenedel'nik*, no. 4 (1914): 46–48; and no. 19 (1915): 217–19.

23. Specifications of the Kiev (formerly Briansk) Railroad Station are presented in G. M. Shchebro, "I. Rerberg," in M. I. Astaf'eva-Dlugach and Iu. P. Volshok, eds., *Zodchie Moskvy: XX vek* (Moscow: Moskovskii rabochii, 1988), pp. 65–66.

Figure 10.1. *Historical Museum, Red Square, 1874–83. Architect: Vladimir Shervud. To the left, this turn-of-the-century view is bounded by the Kremlin walls with the Nikolsky Tower, painted white, and the corner Arsenal Tower. Visible on the right are the twin towers of the seventeenth-century gates and chapel dedicated to the Icon of the Iversk Mother of God. Razed in 1929–30, the gates and chapel have now been rebuilt.*

Figure 10.2. *Moscow City Hall, 1890–92. Architect: Dmitry Chichagov. This view of the north facade, with its seventeenth-century decorative motifs, is similar to the adjacent Historical Museum. They were separated by the Iversk Gates to the right (not visible).*

Figure 10.3. *Upper Trading Rows, 1889–93. Architect: Vladimir Pomerantsev. Facing the east wall of the Kremlin, the Upper Trading Rows represent the culmination of the florid historicist style of the late nineteenth century.*

Figure 10.4. *Upper Trading Rows. View of the central galleria from a walkway on the third level. The ferrovitreous skylight that protects and illuminates the passage was designed by the most prominent Russian engineer of the period, Vladimir Shukhov.*

Figure 10.5. *Hotel Metropole, 1899–1905. Architect: William Walcot, with substantial modifications by Lev Kekushev and others. This view is of the shorter, west facade, which contained the main entrance.*

Figure 10.6. *Moscow Insurance Society Building, completed in 1901. Architect: Feodor Shekhtel. More commonly known as Boyar's Court, for the hotel of the same name, the building faced the Kitai Gorod wall (to the right, not visible) along its main facade, while the shorter facade proceeded up an incline to the early seventeenth-century merchant Church of the Trinity in Nikitniki (partially visible).*

Figure 10.7. *Moscow Merchants' Society Building, 1909. Architect: Feodor Shekhtel. Containing offices for mercantile firms, the building is located two blocks north of the Boyar's Court building. Illustrative of the new commercial architecture, the main facades of this structure contain a reinforced concrete grid with plate glass infill.*

Figure 10.8. *Business Court (Delovoi dvor), 1912–13. Architect: Ivan Kuznetsov. The largest of Moscow's new business complexes, combining modern structural techniques with classicizing details that create an imposing ambience for business activity.*

Figure 10.9. *Muir and Mirrielees department store, 1906–8. Architect: Roman Klein. The first major retail emporium in Moscow to adopt the principle of open floor arrangement of shopping, rather than the galleria, or arcade, system of the preceding decades.*

Figure 10.10. *Moscow Art Theater, completed in 1902. Architect: Feodor Shekhtel. View of the proscenium. The abstract, modernistic quality of Shekhtel's interior design focused attention on the stage, one of the most advanced in Europe. (Photo by William Craft Brumfield.)*

Figure 10.11. *Sytin Printing House, 1905–7. Architect: Adolf Erikhson. Situated on Tverskaia, one of the city's busiest commercial thoroughfares, the Sytin building represented a bold statement of Central European artistic design in the center of Moscow. Its harmoniously balanced frame was decorated by a brightly colored ceramic band visible above the second story. The most recent use of the building is as a showcase for luxury automobiles by General Motors.*

Figure 10.12. *Tretiakov Art Gallery, 1900–1905(?). Architect: Viktor Vasnetsov. Most of the museum space consisted of earlier structures in the Tretiakov family compound. Vasnetsov converted them and added the famous entrance building, with its polychrome arts and crafts decoration. Strangely, there is no consensus on the exact date of construction of this building.*

Figure 10.13. *Apartment complex for the Rossiia Insurance Company, 1899–1902. Architect: N. M. Proskurin. Located near the corner of Sretensky Boulevard and Miasnitskaia Street, these two apartment buildings, decorated with a mixture of medieval and Renaissance elements, actually formed a small city with self-contained utilities.*

Figure 10.14. F. I. Afremov apartment house, 1904. Architect: L. Shishkovsky. Still one of the larger structures on Moscow's Garden Ring, the Afremov building was made economically viable by the extension of the tramway to the Ring. As with urban buildings elsewhere in Europe and in America, additional revenue was obtained by renting the side, blind walls for advertising space.

Figure 10.15. Apartment house on Vvedensky (now Podsosensky) Lane, 1905. Architect: Georg Makaev. Located in a quiet neighborhood in east central Moscow a few blocks from the Garden Ring, this building would have attracted a relatively prosperous clientele with its elaborate Art Nouveau decoration. (Photo by William Craft Brumfield.)

Figure 10.16. *N. P. Pertsov apartment house, 1905–7. Architect-artist: Sergei Maliutin. The most fanciful application of arts and crafts motifs to a modern urban building, the Pertsov building stood a block away from the massive, neo-Byzantine Cathedral of Christ the Redeemer, demolished by the Soviets, now being rebuilt.*

Figure 10.17. *Iaroslavl Railroad Station, 1902. Architect: Fedor Shekhtel. Located on Kalanchevsky Square with two other major rail stations, the Iaroslavl Station represented the boldest application of* style moderne *curves with motifs expressive of picturesque medieval forms.*

Figure 10.18. *Briansk (Kiev) Railway Station, 1914–20. Architect: Ivan Rerberg. This grand terminal, Moscow's main station for the southwest, demonstrates the return to classical forms for major public architecture in Russia just prior to the war and the Revolution.*

CHAPTER 11

Merchant Moscow After Hours: Voluntary Associations and Leisure

Joseph C. Bradley

Conventional wisdom tells us that in the nineteenth century Moscow's merchants shunned the public eye. They were reticent and absorbed in their businesses. Of course, we know that businesspeople everywhere were a reticent lot in those days, and in this, Russia's were no exception. But there is something more to this in the Russian case: for the merchants an entire "kingdom of darkness" was constructed from the bricks of places and homes and the mortar of personal characteristics. Merchant life was *zamknutyi*—closed, walled off, particularistic. In the mid-nineteenth century merchants allegedly did not enter the civic realm. The impression of the literary critic Vissarion Belinsky was typical of the intelligentsia:[1] "Everybody stays at home and fortifies himself from his neighbor. . . . [In the merchant neighborhoods] curtains cover the windows, the gates are bolted shut; a knock at the gate prompts a mean bark from a guard dog. Everything is dead, or perhaps it is better to say, in slumber. . . . Everywhere you see family life but hardly anywhere the city!"

Yet rapid changes toward the end of the nineteenth century suggest Moscow's merchants participated in an expanding public life; moreover, this participation was increasingly organized and associational, not "walled off" and particularistic. The writer P. D. Boborykin observed that merchants held public office, served on school boards, were board members of many organizations and charitable societies, contributed to philanthropic causes, opened art galleries, and were patrons of learned societies and the arts: "The merchant is everywhere. He is around and in the middle of Moscow life. . . . Probably no one can imagine Moscow without the merchant. Take any institution and you will immediately find a merchant." The chronicler of merchant life, Pavel Buryshkin, claimed: "The merchant was not only in the city council, he was in all of the city's public life [*obshchestvennost'*]."[2] A look at merchant participation in the city's many philanthropic associations will suggest an underappreciated feature of late nineteenth-century entrepreneurial culture: the growing civic consciousness of Merchant Moscow.[3]

To be sure, photographs taken at the turn of the century do reveal a private life, a life of leisure. Merchant families have bought country homes (figure 11.1) and eat meals on their porches in the summer (figure 11.2); the immense gardens that accentuated the private world in the city now form a natural background to country life (figure 11.3). They put on amateur theatricals (figure 11.4). They breed and race horses (figures 11.5–7). They hunt; and those angry curs that guarded the gates of their city mansions are now rather more noble-looking hunting hounds (figures 11.8 and 11.9). And merchants at their leisure were ready to take up new sports at the turn of the century: cycling and tennis (figure 11.10). Pictures of merchant families after hours show new country squires. This is no longer merchant life per se; it is genteel life.

Although genteel life frequently remained familial, it also had a more public, organizational dimension. In fact, the first public organization of the Moscow merchantry, the Club, founded in 1786, served as the venue for leisure and charitable activities. By the early nineteenth century, the Merchants' Club became well known for its balls, masquerades, concerts, card games, and "literary evenings," although its charter forbade discussion of religion or politics. Except for a brief stretch at midcentury, the Merchants' Club's charter permitted membership from all estates, allowing a mingling of merchants, nobles, officials, and professionals. The Merchants' Club was the scene of the banquet organized by Kokorev in 1859, at which merchants expressed sympathy with the idea of emancipation, only to be chastised by the government for meddling in matters not of their concern. Among the better-known elders of the Merchants' Club were Nikolai Ivanovich Shchukin and Mikhail and Ivan Abramovich Morozov.

By the latter part of the nineteenth century, the all-purpose club was joined by more specialized leisure and sporting organizations. The horse breeder and racer Morozov was a member of the Moscow Racing Society, as was his fellow horse breeder Gerasim Ivanovich Khludov. Merchants were even more prominent in the Moscow Hunting Society, founded in 1862 to promote hunting and game management. Its membership list included the famous theater director Konstantin Sergeevich Alekseev-Stanislavsky, the railroad magnate and patron of the arts Savva Ivanovich Mamontov, the art collector Sergei Mikhailovich Tretiakov, and the conductor Nikolai Rubenstein, as well as representatives of the Guchkov, Morozov, Prokhorov, Botkin, Vishniakov, Soldatenkov, Solodovnikov, Khludov, Riabushinsky, and Chetverikov clans and the Alsatians Emile and Camille Zindel.[4] Finally, it should be noted that the ladies' semifinals of the 1909 Club Championship of the Moscow Lawn Tennis Association pitted Alexandra P. Riabushinskaia against Nadezhda P. Riabushinskaia. (Despite a photograph in the Association's newletter suggesting that

Alexandra Pavlovna had a good midcourt game, she lost the match; sadly for the Riabuskinskys, Nadezhda lost in the finals.)

Examples of such genteel leisure and sporting life could be multiplied. They certainly made good photographs. But they are only the most "outdoor" tip of the iceberg of associational activity. The rest of this essay will be devoted to merchants' civic and philanthropic activity. We will see an elite devoted to charities; education; collection, preservation, and display of the national heritage; and advancement of the learning, art, and technology of the future.

Russian charitable giving is legendary. In its "traditional" forms, Russian charity included gifts to the church and monasteries, donations to almshouses, and handouts to beggars; wealthy merchants were among the biggest givers (see the Ulianova essay). This merchant generosity can be traced to various motives: religiosity (many of the merchants came from Old Believer families), guilt about the great wealth accumulated in a society with a dim view of trade and commerce, and desire to gain recognition, status, and culture. By the second half of the nineteenth century, more "modern" organized forms of charity—private and municipal institutions—had appeared, many of which were funded by prominent merchant families. A few examples will suffice.

The candymaker A. A. Abrikosov, a convert to Roman Catholicism after studies at Oxford, gave the money for a municipal maternity home that opened in 1906. The Khludov family founded several free rooming houses and a children's hospital. Mikhail Abramovich Morozov founded a shelter for one hundred homeless, donated to the Moscow cancer clinic, and gave money for the restoration of the Cathedral of the Assumption in the Kremlin. Nikolai Vasilevich and Konstantin Vasilevich Rukavishnikov ran, and later turned over to the city, a correctional home for juvenile delinquents. But perhaps best known for their charities was the Bakhrushin family, "professional philanthropists," in Buryshkin's words. Between 1880 and 1904, the family contributed close to three million rubles to municipal charities, in addition to contributions to nonmunicipal charities and institutions. Their beneficiaries included a city hospital, school, orphanage, and a rooming house for the poor. In recognition of their generosity, the brothers Aleksei Aleksandrovich and Sergei Aleksandrovich were made honorary citizens of Moscow, a rare honor.

In many instances the boundaries between merchant contributions to private and municipal charities and those to education were blurred. A skilled labor force, socialized to the ways of the industrial world, was essential to the health of Russian business and—the merchants argued, not surprisingly—to the health of state and nation. The Rukavishnikov Correctional Home also ran a trade school whose innovative methods of instruction were displayed at the Centennial Exposition in Philadelphia in 1876 and influenced American manual training. In addition to providing famine relief in 1891–92, the Moscow Literacy Committee ran public reading rooms and supplied textbooks to schools; among its merchant members were Anatoly Ivanovich Mamontov and Elizaveta Grigorevna Mamontova, Varvara Morozova, Konstantin Rukavish-nikov, and Kozma Terentevich Soldatenkov. But perhaps the three educational societies where the merchant presence was greatest were the Moscow Section of the Russian Technical Society, the Society to Disseminate Technical Knowledge, and the Society to Promote Commercial Education.

The Russian Technical Society was founded in St. Petersburg in 1866 to promote the development of technical and engineering education by means of papers and lectures on technical subjects, publications, prizes and medals, exhibitions, and studies of educational methods. Throughout the 1870s and 1880s, the society became a national forum for debate over the broader issues of ethical and social concerns in education and provided a meeting place where engineers and other professionals rubbed shoulders with government officials and business leaders. By 1896 it had twenty-three regional chapters, including one in Moscow, founded in 1876. One of the most prominent features of the Moscow Section was the very activist Standing Committee on Technical Education: it sponsored public lectures and in the 1890s organized classes for adult workers and a school for workers' children. In 1901 it opened the Museum for Assistance to Labor, whose educational program for workers was later incorporated into government efforts, known as "police socialism," aimed at preempting a revolutionary labor movement.[5] This venture, as well as the increased interest of the Moscow Section of Technical Society in factory conditions, sanitation, and worker housing, and the increasingly close relationship between the Museum for Assistance to Labor and the city's budding union movement, eventually drove a wedge between the society's merchants and professionals.

The merchant members of the Moscow Section of the Technical Society included G. A. Krestovnikov, T. S. Morozov, V. A. Bakhrushin, several Abriko-sovs, V. P. and N. A. Alekseev, and Varvara Morozova. The latter figure occupied a particularly prominent role in educational philanthropy as well as in liberal political circles. Born into the Khludov family in 1850, Morozova, the "classical progressive Moscow philanthropist," in Buryshkin's words, was one of the founders of the Prechistenka evening courses for workers, a municipal vocational school, and the first public library in Moscow (see the Joffe-Linden-meyr essay). She also chaired the Morozov Women's Club, gave fifty thousand rubles to the Shaniavsky Public University, and was a leader in an association that sought to distribute handicrafts commercially. Although the writer S. P. Melgunov considered her no more than a social climber, other contemporaries held positive views. The Kadet leader Miliukov thought she was modest and unassuming and believed in social progress, reason, and goodness; the theater director Nemirovich-Danchenko, commenting on her affiliation with the liberal daily *Russkie Vedomosti*, whose publisher was her second (common-law) husband, opined that "perhaps she even built her whole life according to the noble and restrained tone of that newspaper."[6]

Similar to the Moscow Section of the Technical Society in mission was the Society to Disseminate Technical Knowledge, founded in 1869. It ran a metal-working school, a vocational school for women, and free classes in technical drawing. Particularly innovative was its Commission for Home Readings, modeled after British and American societies of self-education, which drew up lesson plans and commissioned textbooks. Among the merchant members of the Society were several Abrikosovs, Semen Pavlovich Maliutin, Kozma Sol-datenkov, the Rukavishnikov brothers, several Mamontovs, and Vasily Alek-seevich Khludov. Nina Khludova and Elizaveta Mamontova and her husband, Savva Mamontov, were members of the board of the vocational school for women.

Finally, the Society to Promote Commercial Education, founded by the banker Aleksei S. Vishniakov in 1897, reflects the commitment of Moscow's merchants to business education. In 1907 the society opened the Moscow Commercial Institute, which provided training beyond the secondary level in both economics and engineering to prepare actual and prospective clerks and foremen for careers in business (see the Kalmykov essay). The Society also ran a commercial school for women. Board members from the Moscow merchan-try included several other Vishniakovs, Mikhail I. Alekseev, Ivan A. Morozov, several Mamontovs, and Vladimir P. Riabushinsky.[7]

Disseminating education and technical training represented what we might call today an "investment in the nation's future" and is frequently regarded as a form of national pride. The national pride of Moscow's merchants has been noted by many authors. Both individually and through associations, mer-chants were leading figures in the post-1861 period in a movement to pre-serve, display, and promote the national heritage. To be sure, the merchant contribution was often financial; but merchants were important not only for their deep pockets. In their organizational manifestation, their contributions encompassed a variety of societies and institutions, only a few of which may be surveyed here.

Before the national heritage can be displayed and promoted, it must be collected and preserved. Moscow's merchants were legendary collectors. What must they have picked up and stuffed in their pockets as children! One of them, Aleksei Petrovich Bakhrushin, from a family that might have been called "champion collectors," even wrote a book, *Who Collects What?* (fig-ure 11.11).[8] There were several major collectors. Aleksei Petrovich Bakhru-shin and Petr Ivanovich Shchukin collected antiques and rare books (figures 11.12 and 11.13); the former bequeathed his library to the Rumiantsev Mu-seum (now the Lenin Library); he and Shchukin donated their collection of antiques to the Historical Museum. Aleksei Aleksandrovich Bakhrushin, long-time chair of the Theatrical Society, amassed a famous theater collection and founded the Theater Museum. Aided by the painter A. A. Ivanov, Kozma Soldatenkov (1818–1901) collected Russian paintings. The Old Believer Aleksei Ivanovich Khludov (1818–82) amassed a large collection of pre-Nikonian manuscripts and documents. Finally, several merchants, including Gerasim Ivanovich Khludov and Stepan Pavlovich and Vladimir Pavlovich Riabushinsky, collected what has come to be the symbol of old Russian culture—the icon.

Although we may have now a reverent attitude to valuable artifacts of centuries past, the antique trade had its unsavory side, as anyone who has spent time in Moscow will appreciate. Merchants themselves were well aware of this. In words that could have been written yesterday, the authority on Russian collecting, A. P. Bakhrushin wryly observed: "I don't think any of Moscow's antique dealers has a conscience, and how could they; this trade is worse than Gypsy horse trading, and horse traders, as we know, don't consider it a sin to cheat their own fathers." The famous patron Princess M. K. Tenisheva, like Bakhrushin looking down on her social inferiors, was disdainful of the great Moscow merchant collectors, who were aping fashion and desiring "to possess in order to boast." After a visit to the Petr Shchukin collection at the private Shchukin Museum, Tenisheva rather dryly commented that "the praise for the discriminating collector or patron drives to the background and covers up with a pleasant haze a rather prosaic cloth maker or leather maker." Yet the same Petr Shchukin who earned the disdain of Tenisheva won praise from Bakhrushin for being the "most serious" of all collectors. He did not collect anything "without first compiling a whole bibliography and studying the subject in books."[9]

Several of Moscow's learned societies promoted the collection, preservation, and publication of old Russian documents and manuscripts. Anna Morozova and Petr Shchukin were members of one of Russia's oldest learned societies, the Society of Russian History and Antiquities, founded at Moscow University in 1804. Aleksei I. Kludov and Kozma T. Soldatenkov were among the original members of the Society of Old Russian Art, founded at the Rumiantsev Museum in 1864 to collect and study old Russian art and related materials. Divisions within the society hampered its effectiveness, and in 1877 it merged with the Society of Russian History and Antiquities. But according to one observer, "More valiant than many others was the merchant Soldatenkov, but they elected him only to take advantage of his generosity."[10]

Soldatenkov, Khludov, and Stepan P. Riabushinsky were all members of the more successful Moscow Archaeological Society, founded in 1846. Toward the end of the century, three of its projects in particular interested the city's merchants: the Archaeological Institute, the Historical Museum founded by the society and which became the final repository of many merchant collections, and the Commission to Study Old Moscow. Soldatenkov and Vladimir Riabushinsky, along with Nikolai Pavlovich Maliutin and three Bakhrushins, were members of another learned society affiliated with Moscow University, the Russian Bibliographical Society. Finally, much of the nation's treasury of documents and manuscripts would never have appeared in print had not merchants such as N. A. Naidenov, K. T. Soldatenkov, T. S. Morozov, and Petr I. Shchukin bankrolled their publication. In the words of Konstantin Stanislavsky, "Another Maecenas, Soldatenkov, devoted himself to the publication of books that could not hope for large circulation, but were necessary to science, to social life, to culture, and to education."[11]

In collecting icons and other antiques and in publishing manuscripts, merchants preserved the past; in bequeathing their collections and playing an active role in collection management, such as that played by Petr I. Shchukin at the Historical Museum, merchants displayed the national heritage. However, the business elite did not stop at preservation and display. They strove to revive, promote, and even create the national heritage. Icon collecting was one manifestation of a larger interest in folk industries. Embedded in the icon and similar products of Russia's past was a faith, a community effort, and a sense of national identity that the merchants desired to promote and connect with their names for posterity. A few examples will suffice.

Russia had its own version of the better-known arts and crafts movement in England and America. Savva Mamontov gathered artists, designers, and musicians such as Elena Polenova, Victor M. Vasnetsov, and Mikhail A. Vrubel at his country estate of Abramtsevo. Two Morozov brothers, Sergei and Savva, founded the Moscow Museum of Handicrafts in 1885; along with Varvara Morozova, they were instrumental in financing the commercial production and sale of folk crafts. Sergei Morozov financed the influential journal of the Russian arts and crafts movement, *Mir Iskusstva* (The World of Art).[12] One may see in the activities of the merchants the seeds of the later Soviet efforts to display and promote folk crafts and material culture.

Merchants played a similar role in the development of a national tradition in the fine arts, concert music, theater, and opera. The Society of Lovers of the Arts, founded in 1860, provided a community for patrons, artists, and amateurs. Even before the better-known Society of Traveling Exhibitions (often called the "Itinerants"), the Society of Lovers of the Arts tried to bring art to the people by means of permanent exhibitions, art competitions, and art raffles. To mark the donation of the Tretiakov collection to the city, the Society organized the first national congress of artists. Both Tretiakov brothers served as board members, and Sergei was president from 1888 to 1892. Other members were Kozma Soldatenkov, Dmitry Petrovich Botkin, and several Vishniakovs and Morozovs. Savva Morozov not only financed but played an active role in the Moscow Art Theater, founded by a merchant son, Konstantin S. Alekseev-

Stanislavsky. Savva Mamontov's private opera company introduced Fedor Shaliapin and produced operas on national themes such as *Khovanshchina*, *Boris Godunov*, *Prince Igor*, and *The Tsar's Bride*.

Finally, although the Tretiakov brothers are usually associated with the Tretiakov gallery, they were also great music patrons. Sergei Tretiakov was a founder of the Russian Musical Society in 1859; its first concerts were conducted by his boyhood friend Nikolai Rubenstein, also from a merchant family, and founder of the Moscow Conservatory. During its first two decades the Musical Society performed 139 orchestral works, 115 of which were by Russian composers, an impressive fulfillment of a national agenda, considering that in the 1860s and 1870s Russian orchestral music was still in its infancy.[13]

At first glance there seems to be an anomaly between the merchants' role in economics and politics, on the one hand, and in private life and philanthropies, on the other. In the first—in their businesses, in national politics, or in the Moscow City Council—they aspired to build the future. In the second, in their promotion of the national heritage in particular, they seem to be living in the past. Yet many of their philanthropic and associational activities had another dimension. In their leisure as well as in their business and political activities, the merchants, perhaps not always intentionally, shaped a national identity of the future. In applying their talents in the arts, publishing, and technology, at the turn of the twentieth century Moscow's merchants became visionaries.

Undoubtedly, the most visible and striking manifestation of this role was collection and patronage of modernism in art, literature, and philosophy. While his brothers Petr and Nikolai collected Russian antiques and brother Dmitry collected old European masters, Sergei I. Shchukin collected Matisse, Cezanne, and Picasso, and in 1909 opened his house for free public viewing on Sunday afternoons (figure 11.14). Other major collections were held by Ivan and Mikhail Morozov and, of course, Sergei and Pavel Tretiakov. Nikolai Riabushinsky supported the Art Nouveau decorative movement, collected French postimpressionists and Russian moderns, and edited and financed *Zolotoe runo* (Golden Fleece), a lavishly prepared art journal with silky overlays and bindings of gold thread. Margarita Kirillovna Morozova, born into the Mamontov family and widow of Mikhail A. Morozov, was a member of Vladimir Soloviev's philosophical circle and founder of a literary salon where the poet Valery Briusov, grandson of a merchant, and other decadents reigned.

Merchant patronage of a new postrealist aesthetic was important in the development of Russian photography (see the Neumaier essay). The Moscow-based Russian Photography Society organized the first congress of photography in 1896, and thereafter many local and amateur photography societies sprang up. However, the infant world of photographers was divided between those who argued that photography was a craft, a technique by which to reproduce nature, and those who considered photography an art. The former view dominated the associations, competitions, and journals of St. Petersburg; its best-known spokesman was Prokudin-Gorsky, famous for his "photographs for the tsar." In contrast, the Russian Photography Society, through its organ *Vestnik Fotografii* (Photography Herald), championed the school of "art photography": "art is the goal the photographer is striving for and technical aspects are only the means of achieving that goal." Interestingly, members of several prominent merchant families were members of the Russian Photography Society in Moscow: Vladimir A. Bakhrushin was president, and Aleksei P. Bakhrushin, an amateur photographer, won a bronze medal at an International Exhibition of Photography in Paris. Other members included Aleksei I. Abrikosov, a physician and pathologist and later one of Lenin's embalmers; Savva Nikolaevich and Mikhail Anatolevich Mamontov; Mikhail A. Morozov; and Sergei and Nikolai Shchukin.[14]

Regardless of the artistic claims of some of its proponents, photography had important connections with new technologies, and aerial photography had military implications. In their leisure as well as in their businesses, merchant patronage of expositions, museums, scientific societies, and laboratory research made important contributions to the spread of science and technology. Everywhere in Victorian Europe, grand expositions were major events that displayed the latest developments in science, industry, and the arts, and in 1872 and 1882, Moscow hosted two national expositions of science and industry. Sergei M. Tretiakov, Moscow mayor from 1877 to 1882, was instrumental in organizing the second exposition, an effort acknowledged when he was awarded the rank of State Councillor in 1882. The 1872 exposition led to the creation of the Museum of Science and Industry. Beginning in 1878 the museum sponsored public lectures, discussions, free Sunday tours; later it provided classroom space for the Moscow Public University. By providing meeting halls and auditorium space free of charge to numerous other organizations, the museum became a civic center, contributing substantially to adult education, civic life, and the spread of interest in science. One of its founders was the merchant Semen P. Maliutin, and the architect of the wing housing its displays of military technology was V. A. Gartman, whose patron was Anatoly I. Mamontov.

The parent society of the Museum of Science and Industry was the Moscow Society of Naturalists, Anthropologists, and Ethnographers, founded by several Moscow University professors in 1863. Along with the Moscow Polytechnical Society and the Moscow Higher Technical School, it provided the key institutional spaces for one merchant son's contribution to the great technology of the future—flight. The "father of Russian aviation" was N. E. Zhukovsky (1847–1921). A professor of theoretical and applied mechanics at Moscow University, Zhukovsky also taught at the Moscow Higher Technical School and was a member of the Polytechnical Society. After more than two decades of teaching at the Moscow Higher School, in 1909 Zhukovsky began to teach a course on the theories of aviation. Interest was so great that the students organized an "Aviation Circle." At the same time Zhukovsky was a member of the Physics Division of the Society of Amateur Naturalists, Anthropologists, and Ethnographers and gave public lectures to a general audience on aviation at the Museum of Science and Industry.

One of Zhukovsky's students was Dmitry P. Riabushinsky. His experiments in aerodynamics were the subject of a report before the Aeronautical Section of the Russian Technical Society in 1907, the same year that Zhukovsky's theoretical works on the lifting power of an airplane wing began to appear. Two years earlier, Zhukovsky began to conduct experiments in aerodynamics using the world's first operating wind tunnel at the new aeronautical laboratory founded by him and Dmitry Riabushinsky on the latter's suburban estate at Kuchino (figures 11.15 and 11.16). The Physics Division of the Society of Naturalists created a Committee of Aviation; its chair and deputy chair were Zhukovsky and Riabushinsky, respectively. And in 1910, Zhukovsky and Riabushinsky organized the Society of Aviation. Its agenda was to organize lectures, provide training planes, build an airport, promote interest in aviation, help Russian aviation industry take off, and organize civilian and military flying. This it did by, among other things, organizing exhibitions of aviation, air shows, and aviation congresses, including the first National Aviation Congress in 1911, one of whose organizers was Dmitry Riabushinsky.[15]

Dmitry Riabushkinsky's contribution to Russian aviation could not offer us a better metaphor for the change in Moscow's merchants. Over the course of three generations a group that had been closed, bolted in, and walled off had escaped the real and metaphorical padlocks, walls, cages, and guard dogs. In a burst of civic activity and organizational patronage, it helped preserve the past, mold a national identity, and provide leadership and vision for the future in learning, the arts, and science. At the turn of the twentieth century, the great merchant families literally soared. Yet within a few short years, Dmitry Riabushinsky, like many merchants, was forced to leave Russia soon after the Bolshevik Revolution. The flight of the senses they helped bring about prefigured their own personal flight into emigration and, often, oblivion.

NOTES

1. V. G. Belinsky, "Peterburg i Moskva," *Sobranie sochinenii V. G. Belinskogo v trekh tomakh* (St. Petersburg, 1911), vol. 2, p. 1069.

2. P. A. Buryshkin, *Moskva kupecheskaia* (Moscow: Vysshaia shkola, 1991), pp. 34, 98, 220–21.

3. I discuss the role of Moscow's voluntary organizations in the formation of civil society in "Voluntary Associations, Civic Culture,

and *Obshchestvennost'* in Moscow," in *Between Tsar and People: Educated Society and the Quest for Public Identity in Late Imperial Russia*, ed. Edith W. Clowes, Samuel D. Kassow, and James L. West (Princeton: Princeton University Press, 1991), pp. 131–48. See also my *Muzhik and Muscovite: Urbanization in Late Imperial Russia* (Berkeley and Los Angeles: University of California Press, 1985).

4. Moskovskoe obshchestvo okhoty, *Letopis' deiatel'nosti Obshchestva, 1862–1897* (Moscow, 1898). Annual membership dues at the turn of the century were twenty-five rubles. See N. Zhuravlev, ed., "Iz rospisi lichnykh raskhodov fabrikanta M. A. Morozova," *Krasnyi arkhiv* 83 (1937): 225–27.

5. The standard histories of technical societies in Russia are N. N. Gritsenko et al., *Nauchno-tekhnicheskie obshchestva SSSR* (Moscow, 1968); and N. G. Filippov, *Nauchno-tekhnicheskie obshchestva v Rossii, 1866–1917* (Moscow, 1976).

6. Nemirovich-Danchenko is cited in Buryshkin, *Moskva kupecheskaia*, p. 132; the views of Melgunov and Miliukov are taken from Jo Ann Ruckman, *The Moscow Business Elite: A Social and Cultural Portrait of Two Generations, 1840–1905* (DeKalb: Northern Illinois University Press, 1984), pp. 105–6.

7. *Istoriia Moskvy*, 6 vols. (Moscow: Akademiia nauk SSSR 1952–57), vol. 4, pp. 641, 642; vol. 5, pp. 372, 452–55, 468–69.

8. *Kto chto sobiraet* (Moscow, 1916).

9. Quoted in G. I. Vzdornov, *Istoriia otkrytiia i izucheniia russkoi srednevekovoi zhivopisi:*

XIX vek (Moscow: Iskusstvo, 1986), pp. 196–97, 203.

10. Ibid., pp. 86–87.

11. Constantin Stanislavsky, *My Life in Art*, trans. J. J. Robbins (Boston: Little, Brown, 1933), p. 13; Buryshkin, *Moskva kupecheskaia*, pp. 139, 330; *Istoriia Moskvy*, vol. 4, p. 480, and vol. 5, p. 476.

12. Buryshkin, *Moskva kupecheskaia*, pp. 126–28, 327; Thomas C. Owen, *Capitalism and Politics in Russia: A Social History of the Moscow Merchants, 1855–1905* (Cambridge: Cambridge University Press, 1981), pp. 166–67. On the Mamontov circle see Stuart Grover, "The World of Art Movement in Russia," *Russian Review* 32, no. 1 (1973): 28–42; and Stanislavsky, *My Life in Art*, pp. 141–44.

13. *Istoriia Moskvy*, vol. 4, pp 767–68.

14. *A Portrait of Tsarist Russia: Unknown Photographs from the Soviet Archives*, trans. Michael Robinson (New York: Pantheon Books, 1989), pp. 7–37.

15. *Istoriia Moskvy*, vol. 4, pp. 640; vol. 5, pp. 397–98, 409, 450, 478; Filippov, *Nauchno-tekhnicheskie obshchestva*, pp. 45, 153–57.

Figure 11.1. *The family of Aleksander V. Bary (Bari) at their dacha (see figure 1.6 in the Owen essay). This dacha is hardly a modest log cabin. A two-story structure with a grand entrance, it is closer to a country mansion. The windows are thrown open to accommodate the Russian obsession with fresh country air.*

Figure 11.2. *The Shemshurins at their dacha Kuznechiki. The Shemshurins exhibit the Russian passion for eating meals in the open air in summer.*

Figure 11.3. *Sergei Ivanovich Chetverikov hosting factory personnel at his country estate, Goroditsa. The factory "family" is photographed in the space where one is accustomed to seeing relatives and friends.*

Figure 11.4. *The children of Dmitrii Ivanovich Chetverikov staging a home production of Molière's* Le Misanthrope (The Miser) *at the family estate. Amateur theatrics were another traditional feature of extended-family aristocratic life.*

Figure 11.5. *Vladimir Petrovich Smirnov, Moscow vodka merchant and horse breeder. The rather jaunty pose and confident expression challenge the notion of a group with an inferiority complex.*

Figure 11.6. *The horse farm of V. P. Smirnov on Skakovaia (Racing) Street in Moscow. The pavilion bears a resemblance to the grand buildings of the international exhibitions of the era, especially the Moscow Exposition of Industry and the Arts in 1882.*

Figure 11.7. *The Moscow Hippodrome. Award of the "Grand National Prize" to S. N. Konshin's horse Avos (Just in Case), June 12, 1905.*

Figure 11.8. *Hunters resting. The photo is from the family album of the Chertverikovs. No longer the angry curs guarding merchant warehouses and mansions in the city, the noble hunting hound had become another aristocratic accoutrement of merchant country living.*

Figure 11.9. *Pavel Riabushinsky (center, in white fur hat) and his entourage posing with their kill. The Riabushinsky family ledger records considerable sums paid for the services of a jaeger (hunting guide) and food for the dogs.*

Figure 11.10. *Moscow tennis, from the family album of the Bakhrushins. The Bakhrushins were "professional philanthropists," contributing millions of rubles to private and municipal charities.*

Figure 11.11. *Title page of Aleksei Bakhrushin's book* Who Collects What? *Books and porcelain, two objects of his collecting passion, figure prominently on the title page.*

Figure 11.12. *The private art museum of Petr Ivanovich Shchukin. The owner bequeathed his collection of antiquities to the Historical Museum.*

Figure 11.13. *The library of Aleksei Petrovich Bakhrushin.*

Figure 11.14. *The Picasso Room in the Shchukin Museum. The Shchukin collection was nationalized in 1918 and is currently divided between the Hermitage Museum in Petersburg and the Pushkin Fine Arts Museum in Moscow.*

Figure 11.15. *The Kuchino Aerodynamical Laboratory, built by Dmitry P. Riabushinsky at the family estate in 1904. Riabushinsky, a charter member of the Society for Aviation, helped organize public exhibits, air shows, and the first National Aviation Congress in 1911. Perhaps only in Russia was advanced science practiced in log buildings.*

Figure 11.16. *Interior of Riabushinsky's aerodynamical laboratory. The facility boasted the first operational wind tunnel in Europe. This instrument marks the origin of what came to be known in Soviet times as "TsAGI," the supersecret Central Aero- and Hydrodynamic Institute.*

PART FIVE

Merchant Dreams:
Self-Image and
Utopian Vision

CHAPTER 12

Merchants on Stage and in Life: Theatricality and Public Consciousness

Edith W. Clowes

A consideration of the photographic inheritance of Russia's merchantry suggests two vital observations about merchant culture and leads to a number of broader theoretical claims concerning the interrelationship between cultural self-expression and social status. The first point is that this culture was primarily oriented toward visual self-expression. The second is that merchants as a whole—and even the merchant elite that did much to spur the brilliant renaissance of Russian culture at the turn of the twentieth century—were generally hostile to the overwhelmingly verbal, secularized culture of Russia's intelligentsia, a culture that had been dominant in Russia for almost a century.

This essay will explore the premise that this hostility to writing culture made it extremely difficult for the merchantry to develop a modern public image of self. Lacking a rhetoric of public self, or even a perception that one was needed, merchants were limited to the realm of visual art and architecture. But despite dazzling visual achievements in both public and private life—paintings, murals, buildings, and, of course, photographs that the merchants produced—they failed to legitimize themselves as Russia's new "ruling" elite. Clearly there are compelling historical reasons for this failure, but it is certainly worthwhile to explore the ways in which this emerging elite expressed itself—and the ways in which it did *not* express itself—to evaluate the impact of the public image of the merchants on their social status.

The tentative framing of a positive public image that did take place was stimulated in part through dialogue with writers and intellectuals active in that artistic medium located on the cusp between the verbal and the visual—the theater. In the theater, words are put in the context of nonverbal, primarily visual media. Self is defined at least as much by the physical space one inhabits (see the Brumfield essay), the clothes one wears (see the Ruane essay), and the gestures one makes as it is by the words one speaks. Historically, merchants were strongly attracted to the theater and to directing and acting as a social activity, and they tended to be most responsive to writers who wrote for the theater.

In merchants' lives, "theater" often became an extended metaphor for other nonverbal modes of self-enactment and self-realization. Painting theater sets extended from the aesthetic realm into the social realm, for example, in the decoration of facades of train stations, hotels, and other public buildings. Acting on the stage was replaced with action in the political arena. It is thus possible to invoke the broader cultural concept of "theatricality" to emphasize various kinds of nonverbal presentation of self-mirroring, posing, trying-on of personae. The transference of this idea of theatricality from the stage into social, historical actuality allows us to interpret many of the facets of merchant life that have been addressed in this volume—clothes, houses, city, leisure activities—as signs of a created identity. The roles a (merchant) actor chose to play, the clothes in which a merchant posed for a photograph or a portrait, the way a merchant designed and decorated a house—all take on added significance as inventions of self that we are claiming for the merchant culture of the early twentieth century.

The split between verbal and visual self-expression no doubt has its roots in the traditional economic and cultural policies of the tsarist state. Part of the reason for the deep isolation of the Russian merchantry from the larger society was that until the second half of the nineteenth century, none but its wealthiest members could share in the Westernization experienced by other, much more self-aware and vocal elites, particularly the professional intelligentsia and the gentry. As a group, merchants had a very low level of literacy, and for a variety of reasons most never embraced Enlightenment ideals of secular culture, universal education, and civil society that were the heart of liberal intellectual belief. Legally hamstrung by the state, they were isolated among themselves and from outside influences. In addition, their possibilities for economic development were very narrow indeed: they were long restricted from expanding beyond relatively basic industries such as textiles and tax farming. The merchantry was the victim of a self-fulfilling prophecy on the part of the government. Perceived to be too backward to compete with their Western counterparts, Russian merchants were not *allowed* to compete. As a corollary to this legal situation, the merchant memoirist Pavel Buryshkin notes that public opinion, such as it was, worked against native entrepreneurs: "For an unbelievably long time Russians held to the opinion that their country was agrarian, that manufacturing was superfluous, that Russian industry would never be able to compete with Western European industry, and, finally, that the factory and its whole way of life was corrupting the populace."[1]

In Russia before the Great Reforms the merchantry as a whole was truly the antithesis of Westernized educated society—isolated, backward, anti-Western in appearance as well as views. Its location in the city placed the merchantry on the borderline between Westernized gentry-intellectual culture, in which verbal expression dominated, and old Russian peasant-clergy culture, in which visual expression (icons and *lubki* [popular broadsides], festivals and theatricals) was paramount. Not only in their thinking but in their appearance merchants were perceived as a relic of a pre-Petrine manner. Until as late as the 1870s, photos of merchants as well as artifacts and merchant characters in plays, show both perceived and actual conservatism of dress. Men wore beards and long hair, boots and long coats (figures 12.1 and 12.2), while women wore shawls and covered their heads (figures 12.3 and 12.4). Merchant culture was perceived to support, and indeed did in the main support, a semi-medieval patriarchal order. Generally, merchants were uncritical supporters of the autocracy. As Alfred Rieber puts it, they were "the most passive and submissive *soslovie* [estate] in Russian society."[2] The merchantry was typically suspicious of books, indeed, any form of writing beyond the Gospel and the police gazette. Not surprisingly, they had no literary culture whatsoever until late in the nineteenth century, when a number of young men and women from both the wealthy *kupechestvo* and petty merchantry (*meshchanstvo*) broke abruptly with this antiwriting tradition.

Such benightedness found a sharply critical reflection in classical Russian literature of the second half of the century. Merchants in the great novels—for example, in Tolstoi's *War and Peace* or Dostoevsky's *The Brothers Karamazov*—were depicted very much on the periphery of social consciousness, as "objects," part of the social landscape, but emphatically not as thinking, feeling people. This is interesting particularly in the case of Dostoevsky, whose mother came from a merchant family. Dostoevsky, who was brought up to view himself as gentry, absorbed the Orthodox religious traditions of this milieu, but reviled its concern with money and profit.

In the era of the Great Reforms of the 1860s, as manufacturing and marketing became centrally important, much more attention was paid to the value of the entrepreneurial spirit, money, and personal material wealth. Still, in public discourse these concerns were almost always given negative coloration. There were, of course, more positive treatments, as in the case of the entrepreneur Stolz in Goncharov's novel *Oblomov*, but even here the entrepreneur is not Russian but half-Russian. The bible of radical youth in the 1860s, Chernyshevsky's *What Is to Be Done?* welcomes an entrepreneurial spirit, but only in a collectivist context.

At midcentury, the merchantry was wholly unprepared to defend itself against strongly negative literary and theatrical portrayals, much less to articulate a clear, positive self-image. If they responded at all, they tended to answer with actions rather than words. The canonical example is Pavel Tretiakov with his most impressive private collection of Russian art, which he then donated to the city of Moscow for the enlightenment of its citizens. It is noteworthy that merchants as a group never embraced any contemporary social theory that would put them at the top of a new social order as, for example, did

Andrew Carnegie or Henry Ford in the United States. Nor did they have articulate supporters among intellectuals, an Adam Smith or a Max Weber, who could defend and legitimize entrepreneurial economic behavior. The only attempt in this direction, the effort of merchants and Slavophiles to convince the government of the wisdom of high tariffs in the 1850s and 1860s, failed to lay the foundations of a Russian industrial system independent of European financial control. When finally the Riabushinsky brothers attempted to cobble together a social and economic program in the decade before the October Revolution, the complexity and confusion of its discourse, drawing as it did on so many disparate cultural sources, was too fragmented to function successfully as a legitimizing ideology (see the West essay).

Still, the leading merchants felt increasing pressure to emerge from their isolation and to redefine themselves as enlightened citizens. We can see that this change happened partly in response to criticism from prominent writers and literary critics. For example, Buryshkin in his memoirs winces as he remembers the judgment of Petr Boborykin, a popular (gentry) novelist at the turn of the century, that the "study of philosophy is not something for the merchant mind."[3] The great actor and co-founder of the Moscow Art Theater, Konstantin Stanislavsky, writes in his autobiography, *My Life in Art*, that he and his young Art Theater troupe were "dubbed amateurs and the new venture was considered the hobby of a self-deceiving merchant, this last intended to hurt me personally."[4]

Nonetheless, as Ruane, Brumfield, Bradley, and others have shown, from the 1850s on we do find increasing self-reflection among merchants. Typically their self-expression took on visual and stubbornly nonverbal forms: they collected paintings and built buildings. On a more personal level, they used photography to document "family history." But it was the theater that stood at the center of this emerging cultural consciousness. Merchants took pride in the fact that the first Russian theater had been started in the eighteenth century by a merchant, Fedor Volkov. Merchants, particularly Savva Mamontov and Konstantin Alekseev (Stanislavsky), led the way toward the end of the century to break down bureaucratic barriers to private theater. The merchant Savva Morozov provided the main financial backing for Stanislavsky's Moscow Art Theater, founded in 1898. Bakhrushin, yet another merchant, founded perhaps the most famous theater museum in Russia. Mamontov started an artist colony in Abramtsevo in 1870 and went on in 1885 to create the first private opera. Many of the artists from the colony, for example, Vasnetsov, Vrubel, and Korovin, made sets for the opera productions. Mamontov was also a prime mover in the effort to build the central Russian railroad and financed the construction of three railroad stations in Moscow. The Abramtsevo group helped to design the very dramatic facades of these stations (and, as well, a number of other buildings in turn-of-the-century Moscow, including the Metropole Hotel) (see figure 10.5 in the Brumfield essay).

It is essential to point out that narrative—obviously a verbal activity—was latent but nonetheless present in all this decoration and design. Whether in their theater activity or their architectural design, Mamontov's group dramatized themes from Russian folk legend, such as the story of Sadko, the merchant who visited the sea king and saved the city of Novgorod, or "Snegurochka," the beautiful snow maiden who won the heart of a merchant. The implicit thrust of these narrative motifs was away from the current literary realism of Dostoevsky and Tolstoi, in which merchants were either nonentities or villains, to other cultural "scripts" in which they were the heroes.

In the evolution of merchant images in the public domain, four issues stand out: 1) the treatment of women, 2) the ethics of wealth, 3) the desire for elite social status, and 4) the search for a public space and time of their own. Of central interest here are the following questions: how and to what degree were negative stereotypes of the merchant changed through efforts on the part of the merchantry to present its own image of a public self?

THE STATUS OF MERCHANT WOMEN

The question of gender, as Lindenmeyr and Joffe show, was central to the popular image of the benighted merchant. If in the second half of the nineteenth century merchants as a whole were perceived as unenlightened, it was in part due to the playwright Aleksandr Ostrovsky, who embellished this negative social stereotype. In his early plays, such as *A Family Affair* (written 1849, staged 1858) and *My Drink, Your Hangover* (1856), Ostrovsky popularized the word *samodur* to refer to a petty (merchant) tyrant given to gross abuse of his (and sometimes her) familial authority. And it was Ostrovsky who paid particular attention to the plight of merchant women who were typically singled out as the victims of mindless despotism, as in *The Storm* (1860). This theatrical image is supported in reality by evidence from personal diaries. For example, Anna Volkova wrote in her diary in 1887:

> My family situation and the very conditions of merchant life do not permit me to make use of [conversation as a] means of self-education. The people with whom I might talk do not visit [us], being squeezed out [by those who] do not at all desire "to make minds spin, to sharpen understanding, to enlighten feelings, to awaken and nourish thought"; with these others there is nothing to talk about.[5]

It was rare that merchant women received any education at all, and only the most privileged were tutored at home. In the main, women were brought up only for marriage. Symbols of this fettered condition were the shawl and the head covering that we have already seen in the older generation of merchant women and that were typical of the depiction of them on the stage. In 1878 the famous actress Maria Savina refused to take on the role of Iulia, the appealing young widow in Ostrovsky's *The Last Sacrifice*, because, as she objected, she "could not play these parts with shawls."[6] Ostrovsky had to explain that merchant women had already become more sophisticated and refined, if not exactly liberated. And it is interesting to note that an early portrait of the future merchant-philanthropist Varvara Khludova from the 1850s does indeed show a fashionably dressed young girl, without a shawl (figure 12.5)! In the next generation, shawls appear only in photographs of private theatricals in which women dressed up in ceremonial peasant garb. These costumes may simply have been worn because they were pretty and decorative, or, we might speculate, their use in private theater could show the distance that these young educated merchant women had evolved from their peasant origins (figure 12.6).

Women of the merchant elite from the 1890s and 1900s were leaders in culture and education. For women as for men, the theater became a forum for self-realization. M. Lilina became a well-known actress in the Moscow Art Theater, and A. M. Balashova danced with the Bolshoi Ballet. But some women took the plunge into the world of intellectual discourse and social activism as well. M. K. Morozova formed a literary salon that became the heart of early modernist culture in Moscow. V. A. Morozova (*née* Khludova) played an important role in the development of women's education. Varvara Lepeshkina founded a teachers' college, and V. A. Alekseeva a trade school. All these activities were highly visible evidence of the fact that, at least in the upper reaches of the merchantry, the *samodurstvo* that Ostrovsky had highlighted in his plays was being addressed, if not yet overcome. All the work to establish educational institutions for women was additional assurance that alternatives to being a victim of *samodurstvo* might someday be widely available to merchant women, and to women in the lower reaches of society as well.

THE ETHICS OF WEALTH

The profit motive and the accumulation of private wealth was one of the most intractable sources of tension between merchantry and intelligentsia at the turn of the century. It was an issue that attracted a good deal of public comment. Because merchants took no part in the "Enlightenment" discourse that defined the intelligentsia, they never gained the vocabulary necessary to justify their wealth publicly in a way that was credible to anyone but themselves. In art, literature, and the popular press they were frequently pictured as the epitome of ruthlessness, avarice, and dishonesty—in short, of *un*brotherly behavior (figure 12.7). "Moscow does not believe in tears" was a popular saying that meant that there would be no sympathy for the merchant who lost his shirt in business.[7] A popular gypsy doggerel about the merchantry was openly abusive: "The Moscow merchantry, / A broken yardstick, / What kind of son of your fatherland are you, / You're just a son of a bitch."[8] A common term for a merchant was *tolstosum*, which meant "fat pouch" or "moneybags." By association, while the photographic evidence suggests that they were rarely really fat, merchants were often depicted not only with a bloated stomach, but also with fat lips and a fat face (figures 12.8–10).

Again, the theater was the principal forum in which these loose images became hardened into stereotype. Satires written and performed in the 1890s, for example Prince Aleksandr Sumbatov-Iuzhin's *The Gentleman* (*Dzhentel'men*, 1897) or Boborykin's *The Scum* (*Nakip'*, 1899) show merchants flaunting their wealth in foolish and even immoral ways. In *The Scum*, the wealthy grande dame, Nina Vorobina, argues that money allows one complete freedom "from all kinds of silly taboos, copybook maxims, moldy moralities." Vorobina continues: "Without the power of capital, one cannot be, as Nietzsche puts it, 'beyond good and evil.'"[9] Vorobina uses her money to start a rather frivolous Cabaret Macabre.

It is significant that these plays elicited a negative response from their merchant audiences. Sumbatov remembered that the merchants were affronted by his "lampoon on them."[10] Stanislavsky's and Buryshkin's memoirs claim that these images were without merit, though they were nonetheless hurtful because they reinforced already deeply embedded images of the merchant's mindless squandering of his wealth. Meanwhile, for a generation or more the upper echelons of Merchant Moscow had been building, enriching, and enhancing the lives of everyone in their city—building hospitals, schools, museums, and theaters that were open to all. Pavel Tretiakov, the founder of the famous Tretiakov Gallery, may not have "talked the talk" of social enlightenment, but he certainly "walked the walk" when he fought the bureaucracy to gain the right to open a museum that would educate the populace at large about their national cultural heritage. His civic-mindedness won Tretiakov the distinction of being virtually the only merchant to inspire a positive onstage character, in the Ostrovsky play *The Last Sacrifice*.

Probably the most sympathetic contemporary treatment of merchant wealth came, predictably enough, in the theater, from Anton Chekhov, certainly the greatest writer to emerge from the petty merchant business estate, the *meshchanstvo*. The merchant protagonist, Ermolai Lopakhin (figure 12.12), in Chekhov's final play, *The Cherry Orchard* (1904), raises the crucial problem of articulation of public identity and the need for a public discourse in which the merchants could excel. Lopakhin is an extremely hard worker and a practical and kindhearted if tactless person who has worked his way from serfdom to considerable wealth. His impressive achievement is ignored by most people, and he is given a negative evaluation by the play's raisonneur, the eternal student Trofimov. Trofimov characterizes him as "a rich person, soon [to be] a millionaire" who is "necessary in the way that a beast of prey that eats up everything in its path is necessary for the food chain."[11] Here it is interesting to note that historically it was the intellectual Trofimov's hostile rhetoric that was projected by the play's directors. When the play was first staged in 1904, the director Nemirovich-Danchenko chose to emphasize the traditional *tolstosum* or "fat pouch" image, implied by the character Trofimov, rather than the author Chekhov's explicit vision of a dapper, fashionably but not flashily dressed young businessman. Although Chekhov attempted to breathe life into this more positive character, the traditional negative message won out in the original performance of Lopakhin by Leonidov and persisted for generations thereafter (see figure 12.12).

On a deeper level, the play is about the rifts in social discourse between gentry, intellectual, and entrepreneur caused in part by the issue of wealth. What is odd about Lopakhin's predicament is that he, more than all the rest of the characters in this absurdist play, has no control over his semiotic environment, as he literally neither speaks nor acts in the same social, political, and moral "language" as other primary characters. Certainly it is not surprising that he sometimes uses substandard language and that his speech is a bit awkward. For example, he asks Trofimov, "How do you understand about me?" rather than "What do you think of me?" Like his historical counterparts, he actually means to use his wealth in part to serve the public good, but he is too verbally inept, too tongue-tied, to mount a credible ideological defense and to convince others of the merit of his thinking.

MERCHANT ASPIRATIONS TO ELITE STATUS

The central issue of our discussion is that of the merchants' legitimacy as a social elite and their relation to Russia's other historical elites, the gentry and the intelligentsia. Although intermarriage within the merchantry was long the norm, by the 1880s there was some marriage into the gentry. There were also a number of cooperative ventures between the two groups, such as the co-founding of the Moscow Art Theater in 1898 by the nobleman Nemirovich-Danchenko and the merchant Alekseev-Stanislavsky. Nonetheless, although it has been argued that by the 1890s younger, well-educated merchants began to fit well into the society of intellectuals, there is a great deal of evidence to suggest that gentry and intellectuals alike felt merchants to be just as pretentious, contemptuous, and despotic as before, and that the merchants often felt themselves to be socially inept and intellectually inadequate. For example, Buryshkin notes that:

> on the one hand, Moscow was considered a merchant city where representatives of trade and industry occupied leadership positions, especially in the Moscow city government; on the other hand, in all nonmerchant strata of Muscovite society—among the gentry, the bureaucrats, and in intellectual circles, both on the right and on the left—the attitude toward the "moneybags" [*tolstosum*] was generally not very friendly, mocking, and even a bit condescending.[12]

Liubov Gurevich, the editor of the widely read thick journal, *Severnyi vestnik* (Northern Herald), remembered instances of Stanislavsky's cultural and political shortcomings, for example, that Stanislavsky "did not read the thick journals, and he could become confused by . . . newspapers and their censored political reporting." Stanislavsky apparently remarked to her on one occasion that "I understand nothing of political issues and speak [about them] like a dilettante."[13]

The notion of the *samodur* or petty tyrant faded in word but remained in stereotype. In his memoirs, *My Life in the Russian Theater*, Nemirovich-Danchenko emphasized a despotic quality in Stanislavsky, who was continually seeking to enforce his authority over the actors. The writer Maxim Gorky, who was by no means a dispassionate observer, remarked about the chief patron of the Art Theater, the industrialist Savva Morozov: "You could feel his contempt for people and his habit of having full authority over them."[14] Buryshkin also notes the persistent hostility between the literary intelligentsia and the educated merchantry. Writers, dramatists, and journalists continued to generate stereotypes of wealth without ideological legitimacy. Clearly the attention paid to the merchantry was an acknowledgment of their material wealth and influence, but emphatically not of their moral qualities as leaders.

It is curious that younger merchants at the turn of the century tended not to emphasize their standing as merchants per se, but took another route: they tried to redefine themselves more generally as educated Europeans. Frequently they borrowed symbols and stereotypes from other, higher estates and social groups and imitated their behavior. For example, as such plays as Nemirovich-Danchenko's *The New Business* (1890) or Chekhov's *The Cherry Orchard* suggest, it was common practice among the wealthiest merchants to buy old country estates from destitute gentry and to adopt a gentrified life. The Alekseevs, Stanislavsky's family, for example, purchased a small estate, Liubimovka, not far from Moscow. And yet in his memoirs, Nemirovich-Danchenko, a nobleman, described the furnishings in Liubimovka in a belittling way, as "modest but durable, as was everything belonging to the mercantile class."[15] The tension between those with old money and the nouveaux riches never faded.

In the theater these processes were played out in subtle but suggestive ways, through choice of repertoire, choice of character, and, as we have already seen in the case of Lopakhin, in costuming. Highly revealing is the merchant Stanislavsky's tendency always to choose gentry roles. Having frequently played merchant parts in his early private theatricals, he rarely played them in the Art Theater. He claimed rather disingenuously that he had never had much luck with merchant characters. Chekhov requested that he play Lopakhin in *The Cherry Orchard*, clearly anticipating that Stanislavsky's considerable stage presence would lend needed weight to this new imaging of the merchant. Stanislavsky instead opted to take on the secondary role of Gaev, thus diminishing the position of the merchant protagonist, strengthening the authority of gentry characters, and upsetting the delicate social balance of the play (figure 12.11).

Theater repertoire dealing with the merchantry never developed further in sophistication beyond the considerable achievements of *The Cherry Orchard*. A kind of wooden realism recalling Ostrovsky's samodúr characters persisted in Gorky's plays, *The Petit Bourgeois* (1902) and *Summerfolk* (1904), and Naidenov's *Vaniushin's Children* (1901). Thus, symbolically, the public image of the merchant elite froze in time, even as many real merchants avoided the issue of their merchant identity, never openly confronting or successfully challenging the popular image.

A SPACE OF ONE'S OWN

The most lasting public statements of the merchant elite's self-image appeared in the buildings that they built and the ways in which they transformed the city of Moscow, in short, how they used public space to define a new image. And it is here that "theatricality" finds its way out of the circumscribed world of art and works to transform the larger social ambience of the city. As many essays in this volume point out, in midcentury the merchants had been perceived as being, and indeed were, extremely private, isolated, and ingrown in their social dealings. Merchants lived in *Zamoskvoreche*, a district on the south side of the Moscow River across from central Moscow. Their houses have been described as small fortresses with high walls. A writer from this milieu, Ivan Belousov, remembered that "social life among the merchantry hardly existed. Beside their shops and warehouses, taverns and restaurants, merchants entertained each other but otherwise hardly appeared in public places."[16] The merchant's space was almost completely private, and often privacy threatened merchants with isolation.

It was again the dramatist Ostrovsky who first made merchants "see" the world they lived in. In his comedies he stressed the inside, private spaces of merchant life. The two epoch-making articles of Ostrovsky's most famous critic, Dobroliubov, "In the Kingdom of Darkness" (1859) and "A Ray of Light in the Kingdom of Darkness" (1860), defined merchant space for at least a generation as a *temnoe tsarstvo* or "kingdom of darkness." This narrow, isolated interior realm inhabited by merchants and their families embodied *samodurstvo* with its oppressive exercise of patriarchal authority and its hostility to education, social enlightenment, and individual self-realization. Dobroliubov did almost more than Ostrovsky to interpret the merchant condition and to give it a lasting and very unsympathetic imprint, one that was seized by Soviet historians and critics and transformed into canonical "truth."

It was difficult to break out of this dark spiritual and social space, both real and perceived. Only when a few families from the upper levels of the merchantry moved across the river and up the hill and built in previously gentry neighborhoods did they become effective at redefining their image. By transforming the skyline of Moscow, they did most to transform public perceptions of their social estate. The rather theatrical design of private houses built around 1900 are witness to merchants' efforts to recast private space and to integrate it with public space.

Here we must reiterate that a narrative merchant selfhood was implicit in the decor of these buildings, one that redefined the merchant as hero—no longer the nonperson of realist novels and plays. The Riabushinsky mansion (plate 16; see the West essay), for example, was consciously constructed around the legend of Sadko, the rich merchant of Novgorod who descended into the mythic realm of the sea king (figure 12.13).[17] The act of descending the staircase into the public space of the house represented symbolically this descent into the aquatic kingdom, an empowering experience in which the merchant was the hero. The outside of the house is decorated with mosaics showing irises, flowers that grow at the water's edge. The fence around the house carries a wave motif. On the inside, the library ceiling is decorated with bas-reliefs showing lily pads and other aquatic plants. The stairwell, which is the heart of the architectonic narrative, is painted with ocean colors of green and blue. The balustrade flows down the stairs like a wave, culminating in a swirling newel post topped by a stained glass lamp in the shape of a jellyfish (figure 12.14). The parquet floor below continues the undulating wave motif.

Many of the new merchant houses included extra space for whatever philanthropic or cultural activity the owner had undertaken. For example, Shchukin arranged his entire collection of modern impressionist paintings in a crowded gallery right in his house (figure 12.15). Bakhrushin's museum of theater memorabilia likewise accumulated in his house (figure 12.16). As a next step toward entering and transforming the larger social environment in their favor, some merchants—for example, Tretiakov—built separate museums to house their collections. Thus what had been a private interest became a bridge to the public sphere, giving merchants the opportunity to present themselves in a positive light, as leaders, to the world beyond their houses. With time there appeared apartment houses, banks, clubs, theaters, hotels, railroad stations financed by merchants and built to merchant taste. Many of these combined a sophisticated taste for the *style moderne* with a long-standing love for folk legend and Old Muscovite architecture. It cannot be emphasized too strongly that in this combination of the medieval Muscovite and the ultramodern, merchants were groping for a time and space in which they would act as the hero and enjoy a large measure of legitimacy and authority. And ironically, they lingered on the threshold between pre-Petrine tradition and Westernized modernity, on which they had so long been poised.

If anything helped to give merchants self-esteem and to change people's minds about business, it was this "theatrical" transfiguration of Moscow from

a "large village" into the most vibrant city in Russia. Most of the several merchant memoirs point out this achievement first and foremost as the pride of
the Russian merchants. But perhaps more important was the acknowledgment
in 1913 by Boborykin, one of their sharpest critics, that, much like Florence's
di Medici, the Moscow merchants had made their city into Russia's leader in
cultural and scientific achievement. Here was a real change in public perception. But unfortunately stones are silent and cannot bear witness to the
achievements of their makers. In the Soviet era many of these buildings were
as easily severed from their merchant origins in the public memory as they
were seized and nationalized. The Riabushinsky mansion became the residence of the literary figurehead of the Revolution, Maxim Gorky. Other private homes became embassies and ambassadorial residences, sequestered
from the public. As the many merchant memoirists who wrote after the Revolution finally realized, in order to remember the achievements of the past and
to justify oneself before one's society, one needs words. And words came too
late for Russia's merchants. A verbal defense of capital came only at the eleventh hour, in the last decade of the old regime with the Riabushinskys' journalistic efforts. I. A. Kirillov's *The Truth of Old Belief* (1916), published by the
Riabushinskys, was one of the few justifications of capitalist economic activity
in Russian history.

When we remember Russia's vanished merchantry, we must think again of
an image from the theater, of Chekhov's tongue-tied Lopakhin always looking
at his watch, never allowing himself a here-and-now, a space and time of his
own in which to define and exercise a notion of "good," legitimate authority.
He is forever running away from an opprobrious past as a serf, escaping into
mind-numbing hard work. He cannot take charge of social discourse and define a fitting place for himself as a leader in modern society.

In their historical efforts to establish themselves as leaders and to build
bridges to other elites, Russia's merchants financed a grand cultural renaissance, but they never succeeded in overcoming the strong, peculiarly Russian
resistance to private possession, the profit motive, and economic individualism that was deeply embedded in popular culture and in public taste. Although they had done much to overcome the images of the *samodur*, the *tolstosum*, and the kingdom of darkness, they could not penetrate this bedrock of
nonacceptance. Raw economic power could not be parlayed into social and
political authority without the establishment of some publicly admired, heroic
stereotype of the merchantry that bestowed acceptability not just on separate
individuals but on the group as a whole. The institution of the theater and a
broader cultural theatricality among the high merchantry both did a great deal
to bring the merchants out of their historical isolation and to foreground the
issue of a public persona. Still, the theatrical sensibility itself was too fragile a
vehicle to translate authority from the sphere of cultural innovation to the
social and political stage. The search for a new social script with a merchant

hero was starting to work in the private sphere, in private house design, and to a degree in the planning of public buildings, but a cohesive rhetoric of public self did not emerge. Old stereotypes of greed and benightedness continued to hold sway over both the educated and the popular imagination.

The purpose here has been not to diminish the dazzling achievements of Merchant Moscow but to point out its limitations, and the limitations of visual culture in general, as a vehicle for gaining social legitimacy in a historical age in which verbal culture was dominant. This central question begs for further attention: since the Enlightenment, in which writing culture came to dominate visual expression as the more powerful carrier of ideology, is it possible to become a "ruling class" without a cohesive rhetoric of public self and, to return to the notion of theatricality, without a drama or a narrative of social self in which the emerging elite is represented as the hero?

NOTES

1. Pavel Buryshkin, *Moskva kupecheskaia* (New York: Chekhov Publishing, 1954), p. 38.

2. Alfred J. Rieber, *Merchants and Entrepreneurs in Imperial Russia* (Chapel Hill: University of North Carolina Press, 1982), p. 23.

3. Buryshkin, *Moskva kupecheskaia*, p. 35.

4. Konstantin Stanislavsky, *My Life in Art* (New York: Theater Arts Books, 1952), pp. 304–5.

5. Quoted from Jo Ann Ruckman, *The Moscow Merchant Elite* (DeKalb: Northern Illinois University Press, 1985), p. 86.

6. Quoted from Marjorie Hoover, *Alexander Ostrovsky* (Boston: G. K. Hall, 1981), p. 601.

7. Thomas C. Owen, *Capitalism and Politics in Russia* (Cambridge: Cambridge University Press, 1981), p. 152.

8. Buryshkin, *Moskva kupecheskaia*, p. 47. The Russian jingle went as follows: "Moskovskoe kupechestvo,/Izlomanny arshin,/Kakoi ty syn otechestva?/Ty prosto sukin syn."

9. Petr Boborykin, *Nakip'* (St. Petersburg, 1900), p. 25.

10. Aleksandr Iuzhin-Sumbatov, *Zapiski,*

Stat'i, Pis'ma (Moscow: Iskusstvo, 1951), p. 557.

11. A. P. Chekhov, *Izbrannye proizvedeniia v 3-kh tomakh*, vol. 3 (Moscow: Gosudarstvennoe izdatel'stvo khudozhestvennoi literatury, 1960), p. 589.

12. Buryshkin, *Moskva kupecheskaia*, p. 9.

13. Liubov' Ia. Gurevich, *O Stanislavskom: sbornik vospominanii, 1863–1938* (Moscow, Vserossiiskoe teatral'noe obshchestvo, 1948), p. 136.

14. A. M. Gorky, *Polnoe sobranie sochinenii*, vol. 16 (Moscow: Nauka, 1973), p. 499.

15. Vladimir Nemirovich-Danchenko, *My Life in the Russian Theater* (New York: Theater Arts Books, 1968), p. 84.

16. Ivan Belousov, *Ushedshaia Moskva* (Moscow: Moskovskoe tovarishchestvo pisatelei, 1927), p. 113.

17. William C. Brumfield, *The Origins of Modernism in Russian Architecture* (Berkeley and Los Angeles: University of California Press, 1991).

Figure 12.1. *Well into the 1870s merchants were still perceived to, and often did, dress and wear their hair in a premodern way. Men wore long beards, and women covered their heads. As one can see here, the artifact shows an exaggerated version of the real practice: Andrei Andreevich Dosuzhev, born 1805, photo from the 1870s. Dosuzhev traded in cloth.*

Figure 12.2. *Illustration by P. M. Boklevsky for N. Ostrovsky's play* Scenes from Merchant Life.

Figure 12.3. *Merchant-wife doll from the 1850s or 1860s, made by M. D. Vakarina.*

Figure 12.4. *Merchant wife Bobkova, 1863.*

Figure 12.5. *Portrait of Varvara Alekseevna Khludova, around 1860. Toward the end of the century women from the merchant estate showed their modernity and the breadth of their aspirations in the way they dressed.*

Figure 12.6. *Daughters of merchants in a private theatrical, around 1906. More traditional dress was now used only for costumes, showing the distance that modern merchant women put between themselves and their forebears.*

Figure 12.7. *Caricature of Samuil Solomonovich Poliakov, a builder of the central Russian railroad. Note the writing on the flag, "Vsě moě" ("Everything is mine"), which suggests a stereotype of childish selfishness.*

«Мышокъ завеличался,
Зауличалъ, зазнался».

Figure 12.8. *Cartoon of Petr Ionovich Gubonin, who got rich building railways. Merchants were commonly associated with greed and fatness. The pejorative term for a merchant was* tolstosum *or, literally, "fat pouch."*

Figure 12.9. *Although modern merchants were seldom fat, their reflection in popular caricatures was nearly always so. The cultural philanthropist Nikolai Riabushinsky was a handsome man.*

Figure 12.10. *A caricature of Nikolai Riabushinsky (right) by V. Karrik emphasizes the merchant's fat lips.*

Figure 12.11. *Chekhov asked the Art Theater's founder and premier actor, Stanislavsky, to play the part of the merchant Lopakhin, but Stanislavsky refused, preferring instead the secondary gentry role of Gaev.*

Figure 12.12. *L. M. Leonidov as the entrepreneur Lopakhin in an Art Theater performance in 1904 of Chekhov's The Cherry Orchard. Casting and costuming for the play showed the persistence of old merchant stereotypes, despite the efforts of the author to challenge those very stereotypes. Although Lopakhin is young, energetic, and trim, Leonidov's enactment of Lopakhin clearly hews to the popular image of the merchant as tolstosum or "fat pouch."*

Figure 12.13. *In the Riabushinsky mansion, arguably among the finest examples of early twentieth-century private architecture anywhere in Europe, decoration was used very much as a stage set in which its inhabitants could act out the heroic tale of the medieval merchant Sadko who descended to the bottom of Lake Ilmen to play music at the court of the sea king in order to save the city of Novgorod.*

Figure 12.14. *A stained-glass aquatic creature, in the form of a tentacled jellyfish, seemingly floats on the crest of the frozen wave formed by the marble balustrade of the main staircase. The undulating parquet flooring extends the submarine illusion into the central space by replicating the sandy seabed of the undersea realm.*

Figure 12.15. *The interior of Petr Shchukin's home, which housed the collection of old Russian art, really did look more like a public space than a private one.*

Figure 12.16. *This caricature of Aleksei Bakhrushin, repeating the stereotype of the fat merchant (in his case, with some justification), also shows the interior of his house with its theater museum, thereby indirectly highlighting the importance of cultural and philanthropic work as the way out to the larger world beyond the merchant's traditional "kingdom of darkness."*

CHAPTER 13

Visions of Russia's Entrepreneurial Future:
Pavel Riabushinsky's Utopian Capitalism

James L. West

The political and ideological history of Merchant Moscow presents a disturbing counterpoint to the many positive images that appear in this volume. Whatever successes the merchants were having in adopting modern technologies, business practices, social behaviors, and styles of dress, they experienced considerable difficulty in translating their economic and cultural influence into political power. Entrepreneurial politics in Russia were characterized by late beginnings, false starts, and tragic endings.

The weight of history rested heavily on the entrepreneur in Russia. Laboring in the shadow of the autocratic state, immersed in a primitive and precarious economy, and surrounded by hostile elites and masses alike, merchants long remained politically invisible. Entrepreneurs were given little encouragement to aspire to anything beyond a local public role or to generate any public discourse of their own. Russia produced no writers of the stature of Adam Smith to defend entrepreneurial values, no heroes of the capitalist ethic to legitimize business activity. In a society that viewed self-regarding effort as a betrayal of community values, the most successful merchants sought shelter in the ranks of the aristocracy, while the least successful fell back into the ranks of the petty traders. Those who remained were largely passive and deferential, adopting the camouflage of strident Slavophile patriotism and unquestioned loyalty to the tsar.

If mobility in and out of the *kupechestvo* continuously weakened the entrepreneurial stratum, so too did the many internal divisions along fault lines of region, sector, and scale of activity that ramified through its membership. The merchantry was a weak and fractured *soslovie* long before it was confronted by the imperative of transforming itself into a modern entrepreneurial class.

Merchant Moscow occupied a privileged position in this hierarchy of deference. If there were any traditional single focal point for the splintered allegiances of the Russian merchantry, it was this "city of priests and merchants." The spiritual identification of its merchants with the *gosti*, the Muscovite magnates of ancient times, the relative independence of the region's textile industry from the state, the longevity of its multigenerational industrial "dynasties," and its central location in the empire all imparted an aura of unassailable preeminence to the Moscow merchant establishment. The hoary leadership of the Moscow Exchange Society traditionally claimed to speak for the "All-Russian *kupechestvo*" in its dealings with the government. While Moscow's periodic struggles with the bureaucracy over questions of economic policy as often as not ended in defeat, this tradition of merchant leadership meant that when entrepreneurial Russia at last found its modern political voice, it would speak in Muscovite accents.

As the more advanced elements of Merchant Moscow gained financial security and self-confidence in the late nineteenth century, they assumed the role of a cultural elite as well as an economic one (see the Bradley essay). Yet even as they emerged from behind the factory walls to engage in charity, philanthropy, and art patronage, these new Maecenases still hesitated to enter the verbal discourse of ideas that formed the currency of politics in autocratic Russia (see the Clowes essay). They took little part in the debates over industrialization and capitalism that the economic expansion of the 1890s provoked. While intellectuals, economists, and bureaucrats argued the pros and cons of state-centered versus entrepreneurial models of development, the businessmen remained largely silent. They were professionally insular as well: as other groups, doctors, lawyers, teachers, engineers, and zemstvo workers began to develop modern professional identities and highly politicized organizations, the merchants continued to rely on their narrow and specialized "representative" and estate organizations to plead their special interests before the all-powerful bureaucracy.[1]

Such reticence became increasingly untenable, however, as the new century approached. The state-sponsored industrial expansion of the 1890s created new and aggressive entrepreneurial groupings in Petersburg and on the periphery of the empire whose members resented the pretensions of Merchant Moscow. The prolonged depression of the turn of the century threw the Russian economy into unprecedented crisis, and this upheaval in turn triggered a sharp rise in the militancy of labor. To all this the merchants appeared glacially slow to respond; they took no part in the Union of Unions, the broad oppositional movement that briefly unified many professional groups as the crisis deepened. Instead, they loyally supported the government during the Russo-Japanese War. Only when the Revolution of 1905 erupted, and the hermetic world of the old *kupechestvo* was shattered forever, did the entrepreneurs begin to speak with their own voice.

The Revolution of 1905 was a traumatic and shaping experience for the factory owners and merchants. Its first days found them exposed in the crossfire between the aroused workers and the desperate government. The state, for so long the patron of industry and trade, now showed a marked willingness to pacify the workers at the expense of the employers. Sensing itself abandoned by the government, Merchant Moscow seized the initiative in the spring of 1905 by withdrawing its support from the government, and by summoning all industrial and commercial interests to meet for discussions on political unification.

Within the Moscow Exchange Society, a new group of textile entrepreneurs, led by Pavel Riabushinsky and including Aleksandr Konovalov, Sergei Chetverikov, Sergei Tretiakov, and Nikolai Morozov (figures 13.1–6), took the political high ground.[2] This activist center was dubbed by contemporaries the "Young Group," in recognition more of its collective energy than of the chronological age of its members. These industrialists urged their fellow entrepreneurs to join the liberal opposition to the regime and to demand fundamental constitutional reforms. By summer, the Riabushinsky Circle was discussing overt antigovernment action in support of its position, including nonpayment of taxes, closure of factories, and employer-sanctioned antigovernment strikes.

At the first sign of official retribution, however, all hopes for coordinated political action collapsed. When the police detained a prominent businessman in August, the entrepreneurs quickly scattered for cover. The tsar's October Manifesto, promising reform, broke the back of business opposition, and all entrepreneurial groups, including the "young" faction, rallied in defense of the beleaguered government. The brutal Moscow insurrection of December, in which the factories became battlegrounds in the desperate confrontation between the army and militant workers, served as a bloody benediction on the tumultuous year of 1905.

The new political possibilities opened by the October Manifesto found the entrepreneurs once again divided and in disarray. Deep fissures quickly opened between Moscow and Petersburg, as well as within each business community. In the elections to the First Duma in 1906, entrepreneurs campaigned in no less than four competing parties, with predictable results: all went down to humiliating electoral defeat. In the wake of this debacle, the new political divisions within the entrepreneurial stratum rigidified into several competing organizations, each with its own strategy.

The Petersburg groups, traditionally tied to the state by subsidy and patronage, abandoned the political arena altogether, pursuing instead "the economic side of unity." At their initiative the Association of Industry and Trade was founded, a modernized version of the traditional "representative" organizations of the old *kupechestvo*, but with the ambition of uniting all regions and sectors. Merchant Moscow remained more overtly political but more divided than ever over tactics and goals. The conservative majority, under the leadership of Grigory A. Krestovnikov, retreated into the Moscow Exchange Society, hoping for a return to business as usual. A moderate faction following Aleks-andr Guchkov joined the gentry-dominated Octobrist Union, intent on pursu-ing a policy of collaboration with the tsarist regime as long as it upheld its pledge of moderate reform.

This political retreat left the Riabushinsky group high and dry. Unlike the majority of merchants, who remained content to carve out safe niches within the structure of the old order, Riabushinsky and his associates persisted in charting a more independent course for what they unapologetically called "the Russian bourgeoisie." They had little faith in the reformist promises of the government, for history demonstrated that every tsarist "reform" era was followed by one of "counterreform." Cooperation with the regime merely strengthened the forces of order within it, they insisted, and perpetuated a culture of dependency to which the old *kupechestvo* had been so addicted. Thus the Riabushinsky Circle was as contemptuous of the "petitioning mentality" of the Association as it was of the collaborationist politics of the Octobrists.

The Young Group was unwilling to countenance the prospect of the emerg-ing forces of Russian capitalism perpetually immured within an agrarian and aristocratic old order, however "reformed" it might be. They envisioned in-stead a class-conscious and combative "commercial-industrial bourgeoisie" of European historical mythology, capable of moving beyond the old culture of deference to confront all opponents, including Europe itself, in defense of an entrepreneurial capitalist order in Russia. With its radical outlook, the insur-gent "young" industrialists assumed the forward position of a liberal avant-garde of Russian business politics.

Pavel Riabushinsky occupied a unique cultural position from which to at-tempt this transformation from *kupechestvo* to *burzhuaziia*. In 1900, he be-came the twenty-eight-year-old patriarch of a Moscow industrial dynasty (figure 13.7). He and his brothers Vladimir and Mikhail (figures 13.8 and 13.9) oversaw the rapid expansion and modernization of their family's textile and banking enterprises. Beyond the business realm, the Riabushinskys con-tributed broadly to the cultural flowering of Merchant Moscow in Russia's Silver Age: Stepan (figure 13.10) was a pioneer collector of ancient icons; brother Nikolai (figure 13.11) was an aesthete, art patron, and publisher of the sumptuous Art Nouveau journal *Zolotoe runo*; and Fedor sponsored a scientific expedition to Kamchatka in search of radium. Finally, Dmitry (fig-ure 13.12) was a scientist, creator of Russia's first aerodynamic laboratory at the family estate of Kuchino, outside Moscow (see the Bradley essay).

Yet while the Riabushinskys stood on the frontiers of entrepreneurial, scien-tific, and cultural innovation, they remained true to Russia's ancient culture. They were heirs to the patriotism of the old *kupechestvo*; they were intensely nationalistic, anxious to assert Russia's "place in the sun" among the great powers of Europe. They were, moreover, descendants of Old Believer peasant entrepreneurs: Pavel, still piously observant of the rites of the seventeenth-century pre-Nikonian church, and was the lay leader of his sect, the Belokrinitsa Priestly Old Believers, after 1905 (see "A Note on Old Belief"). The ethics, rituals, and mythology of Old Belief constituted for him a living culture, reminders of a distinctive native way of life that modern Russia might wish to emulate, and even revive; as a bridge between the remote past and an unknown future.

This unique symbiosis of avant-garde modernity and pious tradition was architectonically symbolized in the house Stepan Riabushinsky ordered built by the architect Fedor Shekhtel in 1900 (plate 16). The building's stunningly modernist *style moderne* exterior opened into a central interior space recalling the mythic undersea adventures of Sadko, the ancient Novgorodian merchant hero (see the Clowes essay). Yet the entire structure was conceived by its owner as a showcase for his extensive collection of ancient icons. Secluded under the roof of the building was a meticulously re-created Byzantine chapel, suitable for private worship according to the rites of the seventeenth-century pre-Nikonian Orthodoxy (figures 13.13 and 13.14). Thus in this single architectural space, experimentation, mythology, and ritual existed side by side: nine centuries of Old Orthodox piety encased in a modernist jewel box.

The voice of capitalism as Pavel Riabushinsky conceived it would, like his brother's house, contain within it a combination of forward-looking vision modulated by the distinctive resonances of this ancient cultural heritage. It would be intensely nationalistic, fiercely independent, and permeated with the religious morality of pre-Petrine Russia. As a modern independent entrepreneur, he was impatient with the autocratic pretensions of the tsarist regime. Freedom for private initiative would be his demand, space for creative entrepreneurship to transform Russia. And as an Old Believer, he was determined to put an end to the predatory power of the tsars, which had branded his ancestors "schismatics" and persecuted his faith for more than two centuries. A parliamentary democracy, a constitutional system, and a free entrepreneurial economy were to him the essential prerequisites for the creation of a modern industrial great power, a mythic "Great Russia" of the future.

Riabushinsky entertained no illusions about how difficult such a transformation would be. He had already encountered the hostility of the authorities toward his brand of industrial radicalism and sensed as well the disdain of liberal elites toward "politicking merchants" like himself. But more important, he was keenly aware of how remote his liberal values seemed to the Russian people, and how deep-seated their animosity toward capitalism and the *burzhui* (the pejorative popular pronunciation of "bourgeois") who championed it. The leitmotif of his political career would be the attempt to build coalitions that might overcome this popular resistance, to find new sources of legitimacy for capitalism that the *narod* could recognize and accept.

In the wake of 1905, Riabushinsky and his sympathizers had a private vision, but no public voice: they found themselves isolated among their peers, with neither supporters nor constituents. The "young" industrialists thus temporarily retired from the fray to regroup themselves and rethink their tactics. Fortunately for them, certain prominent liberal intellectuals, among them Petr Struve, Sergei Bulgakov, Nikolai Berdiaev, and the economist Ivan Ozerov, were at that very moment moving on a parallel course. Chastened by the violence of 1905, and the recklessness of the radical intelligentsia in calling the people to revolt, these liberals had begun to reassess the traditional anti-bourgeois animus endemic to Russian intellectual culture. Already preparing their famous *Vekhi* assault on the intelligentsia, this group was now interested in opening dialogue with the industrialists.

Riabushinsky and Konovalov characteristically took the initiative by inviting these "men of science" to join them in a series of "economic discussions" in their homes between 1909 and 1912. Here the Riabushinsky group received something resembling a graduate education in political economy and economic policy, as well as active encouragement from the intellectuals to join the political struggle to complete the unfinished democratic transformation of Russia.

The Riabushinsky group emerged from this interlude in 1912 calling themselves "Progressist" liberals, intent on forming a political party with "the Moscow *kupechestvo*" as its core constituency. Riabushinsky himself devoted considerable private wealth to the creation of his own publishing house for this purpose. His Riabushinsky Press began to issue a wide range of publications setting forth Progressist views: the Moscow daily *Utro Rossii* (The Morn of Russia, 1909–17), the nationalist *Velikaia Rossiia* symposium (Great Russia, 1910–11), the Old Believer journal *Tserkov* (Church, 1909–14), and numerous books and pamphlets championing what he called the "bourgeois idea" (figures 13.15 and 13.16).

These publications, along with the speeches of Riabushinsky and his colleagues in various industrial, parliamentary, and Old Believer venues, represent perhaps the most concerted attempt by any businessmen in prerevolutionary Russia to deploy a verbal discourse in defense of entrepreneurial capitalism. With this new voice they sought to seize control of the debate over Russia's future from the intellectuals and bureaucrats, as well as from rival entrepreneurial groups.

The outlook of the "young" industrialists both originated and culminated in a deep-seated nationalist sensibility. Their point of departure was a profound sense of anxiety over the erosion of Russia's great power status. The military debacle of the Russo-Japanese War, and the social chaos of the Revolution of 1905, were to them dire warnings of the growing inability of the tsarist regime to manage the forces of change. The external prestige of the nation, and its internal well-being, were both at grave risk. Imperial Germany, they feared, stood ready at the next moment of vulnerability to extinguish the Russian state, either by direct invasion or persistent economic subversion.

The fate of the nation in the age of imperialist rivalries now depended on the single-minded development of its industrial capacity. A rapid transition to industrial capitalism would have to be undertaken to avert national extinction. But this could no longer be accomplished by the state, as it had been in the past. The existing regime, with its agrarian biases, bureaucratic structures, and paternalistic pretensions, could not initiate or manage the kind of spontaneous and self-sustained expansion that was required. Market economics and entrepreneurial capitalism alone could provide the impetus to awaken and mobilize Russia's productive forces. The protean power of free capitalism, they argued, would act as a multiplier of national wealth, quickly raising the standard of living of the people while it radically enhanced Russia's great power potential.

For capitalism to perform its transformative role, however, it would have to be unshackled. The "young" industrialists were convinced that the tsarist state, long the only engine of change in Russia, was now the chief obstacle to progress. Because the autocracy correctly sensed in the dynamism of the capitalist system a powerful solvent to its centralizing power, they argued, the authorities would always regard private enterprise with hostility. Entrepreneurship required freedom, "like air to breathe." Only parliamentary democracy, constitutional government, and the rule of law could assure the growth and expansion of capitalist institutions in Russia. If the monarchy were to remain at all, its power to obstruct and delay would have to be annulled, or at least checked by constitutional safeguards. The future "Great Russia" would be ruled by an "authoritative" parliament, elected by all citizens and endowed with the power to set new rules of open competition among economic interests, classes, and nationalities.

The coming political struggle would necessarily have be led by those who could wield "material power" and shape that power with their "creative egoism."[3] The Riabushinsky Circle asserted that leadership could no longer be entrusted to the elites that had hitherto challenged the autocracy: the aristocracy and the intelligentsia. These had proven themselves powerless to create anything between governmental immobility and popular anarchy, and neither group seemed prepared to accept the moral and economic legitimacy of capitalist modes of production. The entrepreneurs were the only rising social force with the vision, managerial skill, and economic power to meet this challenge. Together with the new technological and managerial intelligentsia emerging from the process of industrialization itself, the entrepreneurs would be the architects of a new "Great Russia."

Riabushinsky and his associates were painfully aware, however, that the existing industrial and commercial groupings were as yet too divided, too deferential, and too uncertain to fulfill this transformative role. They seemed more inclined to abandon the political field after each crisis, reverting to their own kind of tribal warfare rather than resolutely challenging the opponents of capitalism who fomented those crises. Riabushinsky and his associates argued that these scattered interests must be rapidly "crystallized" into a self-assertive entrepreneurial class, one that shared the "bourgeois idea" that they, alone, were "the creators of material value" in society.[4] Once this common "psychology of the bourgeois" was inculcated, a vigorous entrepreneurial culture would be created around the "powerful young force of the bourgeoisie."[5]

Not just any contingent of Russia's entrepreneurial stratum could claim the standing to lead this new class, the Riabushinsky group asserted. The business elites of Petersburg and the periphery, they maintained, were too recent in origin, too associated with foreigners, and too tied to the state to serve as the core cadres of the emerging *burzhuaziia*. Only Merchant Moscow, "the city of the Russian bourgeoisie," could aspire to this role.[6] Many of the industrial dynasties of the center, having risen directly out of the peasantry, were still "linked by a thousand unseen threads to the people."[7] It was from the people of the heartland, and not the periphery or the Westernized capital, that a new capitalist voice would emanate. Merchant Moscow was for Riabushinsky nothing less than the ancestral seat and future citadel of the Russian national bourgeoisie.

Riabushinsky understood, however, that it would take more than genealogical claims to legitimize the capitalist project in the eyes of the *narod*: it would require a mobilizing ideology, an empowering myth. For this he looked back to the world of the Old Believers, from whose ranks his and many other Moscow merchant families had emerged.[8] Old Belief represented for him the primordial culture of the Russian people: it sustained and nourished in its adherents the collective memory of an "ancient and free Rus" that long predated the tsars.[9] The ways of the schismatics embodied the ancestral values of the uncorrupted *narod*: "the way of life of the Russian people in its authentic purity."[10] Its sober and industrious culture and autonomous traditions embodied qualities that were indigenous to the people of Rus prior to the advent of autocracy: local democracy and an indigenous work ethic.

This legacy, of course, embodied precisely the skills that would be required of the citizens of industrial and democratic "Great Russia." Russian capitalism, suffused with the ethos of a reanimated Old Belief, would unite both worker and employer in a common ethical culture. Entrepreneurship would be understood as a special calling from God, imbued with privileges, but also with responsibilities. Individual initiative would be respected and rewarded, but collective obligations of mutual respect and support among believers would constrain predatory instincts and exploitive behaviors. Elites and masses would once again share the same piety, the same rituals, the same ethos that they had in ages gone by, yet both would now be dedicated to the common task of building a New Russia. The authentic character of the *narod* would then become visible, and "the Russian people will at last stand before the world and God in its own true form," as a free and productive civilization.[11] If Riabushinsky and his associates had had their way, twentieth-century Russian capitalism would have been draped in the ethical vestments of the Muscovite middle ages.

The culmination of Riabushinsky's capitalist and Old Believer vision resided where his inspiration began: in his nationalist hopes for his country. If history followed the course he set, a democratic "Great Russia" would replace the tsarist state. The old empire would give way to a commonwealth of free peoples, all of whom shared and internalized "the psychology of the bourgeois." Free Russia, with her inexhaustible resources, could then expect "a future no less great than that of the United States."[12] On its western frontiers, democratic Russia would at last have the prestige and the power to forge and lead a new condominium of Slavic peoples able to resist "the hand of German imperialism" in Europe.[13] To the east, free and capitalist Russia would act as a culture-bearer, winning the allegiance of native elites by force of example rather than by force of arms. Russia would take its special place among the great and "civilized" powers as a bridge between East and West, as the embodiment of a humane modernity in which the morals, ethics, and mythology of the past informed the conscious creation of a distinctively national future.

These views achieved a modest hearing in the last years of peace, as Aleksandr Konovalov was elected as a Progressist in 1912 to the Fourth State Duma, and Riabushinsky's *Utro Rossii* became one of the largest liberal papers in Moscow. But this combination of parliamentary eloquence and journalistic bravado failed to trigger the hoped-for bourgeois awakening. Indeed, 1914 was a year of near despair for Riabushinsky and his colleagues. The tsarist regime seemed unable to shake off its autocratic ways, and instead seemed to align itself ever more closely with the forces of ascendant reaction. The future of the Duma itself was threatened, and the tsar's ministers had turned away from industry altogether, refusing to consider even the "humble petitions" of the Petersburg Association. In desperation, the "young" industrialists opened clandestine negotiations with Bolsheviks and other radicals to discuss a possible "superorganic," or revolutionary, solution to the deadlock. When this secret initiative collapsed, Riabushinsky spoke ominously of "dark forces" at work in Russia, and his *Utro Rossii* asked plaintively: "We are at the limits of the possible. What can we do?"[14]

It is clear that in the short time available to it, the Riabushinsky Circle failed to make its case either against the Old Regime or with the Russian people. The group even failed to rally fellow entrepreneurs to its vision of a capitalist future for Russia. One reason for this failure may lie in the fact that in their time, Riabushinsky's polyphonic voices—the liberal, the nationalist, the bourgeois, the Old Believer—may have seemed to contemporaries like the cacophonous choirs of the ancient Old Believers, as discordant and fragmented as the class they sought to mobilize.

In retrospect, however, the historian can weave together the dispersed streams of discourse. Taken together, Riabushinsky's ideas might be seen to constitute a "utopian capitalist" vision. Riabushinsky and his people invoked a Russia where all that was wrong was set right, where a free and productive people worked its way out of poverty and backwardness even as it rediscovered its primordial identity. But "utopia" in Greek means "no place." And in reality, at "no place" in the Russia of the time did the elements of his vision exist in any but the most rudimentary form. Time soon ran out, and when it did Riabushinsky's entrepreneurial world was still only a tiny enclave in a vast peasant economy, his *burzhuaziia* still closer to the old *kupechestvo* than to the modern entrepreneurial class he hoped to lead.

For all their flaws, Riabushinsky's utopian constructs might be understood as constituting a founding text for entrepreneurial capitalism in Russia, one that attempted to write an indigenous script for national economic development free of both state control and foreign domination. Even if utopian capitalism plotted only a mythical trajectory for Russian industry, its status in Russian history is nonetheless unique. It represents a pioneering attempt to chart a purely Russian road to democratic modernity, a first effort to imagine capitalism with a Russian, and specifically a Muscovite, face.

NOTES

1. On the political history of the merchants and industrialists before 1905, see Thomas C. Owen, *Capitalism and Politics in Russia: A Social History of the Moscow Merchants, 1855–1905* (Cambridge, Cambridge University Press, 1981).

2. On the history of the Riabushinsky Circle ("Young Group"), see James L. West, "The Rjabusinskij Circle: Russian Industrialists in Search of a Bourgeoisie," *Jahrbücher für Geschichte Osteuropas* 32 (1984): part 3.

3. *Utro Rossii*, May 18, 1910; January 1, 1912.

4. Ibid., January 1, 1912.

5. Ibid., May 18, 1910.

6. Ibid., June 2, 1910; January 1, 1912.

7. Ibid., April 3, 1911.

8. On the attachment of Riabushinsky to Old Belief, see James L. West, "The Neo–Old Believers of Moscow: Religious Revival, Nationalism and Myth in Late Imperial Russia," *Canadian Slavic Studies* 25, nos. 1–4 (1991).

9. *Utro Rossii*, July 5, 1911.

10. *Tserkov*, February 6, 1911.

11. *Slovo Tserkvy*, no. 3 (1914): 61.

12. *Tserkov*, October 19, 1914, p. 970.

13. Ivan Ozerov, *Problèmes économiques et financiers de la Russie moderne* (Paris, 1916), p. 41.

14. *Utro Rossii*, January 12, 1911.

Figure 13.1. *Pavel Pavlovich Riabushinsky, young patriarch of the family, chairman of the family enterprises, Old Believer leader, and Progressist political figure.*

Figure 13.2. *Alexandr Ivanovich Konovalov, Duma leader of the Progressist Party, activist in the War Industry Committees, and minister in the Provisional Government.*

Figure 13.3. *Sergei Ivanovich Chetverikov, in his fifties, the elder of the "Young Group."*

Figure 13.4. *Sergei Nikolaevich Tretiakov.*

Figure 13.5. *Nikolai Davidovich Morozov, member of the famous Old Believer merchant family.*

Figure 13.6. *Pavel Afanasrevich Buryshkin, youngest member of the Riabushinsky Group and memoirist of Merchant Moscow in emigration.*

Figure 13.7. *Company letterhead of P. M. Riabushinsky and Sons textile firm. Illustration shows the sprawling mills at Vishny-Volochek, as well as the gold and silver medals awarded to the company for its high-quality merchandise.*

Figure 13.8. *Mikhail Pavlovich, art collector and banker, director of the Riabushinskys' financial enterprises.*

Figure 13.9. *Vladimir Pavlovich, alter ego of Pavel, icon collector, political activist, nationalist thinker, publisher of* Velikaia Rossiia, *and writer on Old Belief in emigration.*

Figure 13.10. *Stepan Pavlovich, Old Believer leader, collector of ancient icons, and owner of the famous Riabushinsky house designed by Fedor Shekhtel.*

Figure 13.11. *Nikolai Pavlovich, art patron, aesthete, collector, publisher of the Art Nouveau journal* Zolotoe runo (The Golden Fleece), *and Parisian antique dealer in emigration.*

Figure 13.12. *Dmitry Pavlovich, scientist, founder of the Kuchino Aerodynamic Laboratory (the Soviet-era Central Aero- and Hydrodynamic Institute—TsAGI), and member of the French Academy of Sciences in emigration. Photo shows Dmitry's family on the terrace of the Kuchino estate (see the photo in the introduction).*

Figure 13.13. *Fedor Shekhtel's design for Old Believer chapel icon screen in Riabushinsky House.*

Figure 13.14. *The Old Believer Chapel: Byzantine-style dome and frescoes. (Contemporary photo of restoration by William Craft Brumfield.)*

Figure 13.15. *The Utro Rossii publishing house of the Riabushinskys, designed by Fedor Shekhtel, 1907.*

Figure 13.16. *Mastheads reflecting Riabushinsky's liberal and Old Believer publishing empire.*
Top row: left, Morning *(1906); right,* The People's Paper *(1906). Second row:*
left, The Morn of Russia, *(1907, 1909–18); right,* Great Russia *symposium (1910–11).*
Third row: left, Church *(1909–14); right,* The Word of the Church *(1914–17).*
Bottom: Friend of the Land *(supplement to* Church*).*

CONCLUSION

Pavel Riabushinsky consulting with Mikhail Rodzianko, August 1917.

The Fate of Merchant Moscow

James L. West

Late in the summer of 1917, Pavel Riabushinsky was photographed in urgent consultation with the former president of the State Duma and former leader of the Provisional Government, Mikhail Rodzianko. This ghostly image, in which liberal industrialist converses on seemingly equal terms with liberal aristocrat, represents the high water mark of entrepreneurial influence in Russia. But whatever the subject of their hurried conversation, real power was rapidly slipping from the hands of both of them. Only a few short months separated the political "rise" of the Russian bourgeoisie from the total collapse of the nascent bourgeois order in Russia. Only a few tumultuous years divided the secure and orderly world of prewar Merchant Moscow from the lived nightmare of arrests, deportations, and executions. The story of this stunning historical reversal draws together the themes, both visual and textual, that form the central narrative of this volume.

The photographs in this book document the remarkable coming-of-age of a unique social and economic elite, as incandescent in the cultural and economic spheres as it was short-lived in the historical one. Yet as the commentaries that accompany the photographs make clear, Merchant Moscow was a microcosmic world of extraordinary complexity and contradiction. Its achievements were impressive, but its flaws and vulnerabilities were deep and intensifying. Even while the "Russian bourgeoisie" struggled to take shape, evidence abounded that this new class was a fragile and vulnerable construct.

These negative factors became increasing apparent under the enormous social and political stress imposed by the Great War. The actual outbreak of hostilities, which the nationalist entrepreneurs had done much to bring to pass, was greeted with joy by Merchant Moscow. The patriotic fervor of the liberal industrialists was tinged with the exhilarating expectation that the altered balance of domestic forces would work in their favor. But the war crisis found the merchant and industrialists in a particularly vulnerable position. Culturally hegemonic in the life of the city, and thus highly visible to the restive and resentful masses, this economic elite remained in the larger national context socially unconsolidated, politically inexperienced, and economically illegitimate in the eyes of many.

The early stages of the wartime emergency seemed at first to enhance the prestige of the Moscow liberal entrepreneurs, for with the fading of their chief rivals, the Duma Octobrists and the Petersburg Association of Industry and Trade, the Riabushinsky group became the principal spokesmen for the aspirations of Russia's "national bourgeoisie." As events unfolded, however, the war crisis actually undermined rather than furthered the entrepreneurial-capitalist project of the Moscow liberals. For one thing, the mobilization effort vastly expanded the role of the state in the economy and lined the pockets and enhanced the standing of those Petersburg magnates of heavy industry who were their principal competitors and antagonists. For another, Merchant Moscow, immobilized by the crisis, momentarily reverted to the passive and deferential posture of old. Its rank and file remained largely indifferent to new wartime political possibilities and appeared unconcerned even by the government's faltering conduct of the war.

Pavel Riabushinsky first challenged this business-as-usual attitude in 1915 by rallying the torpid entrepreneurs to mobilize themselves for the war effort. He proposed a network of War Industry Committees, local and private organizations geared to war production across the empire. While on their face a patriotic effort to assist the government, these new organizations actually represented a thinly concealed attempt to assert Muscovite control over a shadow economy in preparation for a future day of reckoning. When the authorities disdainfully rebuffed these efforts with justified suspicion, Riabushinsky and Konovalov spearheaded an unsuccessful political offensive against regime in the form of a new liberal Duma coalition known as the Progressive Bloc of 1915. At the eleventh hour, early in 1917, Riabushinsky was hard at work on yet another national business organization, this one openly political and under Muscovite control, called the All-Russian Union of Industry and Trade. Some of his Moscow colleagues, most notably Guchkov, actively engaged in various conspiracies to remove the tsar from power.

These herculean efforts put enormous emotional and physical strain on the industrial leaders. By late 1916, Konovalov and Riabushinsky fell into a bitter dispute with each other over the inclusion of "workers' groups" in the War Industry Committees, which Riabushinsky vehemently opposed. These exertions also undermined their health. By early 1917, most of Russia's business figures were suffering major medical problems brought on by overwork and exhaustion. One can almost sense the physical vitality of the business leadership ebbing away even as their social unity and political resolve faltered.

The February Revolution, which saw the demise of what Konovalov now called "the hated old regime," seemed at first to open the way for the entrepreneurs' ascension to power. Indeed, the Muscovites Konovalov and Tretiakov briefly served as ministers in the Provisional Government, and Riabushinsky entered the new State Council. But this political apotheosis was illusory. The still-unconsolidated "bourgeoisie" and its fragile infrastructure were already at the mercy of a spreading chaos. The War Industry Committees faded, and Riabushinsky's Union of Industry and Trade hardly materialized beyond ambitious paper plans. Konovalov sensed early on that Russia was "moving with giant steps toward catastrophe" and called with more foresight than success for an immediate separate peace with Germany.

The situation soon turned irretrievably worse as Russia lurched from absolute monarchy toward total anarchy. At the very moment when the entrepreneurs arrived at the pinnacle of symbolic authority, real power was hemorrhaging away from elites and cities toward rebellious peasants and workers in rural villages and factory courtyards. This momentous shift encouraged the most radical anticapitalist faction in Russia, the Bolsheviks, to attempt the unthinkable: a preemptive strike against a floundering bourgeois government unable to claim the loyalties of the Russian people.

When Konovalov assumed leadership of the Provisional Government as acting prime minister in October 1917, it was only to surrender the Winter Palace to the victorious Bolsheviks. The "bourgeoisie" thus "rose" in Russia, as Riabushinsky had predicted it would, only with the demise of the autocracy. Yet the entrepreneurs were now powerless to resist the suction of the sinking old regime. In the chaos that ensued, Russian capitalism and most of its opponents were swept away together.

The Bolsheviks rode to power on a wave of primeval resentment against the *burzhui* that was shared by workers, peasants, and large portions of the intelligentsia, both radical and reactionary. Entrepreneurial capitalism had clearly failed to make its case with the Russian public. Even in its death throes, the bourgeoisie-that-was-not-to-be could find no unity of purpose. The last archival trace of Riabushinsky's Union of Trade and Industry in 1918, months after its leaders had slipped into hiding or exile, is a vituperative telegraphic exchange between the now-fugitive entrepreneurs of Moscow and Petersburg over who bore the blame for the calamity. As late as the 1930s in exile, Tretiakov still complained about the "fragmentation and division into sects" that characterized the émigré entrepreneur community. Like the Old Believers in whom Riabushinsky set such store, entrepreneurial Russia seemed to dissolve into mutually hostile sects under the shocks of rapid modernization.

I

The fate of the leading lights of Merchant Moscow at the hands of the Bolsheviks was truly wretched. As arrests of prominent capitalists mounted in 1918 and nationalization decrees cascaded down from the Bolshevik regime, the once-proud captains of Russian industry were torn from the charmed lives they had known and thrust toward almost unimaginable extremes of human experience as prisoners, fugitives, refugees, and émigrés.

Sergei Chetverikov recalled a poignant scene that occurred while he was clearing snow from a railroad track under Bolshevik forced labor near the Morozov textile mills in early 1918. Out of the snow came the figure walking the rails clutching a parcel. It was Arseny Ivanovich Morozov, director of the Bogorodsko-Glukhovsk mills. Having just been expropriated from his home and his plant, Morozov was now wandering in the snow, holding the one object he had managed to save: the family icon.

Dmitry Riabushinsky had a more chilling brush with the Bolsheviks. Many prominent figures of Merchant Moscow, such as Konovalov and Pavel Riabushinsky, were arrested for brief periods of time, after which they slipped out of Moscow and Petersburg toward the areas under White control, but Dmitry remained for a time with his beloved aerodynamic laboratory in Kuchino. Sensing the destructive forces growing around him, he successfully petitioned the Bolshevik government in April 1918 to have his scientific facilities nationalized. Now temporarily attached to the Academy of Sciences under the new regime, Dmitry was on institute business in Moscow one day in September 1918 when his family received a terrifying visit. As recounted by his daughter Aleksandra, who was seven years old at the time, their home at Kuchino was invaded by a unit of Red Guard thugs who said they were looking for the *burzhui*. Not finding him, they went on a rampage, tearing down the drapes, destroying the piano, taking shots at the horse cart bringing the French nanny home, and exploding grenades in the Pechora River nearby, killing many fish. After a day-long orgy of destruction, the soldiers tired of the wait and left, saying they would return to get the *burzhui* and would not leave a brick standing on the next visit.

When Dmitry returned that evening and learned what had happened, he dressed his family in workers' clothes and hustled them to Moscow to take shelter with relatives while he arranged passage south for them. The journey was fraught with danger. At one point, the family had to hide in a shipment of straw while Bolshevik soldiers searched for "contrabanders" with pitchforks. One daughter, Marie, was wounded in the hand by one such thrust, but her fortitude in remaining silent saved the family.

Dmitry's travails did not end with the escape of his family, for he was too well known to have any hope of leaving with them. A few months later he made his way north to Petrograd, hoping to go abroad, ostensibly on Academy of Sciences business. There he was detained and brought before the local boss of the secret police, the Bolshevik Moisei Uritsky, who placed him under house arrest at the Hotel Evropa until confirmation arrived from Moscow that he was indeed on official assignment.

Early the next morning, August 30, 1918, he was arrested by Red Guards, and when he protested that he was under Uritsky's protection, they replied:

"Uritsky's dead." The Cheka boss had been killed by an assassin. The same day, Lenin himself was wounded in another assassination attempt. While Dmitry sat in prison, the Cheka compiled a list of five hundred opponents of the regime to be shot in the event of the Bolshevik leader's death. Dmitry recalled that his only comfort during his incarceration was a small icon placed by a former inmate in the corner of his cell. When he was finally released two months later, the Bolshevik official who came for him ripped the icon down and crushed it under his boot. That act of willful desecration was Old Believer Dmitry Riabushinsky's last experience in Russia; he was deported to Denmark upon his release, never to return.

During the Civil War (1918–20) the majority of prominent Moscow businessmen served in various posts with White armies and governments. After the final collapse of anti-Bolshevik resistance, most evacuated to Paris and London, where they set to work forming a network of Russian business organizations in exile. The speeches given at these émigré congresses made clear that they were anxiously awaiting the day when they would return triumphant to a post-Bolshevik Russia to restore free markets and democracy. Some, like the Riabushinskys, tried to reestablish their business operations in Europe, but their entrepreneurial skills were never quite up to the level of their western competitors, and in any case all such ventures that survived the 1920s were swept away by the Great Depression. Only a fortunate few, like the scientist Dmitry Riabushinsky, managed to create successful careers for themselves in the West. Most of Merchant Moscow's prerevolutionary elite died in penury and obscurity, mourned only by an ever-shrinking circle of aging associates.

Others from the rapidly vanishing world of Merchant Moscow were not even that fortunate. Although all the Riabushinsky brothers escaped abroad, two sisters, Nadezhda and Aleksandra, who in 1909 had played each another in the Moscow Lawn Tennis Association championship, were for reasons unknown unable to leave in time. Nadezhda managed for a time to maintain clandestine correspondence with her brothers through operatives in Riga, Latvia, and reported to them goings-on at their old factories, as well as her own situation and that of her sister. By 1921 she wrote that the factory was at a standstill "because of lack of fuel, the machinery is broken, and the roof leaks badly," all of which drove the workers in desperation to "demand the return of the 'boss' Riabushinsky." About her own condition, Nadezhda wrote candidly that by 1921 she was living in four attic rooms in Moscow, her home having been expropriated long before. She described a Moscow without pigeons or other city birds, "for there is nothing to nourish them." In the early NEP, she wrote, "each of us sells something, but of course there are more sellers than buyers." "Our situation is very serious," she concluded, "please send something, if only chocolate or soap."

In 1922, Nadezhda Riabushinskaia's letters ceased. There were rumors of searches for Riabushinskys and other ringleaders of the bourgeoisie still secretly living in Russia. Until very recently, the fate of the Riabushinsky sisters remained a mystery, though one that already precluded any happy denouement. The opening of the secret police archives now permits us to know the pathetic end of their story in some detail. Sometime in 1931, in connection with the investigation of "Counterrevolution, Wrecking, Diversion, and Espionage in the Textile Industry," 165 people were arrested in a police dragnet of former owners and managers in Moscow. Among them were the Riabushinsky sisters, then in their midforties. For their "crimes," both were remanded to the Solovetsk labor camp on the shores of the White Sea. On October 20, 1937, they were condemned by an NKVD tribunal to "the highest measure of punishment." The fate of Alexandra's two young children, born just before the revolution, remains unknown.

II

Any retrospective judgment on people to whom history was so unkind would seem gratuitous. Russian capitalism was allowed a few scant decades to make its mark, whereas Western middle classes enjoyed centuries of continuous development to make their ascent. In the final analysis, it is arguable that no social group, however culturally mature, socially united, or politically astute, could have successfully mastered the terrifying social chaos unleashed in Russia early in this century.

It is ironic that in their efforts to overcome the deficiencies they well understood, the political elites of Merchant Moscow opened the way to their own destruction. In their efforts to find an antidote to fragmentation and isolation in renewed nationalist appeals, the liberal leadership of Merchant Moscow stands implicated in the catastrophe that befell the Old Order in Russia. The "fateful legacy" of merchant patriotism that they reappropriated, their intense and ultimately self-delusional identification with "the people," their efforts to put "a Russian face" on capitalism, and most ominous of all, their nationalistic longing for a "Great Russia" able to confront "the Teutonic hordes" in Europe, all condemned them to play their own small part in setting off the cascade of crises that ended in revolution.

Thus the images in this volume, and the people and institutions that they portray, must be seen in an ambiguous light, suffused at once with the radiance of a new era and the twilight glow of a doomed Old Order. That these people never managed to give birth to a world entirely of their own making in Russia was their tragedy. That they had well begun that creative process was their achievement, as these photos vividly illustrate. It was the ironic historical fate of Merchant Moscow that its culture and politics began to flower in a historical epoch when all such openings proved to be closings, and all such promising beginnings turned out to be tragic endings.

Suggestions for Further Reading

Allhouse, Robert H., ed. *Photographs for the Tsar: Pioneering Photography of Sergei Mikhailovich Prokudin-Gorskii Commissioned by Tsar Nicholas II.* New York: Dial Press, 1980.

Berton, Kathleen. *Moscow: An Architectural History.* New York: St. Martin's Press, 1977.

Bill, Valentine T. *The Forgotten Class.* New York: Praeger, 1959.

Bradley, Joseph. *Muzhik and Muscovite: Urbanization in Late Imperial Russia.* Berkeley and Los Angeles: University of California Press, 1985.

Brower, Daniel R. *The Russian City between Tradition and Modernity, 1850–1900.* Berkeley and Los Angeles: University of California Press, 1990.

Brumfield, William Craft. *History of Russian Architecture.* Cambridge: Cambridge University Press, 1993.

———. *The Origins of Modernism in Russian Architecture.* Berkeley and Los Angeles: University of California Press, 1991.

———, ed. *Reshaping Russian Architecture: Western Technology and Utopian Dreams.* Cambridge: Cambridge University Press, 1990.

Clowes, Edith W., Samuel D. Kassow, and James L. West, eds. *Between Tsar and People: Educated Society and the Quest for Public Identity in Late Imperial Russia.* Princeton: Princeton University Press, 1991.

Guroff, Gregory, and Fred V. Carstensen, eds. *Entrepreneurship in Imperial Russia and the Soviet Union.* Princeton: Princeton University Press, 1983.

Hamm, Michael F., ed. *The City in Late Imperial Russia.* Bloomington: Indiana University Press, 1986.

Hoover, Marjorie. *Alexander Ostrovsky.* Boston: G. K. Hall, 1981.

Nemirovich-Danchenko, Vladimir. *My Life in the Russian Theater.* New York: Theater Arts Books, 1968.

Owen, Thomas C. *Capitalism and Politics in Russia: A Social History of the Moscow Merchants, 1855–1905.* Cambridge: Cambridge University Press, 1981.

———. *The Corporation under Russian Law, 1800–1917: A Study in Tsarist Economic Policy.* Cambridge: Cambridge University Press, 1991.

———. *Russian Corporate Capitalism from Peter the Great to Perestroika.* New York: Oxford University Press, 1995.

Polunin, Vladimir. *Three Generations: Family Life in Russia, 1845–1902.* Trans. A. F. Birch-Jones. London, 1957.

Rieber, Alfred J. *Merchants and Entrepreneurs in Imperial Russia.* Chapel Hill: University of North Carolina Press, 1982.

Robson, Roy R. *Old Believers in Modern Russia.* DeKalb: Northern Illinois University Press, 1995.

Ruckman, Jo Ann. *The Moscow Business Elite: A Social and Cultural Portrait of Two Generations, 1840–1905*. DeKalb: Northern Illinois University Press, 1984.

Ruud, Charles A. *Russian Entrepreneur: Publisher Ivan Sytin of Moscow, 1851–1934*. Montreal: McGill-Queen's University Press, 1990.

Stanislavski, Constantine. *My Life in Art*. Trans. J. J. Robbins. N.P.: Theatre Arts Books, 1948.

Thurston, Robert. *Liberal City, Conservative State: Moscow and Russia's Urban Crisis, 1906–1914*. Oxford: Oxford University Press, 1987.

Contributors

Joseph C. Bradley is Professor of History at the University of Tulsa in Tulsa, Oklahoma.

William C. Brumfield is Professor of Russian Language and Literature at Tulane University in New Orleans, Louisiana.

Edith W. Clowes is Professor of Russian Language and Literature at Purdue University in West Lafayette, Indiana.

Muriel Joffe is a Research Fellow at the Institute for European, Russian, and Eurasian Studies at George Washington University, Washington, D.C.

Sergei V. Kalmykov is a Research Fellow at the Institute of Russian History in Moscow.

Adele Lindenmeyr is Professor of History at Villanova University in Villanova, Pennsylvania.

Diane Neumaier is Professor of Visual Arts at Rutgers University in New Brunswick, New Jersey.

Thomas C. Owen is Professor of History at Louisiana State University in Baton Rouge, Louisiana.

Karen Pennar is Senior Writer at *Business Week* magazine in New York.

Iurii A. Petrov is a Research Fellow at the Institute of Russian History in Moscow.

Irina V. Potkina is a Research Fellow at the Institute of Russian History in Moscow.

Christine Ruane is Visiting Assistant Professor of History at the University of Tulsa in Tulsa, Oklahoma.

Mikhail K. Shatsillo is a Research Fellow at the Institute of Russian History in Moscow.

Galina N. Ulianova is a Research Fellow at the Institute of Russian History in Moscow.

James L. West is Professor of History at Middlebury College in Middlebury, Vermont.

Mikhail Zolotarev is a chemist whose passion for collecting old photographs made this volume possible.

Index

Abramtsevo art colony, 97, 102, 122, 125, 139, 150

Abrikosov, A. A., 135

Abrikosov, Aleksei I., 33, 141

Abrikosov Manufacturing Company (candy and chocolate), 4, 31, 33. *See also* advertising

Abrikosova, Grafina I., 100

Abrikosova, Nadezhda N., 106

advertising, 42ff; for Abrikosov Manufacturing Company, **pl. 22**; for Alexander Bary and Sons Company, **fig. 1.6**; for Brocard Perfume Company, **pl. 21**; for Kalinkin Liquor Company, **pl. 24**; for Singer Sewing Machine Company, **pl. 25**; for Volga Soap Company, **pl. 23**; for Zimin Dress and Costume Company, **pl. 20**

Alekseev family, 155

Alekseev, Konstantin S. (pseud. Stanislavsky), 97, 115, 134; *My Life in Art*, 150, 153

Alekseev, Mikhail I., 137

Alekseev, N. A., 136

Alekseev, V. P., 136

Alekseev, Vladimir S., 55, **fig. 4.1**

Alekseeva, V. A., 152

Alexander I, 111

Alexander II, 69

Alexander III, 100

All-Russian Union of Industry and Trade, 174

Anounce Agency (advertising), streetcar advertising for, **fig. 2.16**

apartment houses (*dokhodnye doma*), 124; Afremov, 126, **fig. 10.14**; Pertsov, 127, **fig. 10.16**; Rossiia Insurance Company complex, 125, **fig. 10.13**; on Vvedensky Lane, 126, **fig. 10.15**

architects: D. Chichagov, 120; A. Erikhson, 124; V. A. Gartman, 141; L. Kekushev, 121; R. I. Klein, 41, 123, 128; I. Kuznetsov, 123; G. Makarev, 126; A. Pomerantsev, 120; N. M. Proskurin, 125; I. Rerberg,

128–29; V. Shervud, 120; L. Shishkovsky, 126; V. Shukhov (engineer), 121, 128; W. Walcot, 121; N. Zhukov, 127. *See also* Shekhtel, Fedor O.

architectural styles: arts and crafts, 120, 122, 128; empire, 129; neoclassicism, 123; Russian revival, 120; *style moderne*, 119, 125ff, 129, 157; Vienna Secession, 120

architecture, 119–29; *Zodchii (Architect)* journal of, 119

Arnold, Charles, 111

art galleries: Shchukin museum, 138, **fig. 11.12**; Tretiakov, 4, 124–25, **fig. 10.12**

art journals: *Mir iskusstva (World of Art)*, 139; *Zolotoe runo (Golden Fleece)*, 140, 164

art patronage, 63, 106

artists: N. Andreev (sculptor), 122; P. Cezanne, 140; N. I. Chechelov, 79; A. Golovin, 122; A. A. Ivanov, 138; K. Korovin, 150; S. Maliutin, 127; H. Matisse, 140; P. Picasso, 140; V. Vasnetsov, 124, 126, 128, 139, 150; M. Vrubel, 77, 122, 139, 150

Association of Industry and Trade, 163

Avanso and Company (paints), 40

Babaev, Iakov I., 58, **fig. 4.12**

Babst, Ivan K., 46

Bakhrushin, Aleksei A., 100, 102, 135, 137; caricature of, **fig. 12.6**; *Kto chto sobiraet? (Who Collects What?)*, 137, **fig. 11.11**; and Moscow Theater Museum, 102

Bakhrushin, Aleksei P., 137, 138, 141

Bakhrushin family, 135

Bakhrushin, Sergei A., 135

Bakhrushin, Vladimir A., 141

Bakhrushina, Vera, 102

Balashova, Aleksandra M. (dancer), 152, **pl. 8**

banks, 45–50; Discount, 6; Moscow Commercial Loan, 46; Moscow International Trade, 49; Moscow Merchant Mutual